Researching London's HOUSES

First published 2005
by Historical Publications Ltd
32 Ellington Street, London N7 8PL
(Tel: 020 7607 1628)

in association with the London Archive Users' Forum

ISBN 1-905286-00-7

British Library Cataloguing-in-Publication Data
A catalogue record for this book is available from the British Library

Production by Liz Morrell and Patrick Donnelly
Printed in Zaragoza, Spain by Edelvives

The Illustrations

We are grateful to the following for permission to reproduce illustrations in their collections: Museum of London *1*; Guildhall Library, Corporation of London *2, 14, 61, 70, 76, 78, 87, 90, 92, 94, 106*; English Heritage/National Monuments Record *6, 9, 11, 16, 30, 33, 45, 109*; London Metropolitan Archives, Corporation of London *4, 5, 8, 10, 12, 15, 19, 20, 21, 24, 26, 27, 35, 36, 38, 39, 43, 44, 46, 47, 48, 49, 50, 52, 53, 55, 57, 58, 60, 71, 72, 73, 79, 83, 84, 91, 95, 96, 98, 99, 100, 105, 107, 108, 111, 112, 113, 116*; National Monuments Record (© Crown copyright.NMR) *25*; London Borough of Hackney, Archives Department *18, 22, 51, 54, 62*; Simmons Aerofilms Ltd *23*; Kingston Museum and Heritage Service *29*; KingsOak Homes Ltd *37*; the British Library *56, 82*; Dr Francis Sheppard *59*; City of Westminster Archives Centre *63, 64, 67*; Camden Local Studies and Archives Centre *65, 97*; London Borough of Lambeth, Archives Department *66, 86, 101*; the National Archives *68, 69, 75, 80*; the British Museum *89*; Guildhall Art Gallery, Corporation of London *93*; Wandsworth Local History Service *114, 115*; Hillingdon Local Studies and Archives *118, 119, 120, 121, 122, 123, 124*.

The cover illustration, a view of the Thames from Hill End, Shooters Hill, is a watercolour of 1940 by S B Mattey. It is reproduced by permission of Greenwich Heritage Centre.

Illustrations *2, 76* and *78* from manuscripts at Guildhall Library are reproduced by kind permission of Christ's Hospital, the Worshipful Company of Cutlers and Aviva plc respectively. Illustration *13* is reproduced by courtesy of the Trustees of Sir John Soane's Museum. Permission to reproduce no. *46* is is granted by HarperCollins Publishers www.collinsbartholomew.com. Every effort has been made to trace other copyright owners.

Other images have been supplied by the author or publishers.

Researching
London's
HOUSES
an archives guide

Colin Thom

HISTORICAL PUBLICATIONS

*This book was produced in collaboration with the
London Archive Users' Forum.
LAUF campaigned on behalf of researchers in London
archives between 1988 and 2005.
It is succeeded by the Users' Section of Archives for London.*

*A graduate of Glasgow University, Colin Thom has lived in
south London for over twenty years, and for the past eighteen
has been a researcher and writer for the highly regarded*
Survey of London *(now part of English Heritage).
He has also appeared as a documents expert on Channel 4's*
Time Team.

Acknowledgements

I am grateful to the staff of all the libraries and archives in London who have helped with the preparation of this book, in particular: Camden Local Studies and Archives Centre; Greenwich Heritage Centre (especially Jonathan Partington); Guildhall Library, Corporation of London; David Mander, and his successors at Hackney Archives Department; Carolynne Cotton and Gwyn Jones at Hillingdon Local Studies Library; Martin Banham and Claire Frankland at Islington Local History Centre; Kensington Local Studies Collection, Kensington Central Library; Lambeth Archives; London Metropolitan Archives, Corporation of London (especially Dave Tennant and Sally Bevan); The National Archives; Alyson Rogers and other staff at English Heritage's National Monuments Record Centre; Tower Hamlets Local History Library and Archives; Julie Gregson and staff at Wandsworth Local History Service; Westminster Archives Centre.

I would also like to thank my colleagues in the Survey of London and English Heritage, especially the Survey's General Editor John Greenacombe for allowing me to use material from the Survey's work; also Alan Cox and Harriet Richardson, who read and commented on the text; and Derek Kendall and Helen Jones, who helped with some of the illustrations.

Special thanks are due to Victor Belcher and Isobel Watson of the London Archive Users' Forum, who gave me the opportunity to write the book, and shared their knowledge freely. Isobel also prepared the index.

Contents

Preface

In recent years, public interest in 'house history' has grown tremendously. Although there are many good published guides to the subject, nearly all are national in scope, and offer little of relevance to those researching the history of a typical London house or street. None addresses the special problems or the complex and sometimes unique documents that relate to the study of London's housing – particularly to houses of the 19th and 20th centuries, which are by far the capital's most common types.

This book is intended to fill that gap, to give researchers and home-owners a guide to documentary sources for London's housing, most of them freely available in the capital's own archives and libraries, with advice on their use and interpretation. Though aimed principally at amateur historians, the book hopefully will also be of use to archivists and librarians, and to professional researchers.

In geographical terms, this guide is confined to London and its suburbs, which means, until about 1914, roughly the area covered by the London County Council and the pre-1965 metropolitan boroughs. In recognition of interwar suburbia's growth beyond the limits of this 'County of London', after about 1918 the study area is extended to include most of modern-day Greater London.

In terms of the types of buildings covered, the focus is on the typical or 'ordinary' – that is, the smaller sorts of houses and flats owned or occupied at one time or another by the vast majority of Londoners. I have not attempted to address the capital's great aristocratic town-houses (though, in some cases, many of the sources described here would be applicable); nor have I covered local-authority or 'public' housing, which is already the subject of a LAUF guide by Alan Cox.

The book is divided into three sections. An introduction considers the wider story of London's houses, their evolution, methods of construction, planning, style and appearance; and also addresses the capital's inexorable growth from medieval times to the present day. The second section is a series of individual chapters on the principal documentary sources, explaining the likely contents of each class of record, their usefulness, recommended research techniques, and possible difficulties. Typical examples are given for guidance, and each chapter ends with a list of recommended further reading. At the end are three case histories, each focusing on a different period, intended to demonstrate how material from the various sources can be brought together to construct a detailed history of a typical London house or street.

Since I began writing this book, online cataloguing has gathered pace and evolved at a phenomenal rate. Historical documents and data are now widely accessible to the public via the internet, to a degree that was unthinkable ten, or even five years ago. Such rapid change is likely to continue, and so I have resisted any detailed discussion of internet sources, as this would have become out of date very quickly. With so much information coming to hand, today's researcher needs more than ever a clear idea of how to identify, evaluate and collate the relevant evidence. For London's houses, I hope this book can be a first step along that path.

INTRODUCTION

'Neither a great mansion nor a hovel': a short history of London's housing

The phrase above was used by John Summerson in his *Georgian London* to describe the kind of housing covered by this book — the houses of the mass of ordinary Londoners — which became increasingly common and important from the late 17th century onwards to accommodate the capital's expanding professional classes. This essay aims to outline briefly the different types of 'ordinary' housing which have evolved in London, and to give some idea of how the capital has changed and grown since medieval times. For more detailed information the reader is referred to the bibliography at the end of this section.

MEDIEVAL AND EARLY-MODERN LONDON HOUSES

Medieval London was concentrated on the walled City, with two other principal centres outside the walls: Westminster to the west, and Southwark across the river. There were also settlements at Lambeth, beside the Archbishop of Canterbury's palace, and on the north bank between Westminster and the City, along Fleet Street and the Strand, near the Archbishop of York's palace and the Inns of Court. Beyond were mostly villages and monastic foundations.

In the city centre, high-status houses were generally set back from the noise and clutter of the street, and followed the medieval ecclesiastical tradition of a range of buildings grouped around a courtyard, with a great hall at one end. Today Crosby Hall, rebuilt in Chelsea, is the only surviving example of this type of City mansion. Of the ordinary medieval housing stock, nothing remains above ground. Early views show small houses built closely packed

together in rows, their gable ends fronting the streets *(ill. 1)*. Most were only one or two rooms deep, sometimes with a small yard and kitchen behind, and the pressure on space in the City and its environs gradually forced builders upward rather than outward. Hence the narrow building plots common on main routes, still discernible in places such as Borough High Street *(see ill. 14)*, St John Street in Clerkenwell, and along the Strand.

As a consequence of the 'intimate union of domesticity and labour' in medieval times,[1] many of these smaller houses had a shop or warehouse on the ground floor, with the main living- or eating-room (sometimes referred to as the 'hall') on the floor above, frequently projecting beyond it into the street. Such overhangs or 'jetties' were often repeated on the upper floors, the rooms becoming progressively larger and projecting further into the street towards the top *(ill. 3)*. This style of building greatly reduced the amount of light and air reaching ground level, and was unpopular with the civic authorities. Access to the long, narrow plots was usually at the rear, via alleyways between the blocks of houses.

By the end of the 16th century London's emergence as a major trading capital had brought an expansion of its population and geographical limits. New mansions for the well-connected were carved from the great monastic and religious properties seized at the Dissolution; but for the mass of poorer new incomers, home was to be found in the rows of houses appearing in growing numbers in suburbs beyond the City walls — for example in Shoreditch, Wapping and Whitechapel to the east; around the Strand to the west, *en route* to

1. *An early 'map view': an extract from the 'Copper Plate' map, c.1558, showing development in the Walbrook and Dowgate areas of the City.*

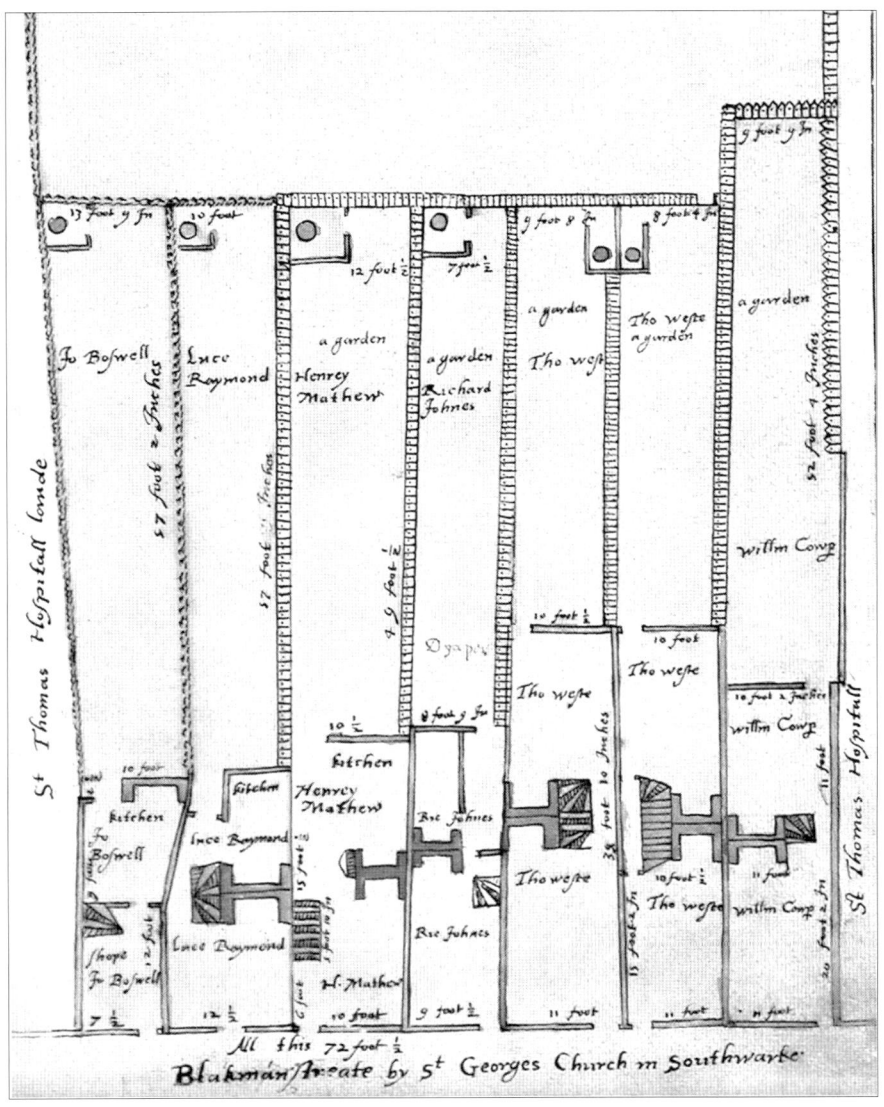

2. Plan of a row of two-room-plan 16th-century houses in Blackman Street, Southwark (later part of Borough High Street), by Ralph Treswell, 1611.

the Court at Westminster; and south of the river in established satellites such as Southwark, Greenwich and Deptford. Although attempts by the Crown to regulate building activity in these areas were by and large ignored, they did increase demand for accommodation in the already crowded city centre, where existing houses were subdivided, gardens and open ground were built over, and buildings began to reach five or six storeys in height.

Surviving documentation reveals a great variety in the size, planning and appearance of early-modern London's housing. Surveys of City buildings undertaken in the early 1600s by Ralph Treswell show houses of one or two rooms on plan, intermingled with larger, often subdivided properties. By this date one particular type of medium-sized house — common in London since the 14th century — was predominant *(ill. 2)*. This had two rooms to a floor and a staircase, with the customary ground-

3. *Early houses: 16th-century buildings in Cheapside, with the train of Marie de Medici (mother of Queen Henrietta Maria).*

4. *Early houses: 16th-century houses on High Holborn, part of Staple Inn, in 1981.*

floor shop and first-floor hall (though by the 1640s the term 'dining-room' was becoming more popular). The kitchen could be situated behind the shop, or, where this space was utilized for warehousing or manufacture, in a rear yard, or upstairs, behind the hall. Other rooms and garrets occupied the floor or floors above. It was this form that was to evolve into the most characteristic of all London buildings, the brick-built terrace-house of the mid-17th century and later.

Until the 17th century London was largely a city of timber. Stone and brick, though essential in modest houses for chimneys and fireplaces, were found in substantial quantities only in churches, public buildings and the mansions of the wealthy. Most houses were composed of a timber frame, filled with lath and plaster, their fronts boarded or plastered, occasionally with decorative pargeting. The Queen's House on Tower Green, of 1540, and Staple Inn, in High Holborn, of the 1580s, though heavily restored, give an impression of the appearance of much of Tudor and Jacobean London *(ill. 4)*. Timber remained a major London building material well after the 17th century, particularly in the outer districts of the

capital — such as Shadwell or Deptford — which remained untouched by influential post-Fire building controls until the 19th century.

Brick houses before c.1670

The devastation wrought by the Great Fire of 1666 has commonly been seen as the single biggest influence on the adoption thereafter of brick as the capital's principal building material. But its use in London houses originated much earlier. Brick was popular as a facing for

5. Typical pre-Fire 17th-century brick house in the City: No. 12 Great St Helen's, Bishopsgate, c.1630, recorded in 1857 (demolished).

6. Nos 52–55 Newington Green in 1993.

aristocratic suburban mansions in the 16th and early 17th centuries: survivals from the period include Sutton House, Hackney (1530s), Eastbury Manor House, Barking (mid- to late-16th century) and Cromwell House, Highgate (1630s). But it was also being used in lower-status housing by the early 1600s, often in conjunction with more traditional materials, such as plaster and weatherboarding, spurred on perhaps by Royal proclamations prescribing brick and stone for new buildings. A study by Roger Leech of the redevelopment of the Bartholomew Fair area, near Smithfield, between *c*.1596 and *c*.1616, revealed about 175 brick houses being erected there as a speculation.[2] Many of these were small houses, with only one room to a floor, built in rows, providing a valuable 'missing link' between medieval building traditions and the 18th-century London terrace-house. And in the parts of the City that escaped the Great Fire, pre-

1660s brick-fronted houses survived and were recorded by topographical artists and antiquarians before being swept away by Victorian improvements *(ill. 5)*.

Brick's increasing popularity among house-builders coincided with the introduction by Inigo Jones and others of classical proportions, styles and motifs from Italy and the Netherlands. Jones had a profound influence on town-planning in London, both as a member of the Commission for Buildings (which sought to encourage a better standard of house construction, in brick and stone), but primarily as the designer of the capital's first fashionable large-scale terrace-house speculative development — the Covent Garden Piazza and surrounding streets, built for the Earl of Bedford in the 1630s. London's first 'town square', the Piazza had two sides lined with terraces of brick-built classical-style houses, raised on open arcades. The façades, designed well in advance of the

7. Aerial view of an early 18th-century estate development: Hanover Square by Sutton Nicholls, 1750.

influential Building Acts of the early 1700s and the dogmatic strictness of Palladianism, do not correspond entirely with our modern perception of a London terrace. Classical motifs, such as decorative pilasters, were combined with elements from medieval and Baroque vernacular architecture, including steeply-pitched roofs, prominent eaves cornices and tall chimney-stacks. High-status houses of a similar style were common in the later 17th century, for example at Lincoln's Inn Fields and Great Queen Street; and, on a more modest scale, hybrid early terrace-houses could be found all across London, mixing the old architectural vocabulary with the new. Survivors of this type are rare: one well-documented example is the row of four 1650s houses at Nos 52–55 Newington Green *(ill. 6)*.

By the 1660s a number of streets and squares of brick-built terraces following Jones's model had appeared on green-field estates to the west of the City, for example in St James's Square, Bloomsbury Square and Leicester Square, presaging the frantic building world of the 18th and 19th centuries.

LONDON AFTER THE FIRE: THE AGE OF THE GEORGIAN HOUSE

The great waves of 18th- and 19th-century house-building, which transformed the intimate London of Pepys's day into the sprawling Metropolis familiar to Charles Dickens and Arnold Bennett, were facilitated by the peculiar system of leasehold land tenure common to the capital. Whether for aristocrats or artisans, inner city or outer suburban, the majority of London's residential streets were developed under this system *(ill. 7)*. Though methods of construction and management varied from estate to estate, even from street to street, in general the typical pattern was similar to that described below.

The leasehold system
A landowner and developer (or 'master builder') would negotiate the lease of a swathe of land for building development. Together they would formulate a contract, or 'articles of agreement', which specified the extent of the ground to be developed; the number, appear-

13

ance and standard of the houses; the date of their completion; the length of the building lease or leases to be granted on completion (usually between 61 and 99 years); and the amount of ground-rent to be paid by the lessee. The most important factor was the retention of the freehold by the landlord, to whom the houses would revert when the leases expired. On the strength of such an agreement the developer could raise capital from investors (sometimes also from the landowner himself) to help finance the laying out of roads or sewers, or for purchasing materials.

Although legally responsible for the entire development, the developer did not always build the houses himself, but would usually sub-let individual house-plots, often in groups of three or four, to smaller builders, who undertook the actual construction. Sometimes the landlord dealt directly with small-scale builders, dispensing with the need for a developer altogether. Usually the smaller builders called upon the aid of other tradesmen and craftsmen, who would barter their services in return for materials or the promise of an interest in some of the plots. Ideally, uniformity of elevation and construction were ensured by careful supervision by the developer and estate surveyor.

Annual ground-rent started at a nominal sum (usually a peppercorn) and rose annually to the full amount after a year or two, allowing the builder to complete his houses and perhaps begin to enjoy some return before having to pay rent. Once houses were completed 'in carcase' (i.e. a brick outer shell with floors and a roof), the promised building leases and sub-leases were issued, enabling mortgages to be raised for further capital, if required. Leases or sub-leases of finished houses were not usually sold to occupiers, but to investors, who in turn rented them out on short-term leases. Thus some four or five interests could be carved out of each property, and even the largest developments on the big estates could involve many builders and men or women of modest capital. Since development in this manner was the privilege of individual landowners, much of London's expansion has been episodic and unplanned.

Each party involved in the system could profit from it, hence its popularity and longevity. A landowner could enhance his ground with houses without a large outlay of capital or the risks involved in developing it himself. He had a secure income from ground-rents, and at the end of the leases the houses would revert to him — or more likely his successors. They could then issue new, short-term repairing leases for the existing houses, or improve their property by clearing the ground and repeating the whole process again with new and up-to-date buildings. The master builder was able to undertake and co-ordinate a large-scale development without the expense of land acquisition, and could enjoy the profits from sub-letting at an increased ground-rent or from selling on his building leases. Smaller builders or sub-lessees were able to participate together in a development which otherwise would have overstretched their individual capabilities, and could look forward to selling their interests to investors or occupiers. And the system of co-operation or barter in operation between the various builders and craftsmen reduced the need for ready cash — frequently scarce at the lower levels of the building industry — to change hands.

However, the system also had its failings. Although it was in the landlord's interest to supervise carefully the construction and management of his estate, where this did not occur the relatively short lease-life of the houses could encourage poor building. Some contractors were eager to complete and dispose of their houses as quickly as possible, thus minimizing expenditure and generating income. Andrew Byrne, in his *London's Georgian Houses*, illustrates an example at No. 32 Albury Street in Deptford, where the facing skin of brickwork was barely attached to the structural bricks behind.[3] Such 'jerry-building' was less frequent on the well-managed hereditary estates, where a secure income through ground-rents depended to an extent on the quality of the fabric, and was more often found when an unscrupulous speculator had acquired freehold land for development.

At greatest risk in the chain of interests were the small-scale builders. The pages of the *London Gazette* in the 18th and 19th centuries frequently listed the bankruptcies of such men.

One way of raising instant capital among needy speculative builders was through the sale of 'improved ground-rents' (i.e. the difference between the rent they paid to the landlord and what they could charge their sub-lessees or tenants); these were often purchased by the landlord himself, eager not to see a builder on his estate in trouble and houses standing incomplete (and unremunerative).

The system persisted into the 20th century, though by the end of the 19th the speculative house-builder was already in retreat in the wake of ambitious private developers with ambition and capital enough to undertake land acquisition, employ direct labour and build and manage estates themselves.

London's Georgian houses

Undoubtedly the greatest impact on London's appearance has been that of the Georgian terrace-house *(ills 8–10)*. A fundamentally simple structure, it offered a degree of flexibility, in terms of form and planning, and profitability to those embarking upon speculative develop-

ment under the leasehold system. Its principles of design and construction were retained and modified by London builders into the 20th century, its appearance updated with the latest brand of architectural ornament. Shorn of its gables, bay windows and coloured tiles, a Victorian or Edwardian London street would differ little from a Georgian terrace.

As we have seen, the idea of a single dwelling with two principal rooms to each floor, which could be repeated in rows, squares or crescents, was not entirely new, but had evolved from the narrow-fronted London townhouse of medieval times, via the classically-inspired, brick-fronted house of the 17th century. The houses could be narrow or wide, tall or short, with staircases placed to one side or centrally, between the rooms; and a small projecting wing (called a closet wing) could be added at the rear. It was largely this adaptability which made the terrace-house ubiquitous, and allowed it to cross the most deeply entrenched of all English divides, that of class: furniture-makers in Shoreditch, watchmakers in Clerkenwell and

8. Typical early 18th-century terrace-houses: Nos 25–33 Great James Street, Holborn, c.1721.

aristocrats in Mayfair and St Marylebone — all lived in terrace-houses.

Post-Fire building legislation ensured that, externally, brick was now the most visible building material, but beneath the outer shell the carcase of the house was still principally of timber. Wood was used everywhere in house construction: in the beams, joists, room-partitions, staircases, sash windows, roof-timbers and internal decoration such as balustrades, panelling, skirting-boards and cornicing. Although the grander type of terrace-house may boast a Portland stone porch, stone, if used at all in lower-class housing, was confined to window dressings, string courses and cornices. Façades wholly or partly of stucco or other composition gained popularity as the Georgian era progressed, but this would have been incised and probably painted to resemble stone, and not the bland wedding-cake icing prevalent today. Roofs were more often of tile than slate, which was more expensive, though this trend changed towards the end of the 18th century, as Welsh slate became more widely available. The other notable external feature was the often decorative wrought or cast iron-work of railings, gates and balconies.

The typical, simple two-room plan was largely dictated by the confines presented by a narrow frontage *(ill. 9)*. All but the poorest terrace-houses had basements, used for storage, or as kitchens and pantries, or, in wealthier areas, as all of these plus rooms for servants. Above ground, room-use was a matter of taste or necessity, but there was usually a pronounced hierarchy. In most smaller houses the two ground-floor rooms would have served as the family's main living-rooms — perhaps a parlour and dining-room — but in trading and manufacturing areas they might be transformed into workshops, counting-houses or offices. On the first floor were sometimes the bedrooms, or, in larger houses (with more storeys), reception or 'withdrawing' rooms, in which case guest and family bedrooms would be placed on the floors above. Even in relatively modest terrace-houses, an attempt would often be made architecturally to emphasise the first-floor front rooms, the equivalent of the *piano nobile* of grander residences. Attic rooms provided extra

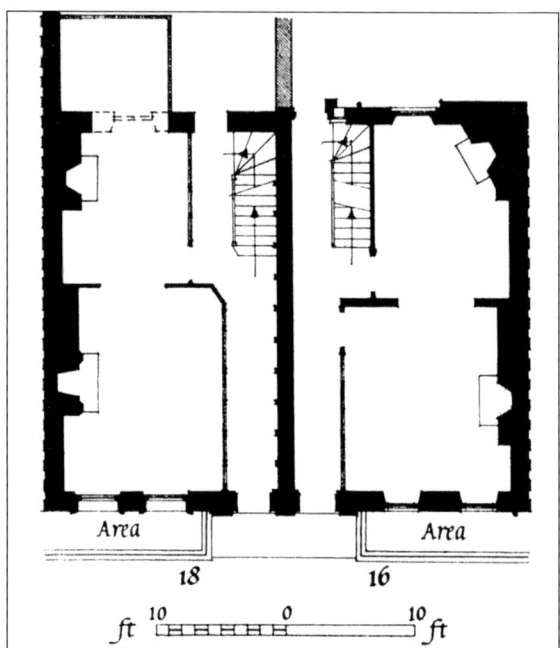

9. Typical early-Georgian house plans: Nos 16 and 18 Fournier Street, 1726.

space for servants, or storage, or served as additional family bedrooms.

Narrow-fronted, and built economically in groups, the terrace-house in appearance comprised one element of a larger whole *(ill. 10)*. The distinctive, regular façades were derived from the type of houses introduced by Inigo Jones at Covent Garden, which were in turn based on Parisian and Italian Renaissance models, most notably the work of Andrea Palladio. Many of the larger terraces had their houses grouped together in a symmetrical palace (or *palazzo*) front, with projecting or pedimented central and end houses. Other influential factors in defining terrace-house style were: the early-18th-century fashion for Palladianism, which coincided with some influential waves of speculative building in central London, and which was disseminated to all levels of the building world in pattern-books of designs and architectural features; and the effect of successive Building Acts of 1667, 1707, 1709, 1724 and 1774, introduced to minimize the risk of fire spreading. For instance, the 1707 Act abolished the prominent wooden eaves cornice popular in the previous century, sub-

10. *Early 18th-century houses: Nos 1–6 Church Row, Wandsworth Plain, c.1723.*

11. *Pre-Building Act late-17th-century houses: Nos 39–43 Old Town, Clapham, c.1690, photographed by Henry Dixon c.1913.*

stituting in its place a parapet of brick *(ill. 11)*; and the 1709 Act demanded that door jambs and window frames be set back in brick reveals, rather than kept flush with the façade. Such stylistic and structural changes, though confined to the inner areas covered by the Acts (i.e. the City, Westminster, St Marylebone, Paddington, Chelsea and St Pancras), were soon being echoed in housing on the fringes, as fashion followed its habitual course, spreading outward from the centre. The early Acts were not rigorously enforced, and to a large extent were more a reflection of contemporary practice than radical reform. But the requirements of the 1774 Act, which divided buildings into different rates or classes dependent on their value and square footage, was more strictly regulated by local teams of district surveyors, a system that persists today.

Two post-Fire building booms, between *c.*1670 and *c.*1690, and from *c.*1710 until the 1730s, saw many open fields of inner London fall to the building speculator. In the first period, most of Holborn was built over, and further west fashionable squares and streets of terraces went up in Soho and St James's. In the second period much of Mayfair was developed, for example Hanover Square, the Savile Row area north of Piccadilly, New Bond Street, Brook Street, Berkeley and Grosvenor Squares; and north of Oxford Street, in St Marylebone, development took place in and around Cavendish Square. Further east, more streets of terrace-houses sprang up in Spitalfields, Shoreditch and Clerkenwell, and similar but free-standing 'rows' of uniform housing also appeared in outlying suburbs, such as Cheyne Row in Chelsea, Church Row in Hampstead, and south of the river at Wandsworth Plain *(ill. 10)* and Clapham Common North Side.

After a lull of nearly thirty years, building took off again in the 1760s on some of the aristocratic west London landholdings: on the Bedford estate in Bloomsbury, and the Portman estate in St Marylebone, for example. These were primarily big houses, aimed at genteel residents. At the same time smaller, middle-class housing began to spread northwards from the older centres of Clerkenwell and Holborn, into Somers Town, Camden Town and parts of Islington. With Napoleon's final defeat in 1815 came peace, relative economic stability, and a London house-building boom lasting some ten years, which saw some large-scale residential developments, such as those by Thomas Cubitt in northern Bloomsbury *(ill. 12)*, Belgravia and Pimlico, and more modest house-building further out.

12. Early 19th-century inner London terrace-houses: Nos 1-6 Gordon Square, Bloomsbury, built c.1820.

The spread of terraces into the suburbs and rural fringes in the late-Georgian period came from the need to house the capital's expanding workforce. From 1700 until 1750 the population remained static at just over 670,000, but by 1831 had more than doubled to over 1,650,000. Landlords of undeveloped land outside the crowded centre saw the chance to enhance their estates with new houses and (hopefully) prosperous tenants. So the same processes and techniques which saw the influential aristocratic estates of central London developed with terraces were repeated in a more modest way on the outskirts, in areas such as Islington, Clerkenwell, Stepney, Kennington or Camberwell. At the same time major transport routes became lined with 'ribbon' developments of houses and shops, for example Camden Road, Liverpool Road, Upper Street and Essex Road in the north, Commercial Road, Mile End Road and Bow Road to the east, and Kennington Road and the Old Kent Road south of the river.

Demographic and socio-economic factors affected the size, status and appearance of each development. During the late 18th and early 19th centuries many wealthy inhabitants moved to new West End estates, close to the Court, and the areas they vacated, such as Holborn, became home to artisans and the lower middle classes. London became in a sense 'ghettoized', with the fashionable parts to the west (Westminster, St James's, Mayfair, Marylebone), formerly fashionable areas further east, towards the City (Bloomsbury, Holborn, Clerkenwell), and the districts connected with industry (and therefore immigration and poverty) confined largely to the south and east (Bermondsey, Rotherhithe, Deptford, Bethnal Green, Wapping, Mile End, Southwark, Lambeth and Poplar). 'Respectable' residential suburbs for the burgeoning middle classes lay further out, or somewhere in-between (for example Hackney, Stepney Green, Clapham or Camberwell).

In terms of house style, by the reign of George III, which began in 1760, the hold of Palladianism on architectural fashion was waning (as was the power of the Whig Oligarchy which favoured it), and a new spirit of political enlightenment in England coincided with the Romantic revolution, and a new interest in the countryside and in archaeology. The result was the introduction of a wider range of architectural styles which, though generally advanced at a higher level, in country houses and public buildings, gradually filtered down to the ordinary house-builders. The revolution in neo-Classical design engineered by Robert Adam, James Wyatt and William Chambers could be seen echoed in doorcases, fanlights and interior décor all over the capital *(ill.13)*. Of even greater influence were the elaborate Regency stucco-fronted houses built by John Nash in Regent's Park and Carlton House Terrace. Nash-inspired Italianate hous-

13. Late-18th-century Adam-influenced neo-classical terrace houses: early 19th-century watercolour of Finsbury Square, west side, built c.1777, designed by George Dance II.

ing dominated the London market for a long time afterwards, and its influence could be seen in the big classical-style Victorian houses erected in the 1850s in Kensington, Knightsbridge and Islington, for example (see *ill. 24*). A neo-Greek idiom also enjoyed popularity in the early 19th century, its simplicity of style making it easily adaptable at the lower end of the social scale, in middle-class houses such as those in and around Sekforde Street, in Clerkenwell, and, more picturesquely, on the nearby Lloyd-Baker estate.

By the end of the 18th century there was a growing desire to bring something of the countryside to urban areas. One seminal scheme was a plan of 1794 to develop the Eyre estate, in St John's Wood, with semi-detached houses. Although not carried out until the 1820s, this was one of the first estate developments to abandon the terrace-house, looking forward to the semi-detached suburbs and villa developments of the later 19th and 20th centuries.

Despite the ubiquity of the two-room plan terrace-house, it would be misleading to think that all of London's Georgian houses were of a similar type or standard. Any attempt to introduce uniformity was undermined by the diversity inherent in a system based frequently on development in small numbers of plots by different builders *(ill.14)*. Late-18th-century houses which were developed piecemeal along

15. *Example of persisting vernacular tradition: back-to-back timber cottages of c.1815 – Ashtree and Rouselle Cottages, Mount Gardens, Sydenham.*

the east side of Kingsland Road, for example, included modest artisans' housing and aspirational suburban residences standing side-by-side.[4] Rows of houses with simple one-room plans were being built in the early 1700s and were still common much later, both in the City and in poorer outer districts to the east and south. In many outer areas older vernacular building traditions persisted hand-in-hand with the latest terrace-housing, even into the 19th century. Timber-framing remained in use, usually covered with plaster, tile-hanging or weatherboarding, providing a picturesque counterpoint to the predominant

14. *Typical high street jumble: Scharf lithograph of Borough High Street, c.1830.*

brickwork (*ill.15*). Although large detached houses were generally the prerogative of the very rich, even in streets and estates of middling pretensions there could be found detached and double-fronted houses, or houses with a double-pile plan rather than the familiar side-passage one.

VICTORIAN AND EDWARDIAN HOUSING: THE 'METROPOLITAN OCTOPUS'

Year by year, almost month by month, the rural scenery of four English shires, Middlesex, Surrey, Kent, and Essex, is swallowed up by the Metropolitan Octopus, the huge congeries of more than half a million closely-built houses, thrusting out of its town buildings, with insidious pretensions to suburban pleasantness, along the main roads of the Home Counties, north and south, east and west, north-west, north-east, south-west and south-east, absorbing the quiet old villages and hamlets, encroaching on their public 'Greens', devouring private parks and gardens, transforming the verdant hills and meadows into hideous brick-fields, and subsequently into a labyrinth of gravelled roads with similar rows of petty villa-dwellings, or streets not much unlike those of any other modern English town.[5]

London's story in the 70-odd years between Victoria's accession to the throne in 1837 and the outbreak of world war in 1914 is one of rapid growth and overwhelming social transformation. A city of 1,650,000 souls in 1831, its population had increased dramatically to a peak of 4,546,000 by 1901. By 1914 London had mushroomed into a conurbation some 18 miles across, extending from Acton to Woolwich, and from Edmonton to Croydon. Victorian and Edwardian London was the world's biggest and most complex human creation.

The reasons for this unprecedented growth are many, but the principal factor was the tremendous expansion of the middle classes. London's place at the heart of Britain's empire generated new jobs in industry, commerce, finance and administration, supported by an ever-growing army of doctors, teachers, engineers, builders and others. These better-paid jobs drew people from abroad and all over Britain, particularly from rural areas, where agricultural production had been depressed by colonial competition. More and more people joined the middle classes, until the term could be used to describe any stratum of society between artisan and aristocrat.

The new middle classes had to be housed, and architecturally the period is characterized by wave after wave of piecemeal, speculative suburban developments, beginning in inner areas, with terraces and villas for the better-off clerical workers, but gradually pushing further outward and embracing lower-paid workers, as public transport improved and became cheaper.

Transport improvements

Most early-Victorian suburbs, such as Brixton or Hackney, were located within two to three miles easy walk for the City clerk. The better-off merchants and bankers — the 'carriage folk' — could travel from further afield in private carriages, as did the artist John Ruskin's father, who journeyed daily from Herne Hill to his office in the City.[6] By the 1830s horse-drawn omnibuses offered a limited service for those who could afford the daily fare; but it was the coming of the railways in the mid-19th century that changed London's social topography, removing the need for the middle classes to live close by their place of work.

In the first railway building boom of the 1830s and '40s new trunk routes reached central London — for example, the London & Birmingham (later the London & North Western) Railway to Euston (opened 1837), and the London & South Western Railway to Nine Elms (1838, extended to Waterloo in 1848). But these were intended principally for freight carriage and long-distance travel, and had few suburban commuter stations. It was the second boom of the 1860s which saw suburban branch and feeder lines added to the main ones, and more and more new routes and termini enveloping the city centre — St Pancras, Victoria, Charing Cross and Cannon Street stations all opened in the 1860s. This momentous decade also witnessed the construction of London's first un-

16. A typical mid-Victorian engineering improvement: Holborn Viaduct, 1869.

derground railway, the Metropolitan, which opened in 1863 from Paddington to Farringdon, but was soon extended and expanded, and by 1884 formed part of an 'Inner Circle' around central London (now the Circle Line).

As a result of these remarkable engineering improvements, much of inner London was for a time in turmoil, a waste land of condemned housing and ugly demolition scars, swarming with labourers and navigators *(ill. 16)*. More buses and better roads were needed to ferry commuters and goods from place to place, and from 1855 the Metropolitan Board of Works, the capital's first London-wide government authority, initiated a host of street improvements to accommodate the increased traffic. Gradually the central area became increasingly depopulated and devoted to commerce and manufacture, as the expanding transport network encouraged the middle-class worker to escape the dirt and grime by travelling to the West End or City from a new home some seven or eight miles further out. Suburban development took off in outer districts that hitherto were little more than villages *(ill. 17)*. Two examples should

17. New housing viewed from Telegraph Hill, near New Cross, c.1893.

suffice. In the south, Penge, a straggling hamlet at the dawn of Victoria's reign, had by 1876 become 'a town in size in population...a waste of modern tenements, mean, monotonous, and wearisome', with churches, schools, offices and shops, and 'whatever may be looked for in a new suburban rly. town'.[7] In the north, Willesden, according to Percy Fitzgerald in 1893, had been a 'genuine rustic village', but 'Word went forth...that there was to be "Willesden Junction", the builders have rushed in, and it has become a sort of town'.[8] In many formerly middle-class districts of inner London, generally the working-class, casual poor and the destitute were all that were left behind. Eventually the better-paid workers were able to join the exodus. In the 1870s cheap horse-drawn trams were introduced, ferrying passengers from the inner suburbs to the outskirts of central London; and by the 1880s cheap workmen's train tickets, provided by companies such as the Great Eastern Railway Company, had become widespread, bringing suburban commuter train travel within the reach of the working man. It was this policy that prompted the building of special working-class suburbs to the north-east of London, along the Great Eastern's route, in places like Stoke Newington, Walthamstow and West Ham.

Social concern

The Victorian age was one of improvement, and this is perhaps truest of all in the realm of public health and sanitation. Public shock at the terrible cholera outbreaks of the 1830s and '40s ushered in a new era of social responsibility and municipal government, made concrete in 1855 with the creation of the Metropolitan Board of Works, a regulatory body empowered to control the capital's sanitation and drainage, road improvements and building regulations.

Investigations into the cholera outbreaks revealed the truly appalling living conditions of the city's working class. Thousands of poor Londoners were crowded into ramshackle,

18. Interior of a slum house in Shoreditch; one room shared by two families, 1919.

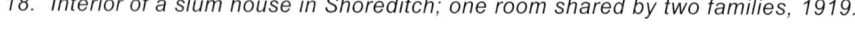

19. Typical turn-of-the-century Clerkenwell slum: Jerusalem Place, photo of June 1899 by H. W. Fincham.

insanitary housing, served by uncovered sewers and putrefying cesspools, with little in the way of fresh water, and incidences of disease and criminality were high *(ills 18, 19)*. Some of the worst ghettos, often viewed as 'no-go' areas by the local police — such as the St Giles' district of the West End and the Saffron Hill area of Holborn and Clerkenwell — were eventually cleared as part of new road and rail improvements, the routes being selected to drive through slum housing.

A fairly typical picture of mid-19th-century working-class living conditions is provided by Wild Court, near Drury Lane. The area — thought to be considerably better than riverside or eastern districts — had 200 families living in 15 old houses there, and an additional nocturnal population of casual poor who slept on the staircases, amounting to a nightly total of about 1,000 people. Open 'troughs of ordure' were found passing through the middle of the upper rooms into a stagnant open sewer in the parapet. When the court was improved in the 1850s, it took 150 truck-loads to remove the contents of 16 cesspools beneath the houses, and another 330 cart-loads for the 'accumulated filth, animal and vegetable' in the basements, including vermin and 'a ton of bugs'. And this in a court 'not half so savage' as what the East End had to offer.[9]

By the 1840s and '50s philanthropic societies such as the Society for Improving the Condition of the Labouring Classes were building blocks of inner-city dwellings for the better-paid or 'deserving' poor. Perhaps best-known in London today are the many estates erected from the 1860s by the Peabody Trust, which used part of a trust fund set up by George Peabody, a wealthy American banker and philanthropist, to provide cheap and clean working-class housing. As an alternative to these rather grim inner-city 'model dwellings', in the 1870s some modest streets of houses were built for artisans on cheaper suburban land at Battersea and Queen's Park by the Artizans & Labourers General Dwellings Company, and occasionally an enlightened employer provided houses for his or her workers — see for example the group of cottages built in 1865 at Holly Village, Highgate, by Baroness

Burdett-Coutts for her servants.

But few if any of the above schemes catered for the poorer sections of the working-class and the casual labourers, who once cleared from their rookeries tended to drift off to already overpopulated slum areas such as the East End. The London County Council built some pioneering housing schemes in the 1890s, such as those at Millbank and Boundary Street, but the over-crowding problem was not tackled adequately until after 1900, when the provision of housing for the poor became principally the responsibility of local authorities.

One effect of this increasing social concern on ordinary private housing was the introduction of more stringent controls on standards of construction, through legislation. The Metropolitan Building Act of 1844 defined the minimum width of new streets, prescribed new rules on drains and cesspools and the size of backyards, and widened the district surveyors' area of jurisdiction as far afield as Tottenham, Poplar, Lewisham and Wandsworth.[10] The 1848 Public Health Act attempted to improve water supply, sewage and general sanitation (for example by suggesting that every new house should have a fixed 'sanitary arrangement' of some kind); and the great Public Health Act of 1875 gave local authorities further powers to control building construction, through 'model bye-laws', and brought together a range of laws relating to drainage, housing, sanitation and disease. As a result of all this legislation, houses became more standardized in construction, and generally more soundly built and salubrious. Each parish vestry or local board of works had its own team of district surveyors to monitor any new building work, and check it conformed to the latest building legislation, and each district had its own medical officer of health.

The Garden City movement

By the early 1900s some new theories on social reform and town planning had been devised to counter the problems associated with urban life. Of these the most radical and influential was the Garden City ideal, expounded in Ebenezer Howard's *Garden Cities of Tomorrow* (1902). In essence, Howard's plan was to build new towns, each of fewer than 30,000 people, separated from London by a green ring or 'belt' of open land. Each 'garden city' would combine industry, housing, shops and other services in a rigorously planned environment, with five-sixths of the area devoted to open space, combining the best of town and country. Houses were to be arranged to allow a maximum of light and air to penetrate, with generous gardens, on irregular or sinuous boulevards, in contrast to the monotonous regularity of inner-city streets. Howard's vision was realized at Letchworth (begun 1903) and Welwyn (1920), both in Hertfordshire. But the movement's influence was also felt in London suburban development, in 'garden suburbs' such as those at Hampstead (begun 1907), Brentham, near Ealing (begun 1901), and Wembley Hill (*c.*1924), all laid out along Garden City lines *(ills 20, 21)*. Howard's ideas were to dominate town planning after the First World War, helping to shape London's interwar suburbia, and his influence was still being felt after the Second, in the post-1945 scheme to re-house Londoners in 'New Towns' beyond a Green Belt.

Principal periods and areas of growth

London's suburban expansion between the 1830s and 1914 can be divided loosely into two periods, before and after *c.*1860, after which the effects of the second great railway boom began to be felt.

Before about 1860 the greatest growth was in the commutable districts some three to four miles from the City. In the north and north-east, Islington's population rose from 10,000 in 1801 to 56,000 by 1841, with rows of terraces and villas appearing in Barnsbury in the 1820s and '30s, followed by bigger Italianate houses in Canonbury Park, Highbury Crescent and Gloucester Crescent by the 1840s. Holloway, too, became a district of semi-detached middle-class villas, best characterized by the aspirational Mr Pooter's home, 'The Laurels'. Similarly, St Pancras grew from 32,000 to 130,000 over the same period. Further east, Hackney, a village in the 1800s, was part of built-up London by the 1850s, with terraces and villas for City workers in Dalston Lane and De Beauvoir Town, for example. And to the north-west, the Finchley Road area, Belsize

Park and Primrose Hill were developed from the 1850s, and villas were also going up in Tufnell Park, St John's Wood and Maida Vale in the 1850s and '60s.

In the west, Hyde Park had for a long time formed the boundary of fashionable London. In the 1830s Georgian-style developments (mostly by George Gutch) covered much of Tyburnia, attracting the better-off commercial classes, followed by similar improvements of the 1840s in Bayswater, and a more moderate class of villa in Paddington, along Westbourne Park and Lancaster Gate, and even as far out as Ealing and Acton. The Great Exhibition of 1851 finally dragged the West End further west, bringing large-scale fashionable housing to Brompton, South Kensington and Knightsbridge.

South of the river, the new bridges of the early 19th century at Vauxhall, Waterloo and Southwark had opened up south London to the City commuter, and well-to-do villa developments sprang up around small existing settlements such as Brixton, Camberwell, Denmark Hill, Herne Hill, Tulse Hill, Champion Hill and Peckham Rye. More middle-class villas could be found to the south-east, in Blackheath and Greenwich.

After about 1860 the suburban railway and tube networks pushed out the boundaries of suburbia, which expanded at a rapid rate alongside the tracks. To the north and north-west, the 1860s and '70s saw growth in Gospel Oak, Kentish Town, Downshire Hill, Chalk Farm, Finsbury Park, Kilburn and Hampstead. Concerted residential development also began in Crouch End, Hornsey, North Harringey and Noel Park, but these were not really built up until after the 1880s. Willesden developed into a reasonably well-to-do suburb between about 1880 and 1900, and at the same time West Hampstead and Kensal Green provided cheaper but still respectable homes for the lower middle classes. In east London, Hackney continued to expand, with more building in Clapton, Dalston and Victoria Park in the 1860s, '70s and '80s *(ill. 22)*.

Most of the suburbs mentioned so far were middle-class in character. Between the 1880s and about 1900 north-eastern districts such as

20. Aerial view of part of Hampstead Garden Suburb, 1950s.

21. Elevations and plans of houses in Erskine Hill, designed by Geoffry Lucas, 1908.

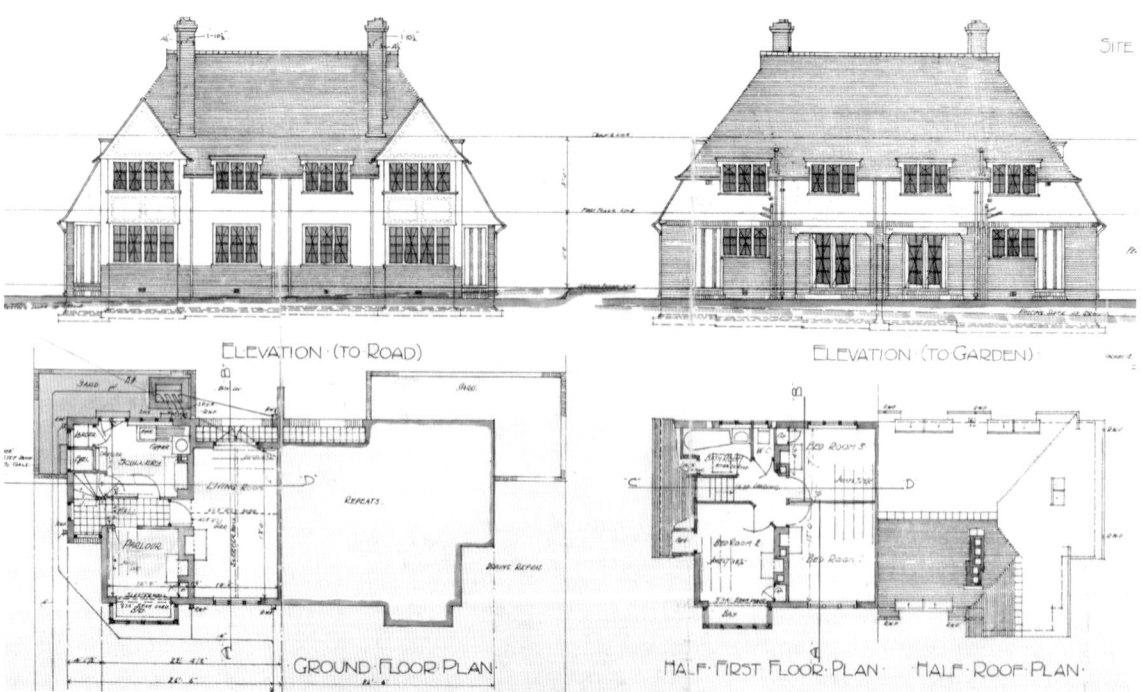

22. Builders taking a break from the final stages of house construction on the north side of Clapton Passage, 1882.

Stamford Hill, Walthamstow, East and West Ham, Edmonton and Ilford grew into substantial working-class suburbs, aided by the introduction of cheap workmen's rail tickets. As for west London, there was more intensive development in established areas like Kensington and Notting Hill; while, beyond, less fashionable districts such as Hammersmith, West Kensington, Shepherd's Bush, Fulham, Acton and Ealing grew considerably from the 1860s onwards.

South of the river, Brixton and Camberwell began to be swamped by speculative terraces. By the 1870s and '80s dramatic change had also taken place in Dulwich, Crystal Palace and Penge — again mostly lower-middle-class developments — and Norwood's once 'oak-clad' hill was now irreversibly 'brick-clad'. To the south-west, Streatham, Tooting, Balham and Battersea became solid areas of urban development, whilst in the south-east districts such as Beckenham and Mottingham also fell to the building speculators.

Between about 1900 and 1914 the built-up area of London almost doubled again, with even more residential suburbs of terraces, semi-

detached or detached houses, spurred on by the continuing expansion of the underground and main-line railway systems. Golders Green, for example, was built up after the Northern Line station opened in 1907, and the population of Hendon grew by 75% between 1909 and 1911. South of the river, the more affluent among the middle classes began to move from Balham and other 'inner' suburbs to new estates in Raynes Park, Merton Park, Sutton and Cheam. Between 1901 and 1911 Merton and Morden witnessed an astonishing 156% growth. However, after 1909 this great peak in house-building began to tail off as war loomed, and by 1914 the country was facing a housing shortage.

Victorian and Edwardian house types
Although Victorian and Edwardian middle-class houses shared much in common structurally with their Georgian predecessors, on the outside they often looked very different. By the 1860s and '70s a wider range of building materials was available than ever before. London, a city built on clay, had always produced its own bricks, and was also a big importer of regionally-made bricks. However, with the

23. Victorian terrace-house monotony: Kensal Rise in 1921.

repeal of the brick tax in 1850, the expansion of the railways, and changing architectural fashions, bricks of all textures and colours could be brought quickly, cheaply and in large numbers to the London market. The same was true of other common building materials, such as glass and timber, and roof slate, and the introduction of mass-produced materials and fittings brought greater standardization in house construction. Another big difference was in street-planning. The sheer volume of cheap housing erected in the late 19th century brought inevitable monotony *(ill. 23)*. In many areas the repetitive grids of identical terraces had little of the elegance of the more humanely-scaled Georgian developments.

In terms of house style, at first there was considerable continuity, with the persistence of the classical tradition in the early Victorian period. It was only after about 1860 that other styles, such as Gothic, Queen Anne, French and Netherlandish, began to appear regularly in London houses, and the cheaper middle-class terraces of the outer suburbs gradually adopted scaled-down versions of the polychrome brickwork, bay windows, pointed Gothic arches and other decorative features of larger properties. The late Victorians' increasing dislike of classical design was apparent in unsympathetic additions and alterations to existing Georgian terraces such as those in Gower Street and Adelphi Terrace (now demolished). In Edwardian times the popularity of English

domestic modes of architecture that had been popular with wealthier patrons — such as the Arts & Crafts and Aesthetic styles — persisted among the middle classes, and were a major influence on the appearance of semi-detached suburbia. Books and journals illustrating and describing the latest types of house and guides for homemakers became more and more widely available.

Although the big contracting firms like those of Thomas Cubitt or James Burton were here to stay, most ordinary house-construction remained in the hands of small-scale speculative builders, who continued to erect houses in relatively small numbers, probably relying on their experience when it came to planning and layout, rather than employing the services of an architect. And most of the houses they built were not owned, but rented by their occupants, usually for short terms of three or five years, as this was still the easiest and most economic form of residence for the middle classes, at a time of unfavourable mortgage rates. Home ownership was not yet a status symbol.

By about 1900 home life for the ordinary Londoner had improved considerably from advances in domestic technology. Pre-payment slot gas-meters brought a new and cheap source of energy to workers who could not afford quarterly bills, and gas soon began to replace coal and paraffin for heating and lighting. By the mid-1920s electricity was becoming standard in new private and local authority housing, and after 1936 all new dwellings, private or public, were required to have a fixed bath in a bathroom.

Terrace-houses
The self-contained terrace-house remained London's principal form of middle- and lower-class private housing in the 19th and early 20th centuries. Most early Victorian terraces followed the established Georgian tradition: two rooms deep, one room wide, flat-fronted and regular in elevation, of brick and stucco, with arched windows, fanlight and a parapet concealing the roof. For the speculative builder, innovation was a financial risk, and, in any case, aspirational middle-class taste yearned for the type of London house associated with its bet-

24. *Victorian Classical terrace-house style: Nos 23–38 Royal Crescent, Kensington, 1842–3.*

ters, i.e. the uniform classical terrace of the great estates, grouped in grids, squares or crescents *(ill. 24)*. In the 1840s and '50s big, richly-decorated stucco terraces went up in Bayswater, Belgravia, Brompton, Kensington and other fashionable west London suburbs, and were soon repeated in a simpler form in the streets of more distant suburbs — in 'Cubitopolis, or Tyburnia; in suburban Islington, or Hackney; in transpontine Camberwell, or distant Greenwich,... the cement-man has given much, and the artist and architect nothing save what has become distorted in transmission', reported *The Builder*.[11]

By the late-Victorian period various developments in planning and construction had changed some aspects of terrace-house design. By then basements, which in many Georgian and early Victorian terraces housed the kitchen (and sometimes the servants' quarters), were becoming less and less common. It became more usual for the kitchen and scullery, and sometimes an outside lavatory, to be placed in a rear wing, or 'back extension', with a coal cellar under the main part of the house. The rear wings gave these later terraces their nickname

of 'back-extension' or 'tunnel-back' houses. At the front of the house, improvements in glass-making brought bigger sash-windows with fewer glazing bars, and from the 1870s the bay window became a common feature, breaking up the monotony of the continuous terrace, and catching the sun *(ill. 25)*.

Standard bay-windowed 'back-addition'

25. *Late-Victorian Gothic terrace-house style: Nos 3–15 Victoria Avenue, Finchley.*

terrace-houses continued to be built by the thousand in London's outer suburbs in the late 1880s and early 1900s, for example in Tottenham, Walthamstow and Neasden. By this date many were being enlivened by wooden porches and balconies, stained-glass window-lights around the front door, tiled forecourts, low brick front walls and iron railings.

Other types of house

'Villas'. The aspiring upper-middle-class professional man often desired something more than a standard terrace-house to express his family's prosperity and position in society. Small detached or semi-detached suburban houses — known as 'villas' — were popular with this class in the Victorian and Edwardian periods, as they had been with their Regency predecessors, offering a diluted version of the aristocratic lifestyle. Housing of this sort was being built in inner middle-class suburbs of the 1840s–60s, such as Westbourne Park, Islington and Putney, and also began to populate the outer suburbs, particularly to the south, in Herne Hill and Lewisham, for example *(ill. 26)*.

Initially the Italianate style of architecture was the most popular for the middle-class villa — a style symbolic of wealth and power, and given royal approval in the 1840s by Queen Victoria and Prince Albert at Osborne House. Often in pale stock brick, with stucco quoins and other decorations, or occasionally of red brick with string courses and dressings in contrasting yellow brick, the Italianate villa is immediately recognizable from its low-pitched roof, overhanging eaves resting on brackets, rounded window-heads, and, in some of the grander examples, an attached tower or campanile à la Osborne. Well-documented examples include those erected in the 1840s and '50s by Samuel Cuming and others on Eton College's Chalcots estate, near Primrose Hill: respectable, semi-detached and reassuringly classical, but otherwise fairly unremarkable.[12]

Pattern books were an invaluable source of inspiration for the early Victorian speculative builder or surveyor at this lower end of the architectural scale: for example, Charles Parker's *Villa Rustica* (1832), Richard Brown's *Domestic Architecture* (1841), and especially the architect

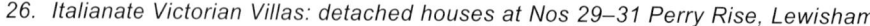

26. Italianate Victorian Villas: detached houses at Nos 29–31 Perry Rise, Lewisham

27. Gothic Victorian Villas: De Beauvoir Square, Hackney.

and landscape gardener J. C. Loudon's *Encyclopaedia of Cottage, Farm and Villa Architecture* (1833). By the 1860s, with the increasing popularity of Gothic, Cottage, and French Second Empire styles in domestic architecture, suburban builders were knocking up villas in any or all of the available styles, sometimes mixing and blending motifs from here and there in a heady, eclectic brew *(ill. 27)*.

By the 1870s, '80s and '90s, the suburban branches of the growing train and tube networks were soon followed by pockets of smaller, lower-class semi-detached villas, which blossomed into new, outer suburbs, in Fulham, Lewisham and Streatham, for example. These houses were mostly in a simplistic English vernacular style of architecture: in red brick and tile, with gables and bay windows, heavily influenced by the recent work of architects like J. J. Stevenson, E. W. Godwin and Norman Shaw in Chelsea, Bedford Park and other upper-middle-class districts.

Maisonettes or 'cottage flats'. Also known as 'half-houses', 'terrace-flats' or 'one-up, one-downs', this was a form of low-rent housing built in large numbers from the 1880s into the early 1900s in working-class or lower-middle-class areas such as Tooting or Walthamstow.

Maisonettes looked very much like standard two-storey terrace-houses from the outside, but were designed to accommodate one family in a self-contained ground-floor apartment, and another on the first floor (see *ill. 98*). Usually separate entrance doors were placed side-by-side within the same porch, sometimes a single front door was shared. Many lower-class terrace-houses were intended for occupation by more than one family, and the development of the maisonette simply reflected this trend.

Flats. In London the first blocks of flats aimed specifically at the middle classes were erected in the 1850s in Victoria Street by a Mr Mackenzie, an Irish developer and self-styled engineer, but to little initial success.[13] Until the 1880s flats of this type were still relatively rare in London, viewed with suspicion by the middle classes and the speculative building profession. Flats were too reminiscent of the 'model dwellings' of the artisan class, and their size and layout was usually unsuitable for the typically large Victorian middle-class family, with its array of live-in domestics. They were also closely associated in the public consciousness with a continental way of life — and with France in particular — and found little favour with some of the more xenophobic elements in middle-class London society. One commentator, comparing the amount of living space required by a Londoner to that of a Parisian, accused the French of using 'very little water, and believing that they can wash themselves with the corner of a wet towel, they do not see the necessity for a bath'.[14]

However, much of the culture of Napoleon III's Second French Empire was absorbed by London's social élite, and with the growing influence of American culture, and the decrease from about 1890 in domestic service — known as the 'servant problem' — central London flats found increasing popularity with the upper classes. Of course it was the luxurious west London apartment blocks which proved most successful, with their high ceilings and generous living spaces, and by 1900 these could be found all over Kensington, Brompton, Knightsbridge and Belgravia. The rural gentry took to them gladly, saving the cost of maintaining an expensive house in town, and they were popular too with retired military men, the young unmarried set, and businessmen. But given the lack of space in the developed inner suburbs for new housing after about 1900, middle-class 'mansion flats' provided an economical alternative to traditional rented housing, and became popular with young professionals and childless couples. Some of these blocks had large suites, servants' quarters, and communal facilities such as a public restaurant. Sandringham Court, in Maida Vale, designed by Boehmer & Gibbs, is a typical example of a block of middle-class Edwardian flats *(ill. 28)*.

However, despite their increasing popularity in central London, by 1911 flats made up only 3% of the total housing stock in England and Wales.

28. A typical middle-class block of flats: Sandringham Court, Maida Vale, by Boehmer & Gibbs, c.1906.

THE MODERN ERA:
LONDON'S HOUSING SINCE 1918

1918 to 1939: London's housing between the Wars

When the First World War began in 1914, London's ordinary housing stock, like that of most English cities, was dominated by small private houses for rent by the better-paid working class and middle class, erected by speculative builders on cheap land and sold in the private property market as an investment. The style and construction of private houses built in the very early years of the 20th century differed little from those built before. The ranks of new terraces on London's fringes — for example in Ilford and Winchmore Hill to the north, Tooting and Streatham to the south — looked much the same as the suburban streets of the 1880s and '90s. But after 1918 the situation changed dramatically. There was an enormous increase in house-building, prompted by the coincidence of various social and economic factors at the end of the war. The chief of these were population growth, a shortage of affordable working-class housing, increasing wealth and aspirations among the middle classes, improved public transport, and government endorsement of the 'garden city' model of residential development. In the public sector, the state-funded 'council' house was finally introduced *en masse*, firstly in cottage estates, later in inner-city blocks, and became a permanent feature of 20th-century English society. In the world of private enterprise, a new kind of middle-class house evolved, which was to dominate the inter-war era. This was the semi-detached suburban villa, built by the thousand in new communities beyond the limits of built-up London. Most of these new suburban houses were rented from developer-landlords, but increasing numbers of the middle-class occupants could afford to buy their own house, usually with the help of a building society mortgage.

The new suburbia: its roots and growth
It was the government's response to the housing shortage of 1914–19 that changed the shape of English housing for the next 30 years.

Wartime rent restrictions discouraged private investment in lower-class rented-house construction, making state intervention inevitable. Between 1919 and 1925 government subsidies enabled local authorities to build this sort of housing in large numbers, without fear of financial ruin (about 200,000 council houses were built in the five years after the war).

Much of the private building trade turned its attention to the newly affluent and growing middle classes, the white-collar workers — civil servants, managers, technicians, doctors, lawyers — many of whom now earned enough money to be able to buy their own property. This social transformation is clear in the statistics: the number of private houses built in Greater London leapt from 4,860 in 1922, to 72,756 in 1934.[15]

The inter-war suburbia of semi-detached houses with front and back gardens, arranged along winding roads, was not entirely new in concept. It followed on from the Garden City movement of the pre-war era, offering an escape from the overcrowded industrial centre and a new life close to the countryside. This was made possible by improvements in transport. Railway and tube lines were extended into the surrounding countryside, allowing workers to commute from ever further afield; and new roads and arteries — such as the Western Avenue, Great West Road and the Kingston By-pass — spawned new ribbons of building development, both industrial and residential *(ill. 29)*.

29. *Suburbia: aerial view of the Tolworth Rise section of the Kingston By-pass, late 1930s.*

This rapid outer growth changed entirely the shape and size of the capital. Late-Victorian suburban expansion had reached Tottenham and Hornsey to the north, Balham and Streatham to the south, East Ham and Stoke Newington to the east, and Ealing and Acton to the west, making London the largest developed area in the world. But between the wars the outer boundaries of built-up London were pushed further out, engulfing many once outlying villages of rural Essex, Middlesex, Kent and Surrey. In the south, there was enormous growth in places such as Bexley, Beckenham, Bromley and Sidcup in Kent, and Merton, Croydon and Surbiton in Surrey. But it was to the north of London that the transformation was most dramatic. New underground and electric trains now transported London's workers to and from neighbouring parts of Essex — in particular Barking, Billericay, Dagenham, Ilford and Romford. And in Middlesex, where the Metropolitan Company built its own housing estates along its extended underground railway network, the entire county mutated into one vast residential and industrial zone, with a population of over 2 million. By 1939 nearly all of the Middlesex countryside had disappeared beneath a sea of concrete and tarmacadam. Names once associated with rural peace — Enfield, Edmonton, Hayes, Harlington, Uxbridge, Harrow, Ruislip and Northwood — became forever synonymous with the suburban way of life.

At the time, this unplanned, sprawling growth seemed unstoppable. Attempts were made to check it, most notably by Herbert Morrison and the London County Council in the 1930s, when they offered to assist local boroughs in acquiring open land for a protective 'girdle' around the built-up area. But this inviolable 'Green Belt' was not firmly established until 1947. Instead, it was the outbreak of war in 1939 which finally brought to an end the march of semi-detached houses across the countryside. In the financial uncertainty of a world war, building societies withdrew their loans, prospective purchasers withdrew their offers, and builders were forced to close down. This sudden halt is still evident today in parts of outer London, for example at Hayes (near West Wickham) and at Mill Hill and Edgware, where the rows of houses stop suddenly and fields begin, as if the builders had downed tools for a break in 1939 and never came back.

The builders of suburbia

At the beginning of the inter-war era, the building industry had changed little from pre-war years: traditional materials and methods of construction persisted, as did the predominance of small firms and individuals. But the boom of the late 1920s and early '30s saw the emergence of bigger firms of builder-developers, who became involved in the entire business of suburban estate development, from buying sites and laying out roads, to marketing and selling the finished houses. Their ability to purchase land and materials in bulk, and to borrow money cheaply, enabled them to dominate the residential market, and many of the larger, successful inter-war firms are still with us today (for example Costain, Laings, Wates and Wimpey). A few of these big concerns had the manpower and business capacity to operate all over London, but generally the suburban house-builder limited himself to a local sphere of influence: Leo Meyers' New Ideal Homesteads built heavily in Bexley and Sidcup; Wates, a Streatham firm, were big builders in south London; and there was a host of others — Haymills in Hendon, D. C. Bowyer in Bexley, T. F. Nash in Harrow and Rayners Lane, to name but a few. Many used the latest sales techniques, placing advertisements in the press, in mass newspapers like the *Evening News* and *Evening Standard* (which regularly carried homebuyers' guides), as well as in new specialist publications such as *New House*, *National Builder* and *Metroland (*see *ill. 32).* Buyers were also tempted by full-scale show houses at the annual Ideal Home Exhibition at Olympia, which first opened in 1908. Laings even went so far as to build a show house outside King's Cross railway station, to entice commuters.[16] On new and partially-completed estates, cars were on hand to ferry prospective purchasers from the train stations to the site offices. Some firms, like Wates, also opened offices in run-down inner areas. Other inducements included free season tickets (for an initial period); hire-purchase agreements (enabling buyers to acquire a house for a relatively small deposit and weekly repayments); and some builders even offered to lend deposits to poorer households, encouraging them to move from the rental market. By the mid-1930s a three-bedroom suburban house outside London could be purchased for about £500, or repayments of around 13s a week — within the reach of the 'normal' workers weekly wage of £3 15s.[17]

The inter-war suburban house: its style and construction

The speculative builders and architects who created the new suburbia knew well their customers' tastes and aspirations. Architecturally conservative and suspicious of continental 'modern' styles, the English middle-class house-buyer of the 1920s and '30s had a strong idea of what a house should look like. So a traditional English domestic idiom prevailed. Builders raided the vocabulary of an earlier generation of vernacular architects — Norman Shaw, Voysey, Lutyens — and applied cut-price versions in a mix of red brick, pebble-dash, hung-tiling, half-timbering, leaded panes and roof tiles to their new semi-detached houses *(ills 30, 31)*. There was great variety in exterior styling — Jacobethan, Queen Anne, Arts-and-

31. Advert for Haymills' 'Beautiful Barn Hill'.

30. Suburban houses: J. Scheerboom photo of a suburban street scene in Lakenheath, Oakwood, in Enfield.

"COSTIN' HOUSES
AT KENTON –
BUILT TO LAST!
27 Years Recommendations

ENTIRELY NEW FEATURES

★ No road charges

★ No law charges

★ No stamp duties

★ Electric – Light fittings included

★ Small deposits by arrangement

★ Both new Estates

WOODCOCK DELL
£865 ~
£1200
FREEHOLD

LYON FARM
£1050 ~
£2500
FREEHOLD

SEND FOR ILLUSTRATED BOOKLET NOW –

F.&C.COSTIN LTD.
Dept. A.I. Kenton Rd., Harrow.

32. Advert for Costin houses in Kenton, typical of 'Metroland'.

Crafts, and of course the much-derided Olde English 'stockbroker Tudor', with its mock timbering. In each case the intention was the same: to lend an air of picturesque individuality to housing which was otherwise regular and monotonous, and to evoke a 'cottagey' atmosphere of rural tranquillity to contrast with the densely built-up inner-city streets that most of the new suburbanites were leaving behind. Suburban architectural style, though derided by the architectural establishment, helped the expanding middle class to express its identity and individuality. Unsurprisingly, the two styles favoured by the establishment — Neo-Georgian and functional modernism — were rarely found in suburbia: the first smacked too

much of the council estate, the latter was too highbrow and un-English.

In terms of their planning, the thousands of suburban semi-detached houses offered variations of a standard arrangement of entrance hall, living-room, separate dining-room or parlour and kitchen on the ground floor, and two or three bedrooms and a bathroom upstairs. It is easy now to underestimate the impact that brand-new housing of this type, with separate bedrooms, kitchens and bathrooms, would have had on families reared in the crowded streets of central London. The popularity of the 'semi' with builder and buyer alike came largely from its dual nature. Part detached house, it had a modicum of the privacy and kudos associated with that form; part terrace, it also offered some of the old spirit of neighbourliness and community. Perhaps most importantly of all, it stood in a relatively generous, open site, with front and back gardens — a new experience for former inner-city dwellers, used to grim back 'yards' — yet it still offered the builder a degree of economy, with a shared party wall and standard fixtures and fittings.

There were, of course, variants to the semi-detached orthodoxy. On some estates a few detached houses were provided for better-off residents — well-paid professionals, such as doctors, for instance — and occasionally houses were built in groups of four or six — like short terraces — for those who wished to economize, or were less concerned with privacy. Externally, these looked like larger or smaller versions of their semi-detached neighbours, and were clothed in the same architectural styles. During the inter-war period bungalows also enjoyed something of a vogue, particularly with retired couples or others who found their arrangement (and lack of stairs) convenient. 'chalet-style' houses — basically bungalows with extra bedrooms in the roof-space — offered a compromise for those who needed more room or disliked sleeping at ground level.

Inter-war flats
For those who did not wish to live in a suburban house on a tree-lined street, blocks of private service flats offered a modern and styl-

33. Interwar flats: Haymills Flats, Hanger Lane, 1933.

ish alternative *(ill. 33)*. The inter-war period witnessed a boom in private flat-building, particularly in the 1930s, by which time the building economy had recovered from its post-war slump and investment in rental property had again become viable. Flats suited the modern way of life. Smaller family units required fewer rooms than their Victorian and Edwardian forebears, particularly given the decline in domestic service; and for the new army of single professionals, businessmen and childless professional couples, apartment blocks offered a convenient form of commuter life, without having to conform to the suburban norm. 'Convenience' above all describes the essence of inter-war flat-living. The flats were often located on main roads (see for example the number of apartment blocks lining Finchley Road, Edgware Road or Streatham Hill), and were usually close to train or tube stations, or above a parade of shops. At the upper end of the market, high-class West End flats were advertised with the latest labour-saving gadgets and luxury devices, such as facilities for television reception, or air-conditioning.

Stylistically, the 1930s flats expressed a different approach to life from the suburban housing estates. Even the standard, low-cost 1930s blocks, found all over the capital, usually gave off a whiff of the Jazz Age, with flat roofs, metal windows, and the odd piece of Deco decoration. But it was the more expensive, luxury apartment blocks that provided progressive architects with a suitable vehicle for modern design, sometimes with exceptional results (as at Highpoint I and II in Highgate, of 1936–8, by Berthold Lubetkin). Many of these blocks were built and managed by big property companies, not the firms of local builders engaged in suburban house-building.

The outbreak of the war in 1939 brought the rented flat-building boom to an abrupt halt; like the suburban housing market, it never recovered.

Since 1945
In terms of house-building and town planning, the aftermath of the Second World War witnessed a transformation even more radical than that which followed the First World War, and very different in form.

Post-war planning for London

During and after the Second World War, extensive bomb damage and demolition provided London's planners with an unmissable opportunity to impose their town-planning theories on a largely unwilling public. Under Sir Patrick Abercrombie, a committee of London County Council and Home Counties representatives was formed to consider London's future, and produced a series of plans which were to form the basis of an official County of London Plan in 1951.

Some 20 years before the creation of the Greater London Council, the post-war planners understood the need to plan for a capital which had extended far beyond the London County Council's boundaries. Firstly, new planning controls were introduced to prevent any further spread of London's enveloping suburbia, creating the protective Green Belt of countryside around the metropolis (as suggested in the 1930s), which to a large extent still exists today. New housing was to be erected in the existing built-up area, on bomb-damaged, slum-clearance or infill sites, in densities which were to increase towards the centre. Any surplus or 'overspill' population was to be housed in a number of 'New Towns' situated well beyond the Green Belt. A notoriously organic, unplanned city before the war, London became a much more rigorously planned one afterwards, as the authorities struggled to cope with the chronic housing shortage against a backdrop of increasing social change and diversity, decline in manufacture and heavy industry, and a rise in car-ownership.

The dire need for new homes in London after the war dictated that most of the post-war schemes were for public housing, carried out by the LCC or the metropolitan borough authorities (or a combination of the two), and so by and large do not concern us here. The greatest transformation took place in the City, and in the poorer districts to the south and east, where bomb damage had been most intensive. Mass housing became an important arena for architectural and social experimentation, and over the next 20 to 30 years large new housing estates of concrete and glass sprouted all over these parts of London, in many cases obliterating the old street patterns.

34. *Houses by SPAN at Corner Green in Blackheath, in 2005.*

In the world of private enterprise, there was little speculative building immediately after the war. With money and materials in short supply, until 1954 government licences were required to build private housing. The few private schemes that were built were usually planned in small groups, and were noted at the time for their functionalism and plainness of appearance in comparison to earlier developments, though this was often a consequence of post-war economic stringency as much as an expression of modern design principles. Some of the most highly regarded are the SPAN estates of the late 1950s and '60s, designed by Eric Lyons (for example Parkleys in Richmond, and Corner Green in Blackheath). Although modern in terms of their architectural design, the SPAN estates were friendlier in scale and form than the great council estates, with houses and flats set in small groups around courtyards and green spaces *(ill. 34)*.

New materials and techniques

The severity of the 1940s housing crisis encouraged experimentation with new building materials and production-line manufacturing techniques. In 1944, before the end of the War, the Ministry of Works built a small experimental housing estate in Northolt, to demonstrate to local authorities the possibilities of building standard types of houses in steel or concrete.[18] In the four years after the War, over 150,000 two-bedroom prefabricated temporary bungalows (or 'prefabs') were provided under a government Temporary Housing Programme.

These were specially designed with little or no brick and timber, using instead materials such as steel, asbestos cement and reinforced concrete, and some previously unknown to house-building, such as aluminium.

Prefabs apart, the use of modern materials like steel, concrete and glass was often viewed by the general public as better suited to large, public structures — such as hospitals or schools — than to the more intimate domestic spaces of the average family home. Traditional brick-built houses remained popular with builders and the public, and updated versions of them were a major part of some of the New Towns built outside London, and of the housing designed to coincide with the 1951 Festival of Britain, such as the Lansbury Estate in Poplar.

Even where traditional methods were employed, standardization and mass-production gave post-war houses a different character from their pre-war predecessors. Interior walls were generally of concrete blocks, not lath and plaster or timber partition. Timbers where used were much thinner than before, and joined with connectors rather than complex carpentry joints. Windows had fewer glazing bars, and bigger panes of glass.

The rise and fall of high-rise

A central element in residential planning of the post-war era was the multi-storey, or high-rise tower-block. The peak period of high-rise building was the 1960s, when some 600 blocks were erected in Greater London. To the planners, high-rise towers suited the needs of the time. Their introduction coincided with government calls for economy in new developments and the use of industrial building techniques, which led to larger estates and taller, thicker tower blocks. They also suited the stylistic movement known as 'New Brutalism', an austerely modern alternative to the more vernacular-derived 'New Humanism' of the 1950s. By the 1960s the GLC and the local borough authorities were building huge concrete and glass blocks of flats — see for instance the Warwick estate in Paddington, and the Pepys estate in Deptford (with towers 24 storeys high). But such enormous structures showed little respect for and eroded the traditional character of their surrounding area, and were generally indistinguishable from those elsewhere in Britain or on the continent. Most importantly of all, they were unpopular with the people who had to live in them, particularly families with young children, and became associated with many developing modern urban problems such as vandalism and juvenile street crime. The dramatic collapse of Ronan Point in 1968 brought public dislike of tower blocks to a head, and ushered in a new era of low-rise building.

Recent trends

By the early 1960s the policies of previous decades were being seen as mistakes. To some architects and planners the Garden City ideal of life outside the city centre was unnatural: 'young housewives...missed the warm human comfort that comes with crowded streets'.[19] The recent New Towns were thought to breed similar problems, termed 'New Town loneliness', and suffered from an unnatural segregation, being populated almost entirely by the skilled working class. High-rise tower blocks had not provided an answer, either.

This change of heart coincided in the 1970s with a growing conservationist movement, which argued convincingly for the retention and modernization of the capital's existing Georgian and Victorian housing stock as a viable alternative to wholesale redevelopment. As a result, some historic districts, such as Spitalfields and Covent Garden, were saved from the developers. Also, certain inner suburban areas that had deteriorated since the war — for example Islington and Camden in the north, Battersea and Clapham in the south — underwent 'gentrification', as their old houses were snapped up and refurbished by a younger generation of London workers for whom life in outer suburbia was an unattractive prospect.

This increasing popularity of traditional forms of housing was reflected in new 'mixed-use' developments. In these a more flexible assemblage of tall towers and lower blocks of flats were combined with low-rise housing (often of traditional materials, such as brick and slate), or occasionally with upgraded old terraces, all intended to support an 'integrated' community, preferably with schools and other services

35. *The rear of 14 South Hill Park Gardens, Hampstead, one of a semi-detached pair, replacing bomb-damaged Victorian houses, built in 1951 to different designs. They were themselves replaced c.2000 to a design based closely on the 19th-century elevations. Photograph by the architect Colin Penn.*

36 *Post-war town houses at Church Road, Upper Norwood, constructed by Taylor Woodrow.*

37. Design for houses at Malmesbury Road, Morden for KingsOak Homes, 2005.

near by. Although of concrete, the west side of Brunswick Square, in Holborn, built in 1968–72, is a characteristic and well-known example of this functionally-integrated, low-rise approach to urban living; originally intended for private residents, it was completed by Camden Borough for council tenants.

The oil crisis, economic depression and rising unemployment of the late 1970s and early '80s coincided with a decline in the provision of public housing. The Thatcher government's dislike of planning and social reform was made evident in its abolition of the GLC and in its experiment in market-led regeneration in London's Docklands. The gleaming towers of the Docklands Enterprise Zone's office blocks and prestige apartments stand shoulder to shoulder with some of the capital's most impoverished public housing estates, and today the area bears testament to one of central London's most serious social problems: the polarization of its population into two camps — affluent home-owners and a deprived and poorly-integrated underclass. Of the respectable middle-class and industrious working-class people who traditionally fed the capital's prosperity, many have moved further afield, squeezed out by escalating house-prices and

fear. But one aspect of Docklands' success was as an example of how decayed inner areas could be resurrected by mixing new development with the residential conversion of outdated industrial or commercial buildings, a process which has since been repeated on the fringes of the City, in Shoreditch and Clerkenwell, for instance. Once renowned for their furniture, jewellery and clock-makers' warehouses, these areas are now centres of Manhattan-style 'City Living' — the spiritual homes of the 'loft apartment' — though to what degree this meets Londoners' housing needs is a matter of conjecture.

Today, while urban regeneration in the form of commercial and residential conversion and development takes place in certain inner districts, as their popularity with developers and investors waxes, outer London is still the domain of the private building contractor and speculator. Sizeable estates of new-build houses and apartments by firms such as George Wimpey, Laing, Fairview and Barratt Homes appear with regularity on disused or cleared sites in areas like Brentford, Morden, Kidbrooke and Silvertown; these are the present-day equivalents of the suburban housing estates of the 1920s and '30s *(ill. 37)*.

NOTES AND REFERENCES

1. Lewis Mumford, *The City in History*, 1961, p. 324.

2. Roger H. Leech, 'The Prospect from Rugman's Row: The Row House in Late Sixteenth- and Early Seventeenth-Century London', in *Archaeological Journal*, vol. 153, 1996, pp. 201–42.

3. Andrew Byrne, *London's Georgian Houses*, 1986, p. 124.

4. See Peter Guillery, 'Waste and Place: Late-18th-century development on Kingsland Road', in *Hackney History*, vol. 6, 2000, pp. 19–38.

5. *Illustrated London News*, 23 Aug 1884, p. 187.

6. *Survey of London*, vol. xxv, 1956, pp. 10–11.

7. James Thorne, *Handbook to the Environs of London*, 1876, vol. 2, p. 467.

8. Percy Fitzgerald, *London City Suburbs As They Are To-Day*, 1893, p. 125.

9. *Household Words*, 16 Dec 1854, pp. 409–13; 25 Aug 1855, pp. 85–7.

10. For a detailed summary of the 1844 Act and a list of the parishes under its jurisdiction, see C. C. Knowles and P. H. Pitt, *The history of building regulation in London: 1189–1972*, 1972, pp. 60–4.

11. *The Builder*, 18 Sept 1858, p. 630.

12. For the development of this estate, see Donald J. Olsen, 'House upon House: Estate development in London and Sheffield', in H. J. Dyos and Michael Wolff (eds), *The Victorian City: Images and Realities*, vol. 1, 1973, pp. 333–57; and also John Summerson, 'An Early Victorian Suburb', in *London Topographical Record*, vol. 27, 1995, pp. 1–48.

13. *The Builder*, 26 Nov 1853, pp. 721–2: information kindly provided by Isobel Watson.

14. *The Builder*, 13 Jan 1872, p. 23.

15. *Little Palaces: The suburban House in North London 1919–1939*, 1987, p. 12: Anthony Quiney, *House and Home. A History of the Small English House*, 1986, p. 149.

16. Miles Horsey, 'London Speculative Housebuilding of the 1930s: Official Control and Popular Taste', in *London Journal*, vol. 11, no. 2, 1985, p. 156.

17. Alan A. Jackson, *Semi-Detached London*, 1991 edn, pp. 152–3.

18. *Country Life*, 13 Oct 1944, pp. 634–6.

19. Alice Hope, *Town Houses*, 1963, p. 9.

BIBLIOGRAPHY

General Works

Peter Ackroyd, *London. The Biography* (Chatto & Windus), 2000

Felix Barker and Peter Jackson, *London: 2,000 Years of a City and its People* (Macmillan), 1974

Christopher Hibbert, *London: The Biography of a City* (Penguin edn), 1980

Hermione Hobhouse and Ann Saunders (eds), *Good and Proper Materials. The Fabric of London since the Great Fire* (RCHME / London Topographical Society), 1989

Simon Jenkins, *Landlords to London: The Story of a Capital and its Growth* (Constable), 1975

C. C. Knowles and P. H. Pitt, *The history of building regulation in London: 1189-1972* (Architectural Press), 1972

Anthony Quiney, *House and Home: A History of the Small English House* (BBC), 1986

Nikolaus Pevsner, Bridget Cherry and Simon Bradley, *The Buildings of England* (Penguin/Yale), London volumes

Roy Porter, *London: A Social History* (Hamish Hamilton), 1994

S. E. Rasmussen, *London: The Unique City* (Jonathan Cape), 1937 (revised edns, 1948 & 1982)

A. Saint and G. Darley, *The Chronicles of London* (Weidenfeld & Nicolson), 1994

Ann Saunders, *The Art and Architecture of London. An Illustrated Guide* (Phaidon), 1984

Francis Sheppard, *London: A History* (Oxford University Press), 1998

Survey of London, 45 volumes, 1900–2000

Victoria County History

Ben Weinreb and Christopher Hibbert (eds), *The London Encyclopaedia* (Macmillan), 1983 (revised edns 1987 & 1993)

Ken Young and Patricia Garside, *Metropolitan London: Politics and Urban Change 1837–1981* (Edward Arnold), 1982

Medieval and Early-Modern Periods

Caroline M. Barron, 'Twenty Years of London History 1975–1995: London in the Later Middle Ages 1300–1550', in *London Journal*, vol. 20, no. 2, 1995, pp. 22–33

A. L. Beier and R. Finlay (eds), *The Making of the Metropolis, London 1500–1700* (Longman), 1986

Norman G. Brett-James, *The Growth of Stuart London* (Allen & Unwin), 1935

Paul Griffiths and Mark S. R. Jenner (eds), *Londonopolis. Essays in the cultural and social history of early modern London* (Manchester University Press), 2000

Vanessa Harding, 'Reconstructing London before the Great Fire', *London Topographical Record*, no. 25, 1985, pp. 1–12

Vanessa Harding, 'Twenty Years of London History 1975–1995: Early Modern London 1550–1700', in *London Journal*, vol. 20, no. 2, 1995, pp. 34–45

Derek Keene, 'A new study of London before the Great Fire', in *Urban History Yearbook 1984* (Leicester University Press), 1984, pp. 11–21

Derek Keene, *Cheapside before the Great Fire* (Economic and Social Research Council), 1985

Derek Keene and Vanessa Harding, *A Survey of Documentary Sources for Property Holding in London Before the Great Fire* (London Record Society Publications vol. xxii), 1985

Derek Keene, 'Twenty Years of London History 1975–1995: London in the Early Middle Ages 600–1300', in *London Journal*, vol. 20, no. 2, 1995, pp. 9–21

Frank Kelsall, 'The London House Plan in the Later 17th Century', in *Post-Medieval Archaeology*, vol. 8, 1974, pp. 80–91

Roger H. Leech, 'The Prospect from Rugman's Row:

The Row House in Late Sixteenth- and Early Seventeenth-Century London', in *Archaeological Journal*, vol. 153, 1996, pp. 201–42

E. McKellar, *The birth of modern London: the development and design of the city 1660–1720* (Manchester University Press), 1999

J. F. Merritt (ed.), *Imagining Early Modern London* (Cambridge University Press), 2001

Stephen Porter, *The Great Fire of London* (Sutton), 1996

T. F. Reddaway, *The Rebuilding of London After the Great Fire* (Jonathan Cape), 1940

L. F. Salzman, *Building in England down to 1540: a documentary history*, 1952 (Kraus Reprint edn, 1979)

John Schofield, *The Building of London from the Conquest to the Great Fire* (British Museum Press), 1984 (revised edn, 1993)

John Schofield, *The London Surveys of Ralph Treswell* (LTS Publication No. 135), 1987

John Schofield, *Medieval London Houses* (Yale University Press), 1995

Lawrence Stone, 'The Residential Development of the West End of London in the Seventeenth Century', in Barbara C. Malament (ed.), *After the Reformation* (Manchester University Press), 1980, pp. 167–212

Georgian Period

J. Ayres, *Building the Georgian City* (Yale/Paul Mellon), 1997

Neil Burton (ed.), *Georgian Vernacular* (Georgian Group, symposium papers), 1996

Andrew Byrne, *London's Georgian Houses* (Georgian Press), 1986

Dan Cruikshank and Neil Burton, *Life in the Georgian City* (Viking), 1990

Dan Cruikshank and Peter Wyld, *London: The Art of Georgian Building* (Architectural Press), 1975

Celina Fox (ed.), *London – World City* (Yale / Museum of London), 1992

Dorothy M. George, *London Life in the Eighteenth Century* (Penguin edn), 1966

Peter Guillery, 'Waste and Place: Late-18th-century development on Kingsland Road', in *Hackney History*, vol. 6, 2000, pp. 19–38

Peter Guillery, *The Small House in Eighteenth-Century London* (Yale University Press / English Heritage), 2004

Donald J. Olsen, *Town Planning in London, the eighteenth and nineteenth centuries* (Yale University Press), 1964 (revised edn, 1982)

Hugh Phillips, *Mid-Georgian London* (Collins), 1964

Stanley C. Ramsay and J. D. M. Harvey, *Small Georgian Houses and their Details, 1750–1820* (Architectural Press), 1972

George Rudé, *Hanoverian London, 1714–1808* (Secker & Warburg), 1971

Leonard Schwarz, 'Twenty Years of London History 1975–1995: London, 1700–1850', in *London Journal*, vol. 20, no. 2, 1995, pp. 46–55

John Summerson, *Georgian London* (Pleiades Books),

1945 (and various revised edns; most recently edited by H. M. Colvin, published by Yale University Press, 2003)

Victorian and Edwardian Period

T. C. Barker and Michael Robbins, *A History of London Transport* (George Allen & Unwin), vol. 1 (1963), vol. 2 (1974)

Helena Barrett and John Phillips, *Suburban Style. The British Home, 1840–1960* (Macdonald & Co), 1987

Charles Booth (ed.), *Life and Labour of the People in London* (Macmillan, 17 vols), 1892–1903

Kellow Chesney, *The Victorian Underworld* (Pelican edn), 1972

W. S. Clarke, *The Suburban Homes of London* (Chatto & Windus), 1881

M. J. Daunton, *House and Home in the Victorian City. Working-Class Housing 1850–1914* (Edward Arnold), 1983

John Davis, 'Twenty Years of London History 1975–1995: Modern London 1850–1939', in *London Journal*, vol. 20, no. 2, 1995, pp. 56–90

Roger Dixon and Stefan Muthesius, *Victorian Architecture* (Thames & Hudson), 1978

H. J. Dyos, *Victorian Suburb. A Study of the growth of Camberwell* (Leicester University Press), 1961

H. J. Dyos, 'The Slums of Victorian London', in *Victorian Studies*, vol. XI, no. 1, Sept 1967, pp. 5–40

H. J. Dyos, 'The Speculative Builders and Developers of Victorian London', in *Victorian Studies*, vol. XI, Supplement, Summer 1968, pp. 641–90

H. J. Dyos and Michael Wolff (eds), *The Victorian City. Images and Realities* (Routledge & Kegan Paul), 2 vols, 1973

Arthur M. Edwards, *The Design of Suburbia* (Pembridge Press), 1981

Percy Fitzgerald, *London City Suburbs As They Are To-Day* (Leadenhall Press), 1893

S. Martin Gaskell, 'Housing and the Lower Middle Class, 1870–1914', in Geoffrey Crossick (ed.), *The Lower Middle Class in Britain 1870–1914* (Croom Helm), 1977, pp. 159–83.

Mark Girouard, *Sweetness and Light, the Queen Anne Movement 1860–1910* (Clarendon Press), 1977

P. G. Hall, *The Industries of London since 1861* (Hutchinson & Co), 1962

Peter Hall, 'Industrial London: A General View', in J. T. Coppock and Hugh C. Prince (eds), *Greater London* (Faber & Faber), 1964, pp. 225–45

Henry-Russell Hitchcock, *Early Victorian Architecture in Britain* (Da Capo Press), 2 vols, 1972

Hilary Hockman, *Edwardian House Style* (David & Charles), 1994

Helen C. Long, *The Edwardian House* (Manchester University Press), 1993

John Marshall and Ian Wilcox, *The Victorian House* (Sidgwick & Jackson), 1987

Charles Mayhew, *London Labour and the London Poor* (Griffen Bohn, 4 vols), 1851–62

Priscilla Metcalf, *Victorian London* (Cassell), 1972

Stefan Muthesius, *The English Terraced House* (Yale University Press), 1982

Donald J. Olsen, *Town Planning in London, the eighteenth and nineteenth centuries* (Yale University Press), 1964

Donald J. Olsen, *The Growth of Victorian London*, (Batsford), 1976 (revised 1979)

Linda Osband, *Victorian House Style* (David & Charles), 1991

Sydney Perks, *Residential Flats of All Classes* (Batsford), 1905

R. Price-Williams, 'The Population of London, 1801–81', in *Journal of the Statistical Society of London*, vol. xlviii, 1885, pp. 349-432

D. A. Reeder, 'A Theatre of Suburbs: Some Patterns of Development in West London 1801–1911', in H. J. Dyos (ed.), *The Study of Urban History* (Edward Arnold), 1968, pp. 253–71

Aileen Reid, *Brentham: a history of the pioneer garden suburb 1901–2001* (Brentham Heritage Society), 2000

S. B. Saul, 'House Building in England 1890–1914', in *Economic History Review*, 2nd series, vol. xv, no. 1, 1962, pp. 119–37

Alastair Service, *London, 1900* (Crosby, Lockwood & Staples), 1979

Alastair Service, *Edwardian Interiors* (Barrie & Jenkin), 1982

Francis Sheppard, *Local Government in St. Marylebone 1688–1835. A Study of the Vestry and the Turnpike Trust* (Athlone Press), 1958

Francis Sheppard, *London 1808–1870, The Infernal Wen* (Secker & Warburg), 1971

W. Shaw Sparrow (ed.), *Flats, Urban Houses and Cottage Homes* (Hodder & Stoughton), 1906

John Summerson, 'An Early Victorian Suburb', in *London Topographical Record*, vol. 27, 1995, pp. 1–48

John Summerson, 'The London Suburban Villa 1850–1880', in *The Unromantic Castle* (Thames & Hudson), 1990, pp. 217–34

James Thorne, *Handbook to the Environs of London* (John Murray), 1876

Gavin Weightman and Steven Humphries, *The Making of Modern London, 1815–1914* (Sidgwick & Jackson), 1983

J. A. Yelling, *Slums and Slum Clearance in Victorian London* (Allen & Unwin), 1986

Modern Period

Sir Patrick Abercrombie, *The Greater London Plan 1944* (HMSO), 1945

J. Burnett, *A Social History of Housing 1815–1970* (Methuen), 1978

Hugh Clout (ed.), *Changing London* (University Tutorial Press), 1978

A. M. Edwards, *The design of suburbia: a critical study in environmental history* (Pembridge Press), 1981

Lionel Esher, *A Broken Wave: The Rebuilding of England 1940–1980* (Allen Lane), 1981

Chris Hamnett and Bill Randolph, 'The Rise and Fall of London's Purpose-Built Blocks of Privately Rented Flats: 1853–1983', in *London Journal*, vol. 11, no. 2, 1985, pp. 160–75

Elain Harwood, *Something worth keeping? post-war architecture in England: housing and houses* (English Heritage), 1996

Michael Hibbert, 'Twenty Years of London History 1975–1995: London Recent and Present', in *London Journal*, vol. 20, no. 2, 1995, pp. 91–101

Keith Hoggart and David R. Green (eds), *London. A New Metropolitan Geography* (Edward Arnold), 1991

Alice Hope, *Town Houses* (Batsford), 1963

Miles Horsey, 'London Speculative Housebuilding of the 1930s: Official Control and Popular Taste', in *London Journal*, vol. 11, no. 2, 1985, pp. 147–59

Steve Humphries and John Taylor, *The Making of Modern London 1945–1985* (Sidgwick & Jackson), 1986

Alan A. Jackson, *Semi-Detached London. Suburban Development, Life and Transport, 1900–39* (Wild Swan), 1979, 2nd edn 1991

David Jeremiah, *Architecture and Design for the Family* (Manchester University Press), 2000

Little Palaces: The suburban House in North London 1919–1939 (Middlesex Polytechnic exhibition catalogue), 1987

Paul Oliver, Ian Davis and Ian Bentley, *Dunroamin. The Suburban Semi and its Enemies* (Barrie & Jenkins), 1981

Martin Pawley, *Architecture versus Housing* (Studio Vista), 1971

Colin Penn, *Houses of Today* (Batsford), 1954

Alison Ravetz (with Richard Turkington), *The Place of Home: English domestic environments, 1914–2000* (E. & F. N. Spon), 1995

Andrew Saint (ed.), *London Suburbs* (English Heritage), 1999

L. C. B. Seaman, *Post-Victorian Britain 1902–1951* (Methuen), 1966

Mark Swenarton, *Homes Fit for Heroes: the politics and architecture of early state housing in Britain* (Heinemann), 1981

F. M. L. Thompson (ed.), *The Rise of Suburbia* (Leicester University Press), 1982

Brenda Vale, *Prefabs. A History of the UK Temporary Housing Programme* (E. & F. N. Spon), 1995

Gavin Weightman and Steven Humphries, *The Making of Modern London, 1914–1939* (Sidgwick & Jackson), 1984

Jerry White, *London in the Twentieth Century: A City and its People* (Viking), 2001

J. W. R. Whitehand and Christine M. H. Carr, 'Morphological periods, planning and reality: the case of England's inter-war suburbs', in *Urban History*, vol. 26, 1999, pp. 230–48

J. W. R. Whitehand and Christine M. H. Carr, 'The creators of England's inter-war suburbs' in *Urban History*, vol. 28, 2001, pp. 218–34

CHAPTER ONE

Maps and Plans

Of all the documentary sources available to the house historian, maps and plans are, by their very nature, the most graphic and accessible. They provide an easily understandable visual record of a building, street or area at a specific moment in history; and a group of maps and plans of different dates can reveal much about the changes to houses and their environs.

Indeed, a great deal of London's history and growth can be traced in successive generations of maps: the tightly packed rows of timber houses clustered together in and around the medieval City; the great era of West End estate development by families such as the Russells and Grosvenors in the 17th and 18th centuries; the bustling metropolis of Victorian times, with its expanding networks of roads, railways and suburbs; and the sprawling Greater London of today.

The first step for students and researchers of house history in London should be to locate a large-scale map of the area in question. Accurate, large-scale maps, such as the Ordnance Survey series, will give a reliable indication of the site, size and shape of individual houses, and the layout of surrounding streets.

Ordnance Survey maps

The first Ordnance Survey (OS) maps of southern England were published in the early years of the 19th century at a scale of one inch to one mile. By the middle of the century the OS was issuing nationwide maps of towns and countryside at various scales. The smaller one- and six-inch maps are of limited use to the urban historian; but the two large-scale series covering London, at 25 inches (1:2500) and five feet (1:1056) to one mile, are invaluable. Both scales were first produced in the 1860s and '70s. They were revised and updated in the 1890s, and again in the early years of the 20th century and the 1930s. Their present-day equivalent is the OS National Grid series, at 1:1250 scale (about 50 inches to one mile). Recently the OS has re-surveyed and digitized its data, and users can now search on-line and print modern maps at 1:25000 magnification; these modern maps no longer carry a specific survey date.

It is usually best to begin with the most recent edition of the OS which shows the particular house or street under study. Once the property has been clearly identified a comparison with earlier maps will provide much useful information, such as changes in street name or alterations to boundaries. If the house was erected after the mid-1860s, then a trawl through successive editions of OS maps should suggest an approximate date of construction, which can be corroborated by checking other sources such as ratebooks and local street directories.

The scale of the 25-inch maps makes them ideal for studying the overall development of a particular street or district, whilst at the same time identifying individual properties and boundaries in some detail. For instance, Illustrations 38 & 39 show a small area of Hampstead, to the west of Hampstead Heath railway station, from OS maps of the mid-1860s and mid-1890s. The earlier map shows that the transformation of this leafy retreat into a bourgeois suburb was already well under way: houses and gardens of various sizes line Downshire Hill and John Street, whilst across Haverstock Hill, in Rosslyn Park, incomplete rows of semi-detached houses denote the ongoing develop-

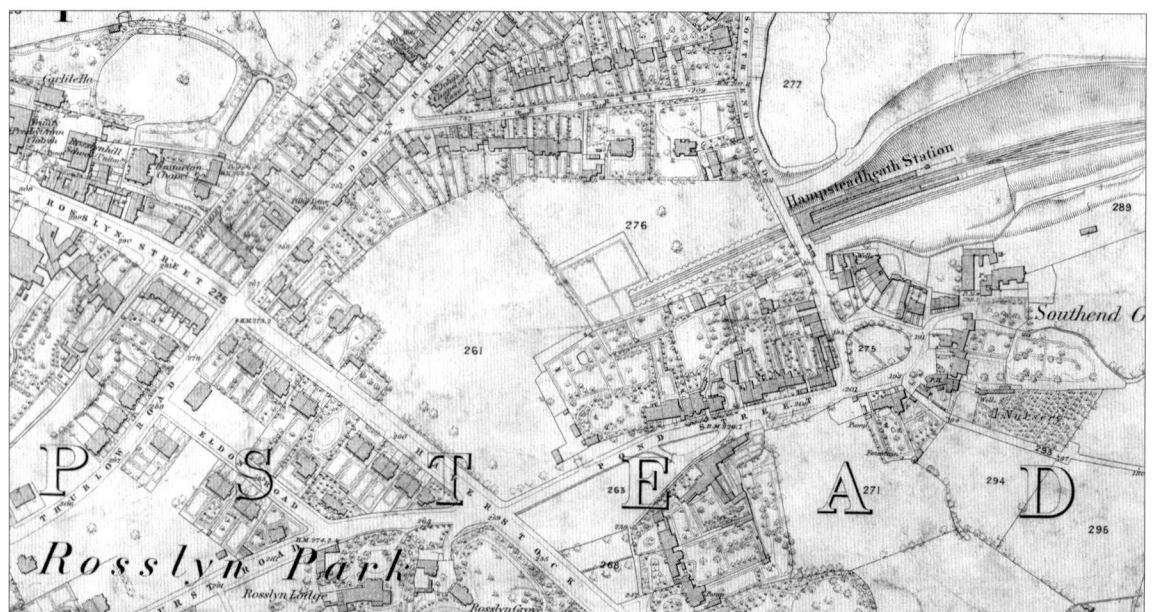

38 & 39. *Comparative Ordnance Survey maps of the area around Hampstead Heath Station, from the 1860s (above) and 1890s.*

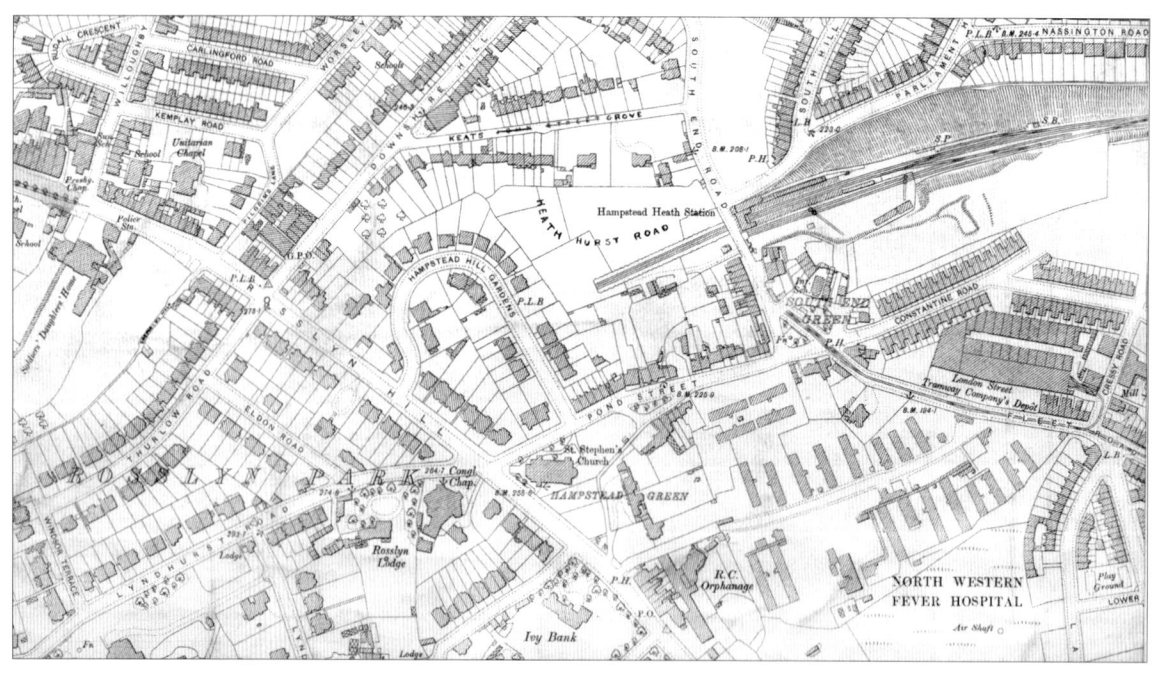

ment in and around Lyndhurst Road and Thurlow Road. These latter streets are shown fully developed in the second map, along with a new street (Lyndhurst Gardens), and two churches (the Congregational Chapel and St Stephen's). But the major difference is the new middle-class enclave of Hampstead Hill Gardens, developed in the 1870s. Note also that this stretch of Haverstock Hill had by then become part of Rosslyn Hill. Further examples of the comparative use of OS maps can be found in the Case Studies at the end of this book (see *ills 111–113, 118, 119*).

A lot more in the way of structural information can be gleaned from the larger-scale five-foot OS maps. Features such as entrance porches, steps, bay windows and rear projections are more clearly identifiable. Changes in outline over the years are often a sign of extension or structural alteration, though it should be borne in mind that a radical difference in size or shape may indicate that a complete rebuilding has taken place. The earlier editions of the five-foot maps were produced only for London, but the 20th-century revisions were extended into parts of Middlesex, Essex, Kent and Surrey as the capital expanded. For some outer areas, therefore, it may be necessary to refer to the relevant OS county maps.

As with many documentary sources, the best place to consult OS maps is in the local borough history library or archive, or county record office, most of which keep a collection of maps for their area. Both the Guildhall Library and the London Metropolitan Archives have large collections. The British Library Map Library has the five-foot London maps in bound volumes on open shelves, but a reader's ticket is required for access.

Many of the OS 25-inch maps of Greater London from the 1860s, 1890s and early 20th century have been reprinted by Alan Godfrey Maps at a reduced scale of 1:4340 (about 15 inches to one mile). These 'Godfrey Edition' maps come in a user-friendly folded format, ideal for use outdoors, and include informative background notes on each area by local historians and archivists. Most local libraries have a stock of Godfrey maps for their district, and a wider selection can be obtained from larger repositories such as the National Archives and the Guildhall Library bookshop. The maps are also available direct from Alan Godfrey Maps.

Pre-Victorian and earlier maps of London

A rich variety of maps is available to researchers who wish to explore the earlier history of London and its buildings. But other than the handful of major examples mentioned below, the majority of these are too small in scale to give reliable information about individual houses; they do, however, illustrate the steady growth outwards of the capital, the development of new residential areas, and the continuous building activity within central London. For the period before the Ordnance Survey, the major maps of London have been reprinted in book form by the London Topographical Society (LTS) in their series of historic 'A to Z's (see *Further reading*, below). The London Metropolitan Archives has a useful self-help store of facsimile versions of all the major London maps, from Braun & Hogenberg's map of mid-16th-century London onwards.

The largest and most important map to show London in the late 18th and early 19th centuries is Richard Horwood's *Plan of the Cities of London and Westminster...and Parts adjoining showing every house*, begun in 1792, published first in 1799, and again, after Horwood's death, in editions of 1807, 1813 and 1819. Horwood ambitiously attempted to record all the properties in London (complete with house-numbers) and each parish boundary, at a large scale of 26 inches to 1 mile (1:2400). The value of the map lies in its detail and extent, covering London from Chelsea and Regent's Park in the west to Deptford and Poplar in the east, enabling Horwood to show formerly rural outer areas — such as Finsbury and Kensington — filling up with houses (see *ill. 106*). There is no better picture of London before the coming of the railways. The third edition of Horwood's map (1813) has been reprinted by the LTS.

For the mid-18th century, John Rocque's *Plan of the Cities of London & Westminster and Borough of Southwark*, published in 1747 at a scale of 26 inches to 1 mile, is the best source. Rocque's map recorded the Georgian demand for fashionable west London townhouses in new developments such as Grosvenor Square and Mayfair, and the large scale enabled him to show 'all the squares, streets, courts and alleys in their true proportions' (though unlike Horwood he dos not show individual house-plots). Rocque's London plan has also been reprinted by the LTS. Rocque also published in 1746 a map of London and the country about it 'Ten Miles Round', at a scale of 5° inches to 1 mile, the first map to cover what is now the Greater London area.

The appearance of 17th-century London was recorded by John Ogilby and William Morgan in their large-scale London plan of 1676, the first detailed and accurate plan of the capital. The undertaking was largely a result of the need for a reliable survey of London property following the Great Fire of 1666. Ogilby and Morgan's map was the first true two-dimensional plan of London. Its large scale (52¾ inch to 1 mile) conveys the persisting medieval character of the City, its narrow house-plots, lanes, courts and alleys. A separate key to the map — the *Explanation* — was published in book form in 1677. Both the map and street index have been reprinted by the LTS.

Pre-Fire maps of London are nearly all 'map-views' — a picturesque hybrid of the panorama and the 'bird's-eye' view — and not plans in the strict two-dimensional sense. Their reliability may be questionable, but they do show the size and appearance of medieval London and the density of its housing. Faithorne & Newcourt's map of *c.*1658 gives a good impression of the City and its surroundings before the Great Fire and the redevelopment of the late 17th century. The two best-known and most useful map-views are the so-called 'Agas' map and Braun & Hogenberg's map: both show London in the mid-16th century and both appear to derive from an earlier copper-plate map, of which only three plates survive (see *ill. 1*). These and many other early maps and plans have also been reprinted by the LTS.

Goad Fire Insurance plans

Recent years have seen a growing awareness among historians of the usefulness of the large-scale fire-insurance plans of British towns and cities produced between the 1880s and 1970 by

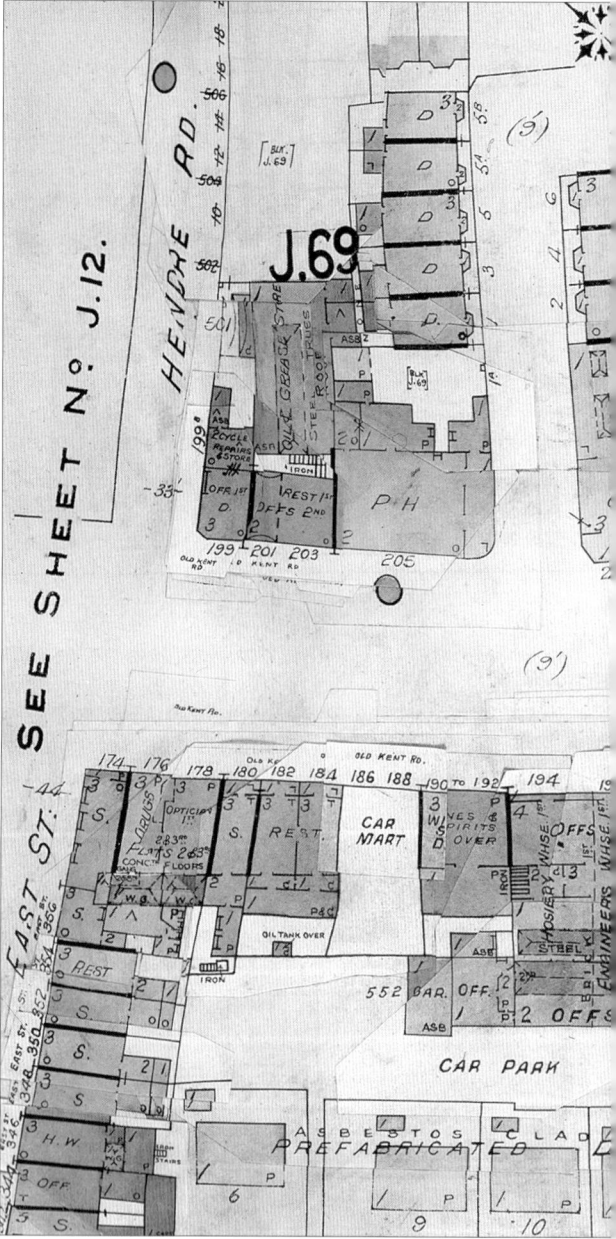

the firm of Charles E. Goad Limited.

These highly-detailed, specialized maps were intended to help insurance companies assess the level of risk to property from fire. They therefore concentrate primarily on indus-

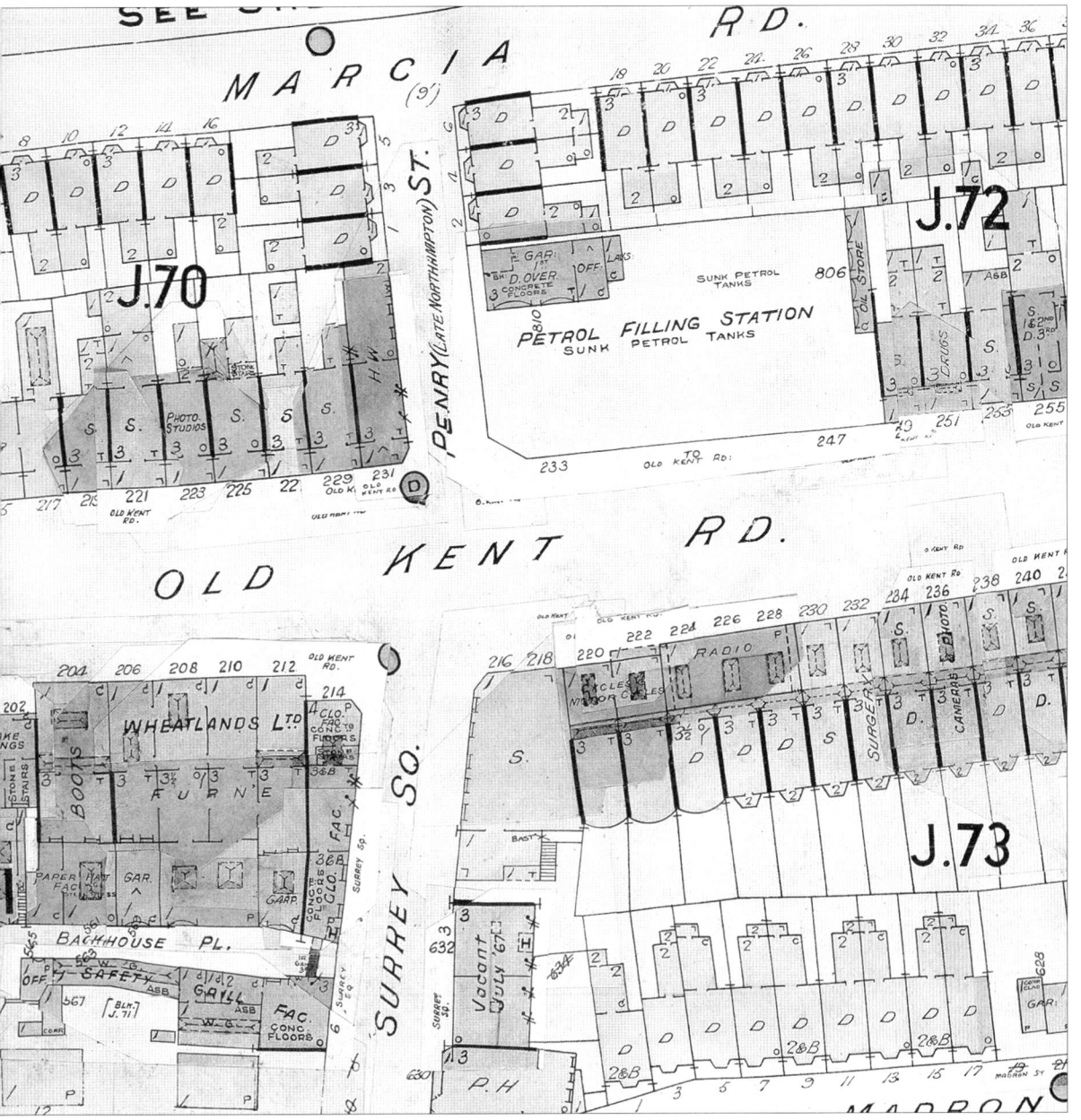

40. *Goad Fire Insurance plan of part of Old Kent Road, c. 1970, showing a predominance of terrace-houses and shops, with some post-war redevelopment.*

trial and commercial districts. But as fire can spread from adjoining buildings, frequently the surrounding residential streets are covered equally thoroughly, offering a wealth of information about London's houses.

There are 22 London volumes: twelve (vols I–XII) cover the central area in some detail, whereas the remaining ten (vols A–K) are more selective, concentrating on the most densely populated parts of outer London. The volumes were updated regularly for fire insurance companies, to whom they were leased, by pasting any changes on to the existing sheets of maps. Thus it is always necessary to check the date of the base map and the date of the last revision. Some volumes, such as those in the British Library, were never revised.

Although they are less extensive in coverage than the Ordnance Survey, the large scale of the Goad plans, at 1:480 (40 feet to 1 mile), offers a more detailed and precise depiction of individual properties. Unlike the OS, street numbers are included, and abbreviations indicate the use of each building. Important structural information is also given, such as the height of buildings, the number of storeys, party walls, skylights, and the location and type of windows. A system of colour-coding shows at a glance the different building materials, such as brick or stone, wood and iron. Illustration 40 shows part of the Old Kent Road from one of the Goad volumes. The petrol station at the corner with Penry Street and the single-storey prefabs of Minnow Street were built on the sites of houses destroyed or damaged by enemy bombing during World War Two (see also *Bomb Damage records,* pages 149-151).

The major collections of Goad fire insurance plans of London are those in the British Library Map Library, the Guildhall Library (Department of Prints, Maps and Drawings), and the London Metropolitan Archives.

Booth poverty maps
A unique picture of London and the life of its inhabitants in late-Victorian times is provided by Charles Booth's mammoth, multi-volumed study, *Labour and Life of the People in London*, researched, written and published between the late 1880s and the early years of the 20th century. Booth and his team of research assistants conducted a painstaking, street-by-street investigation of central London, initially to establish the different social classes of the inhabitants, but later extending the survey to incorporate industry and religion.

Alongside the volumes of text were published what Booth referred to as maps of 'London poverty by streets', based on the initial

research undertaken in 1889. Booth distinguished seven separate classes of inhabitant in the capital, from the wealthy and well-to-do to the 'lowest grade...occasional labourers, loafers, and semi-criminals — the elements of disorder'. The beauty of the maps is their simple system of colour-coding — gold for wealthy, red for well-to-do, dark blue and black for the poorest and semi-criminal classes, etc — which graphically illustrates the economic status of individual districts and streets.

For those interested in discovering the social character of a particular area or street at the end of the 19th century, the Booth maps are a useful companion to the censuses. But unlike the census, a large area can be studied at a glance. Distinct residential areas are easily distinguishable: compare, for example, the swathes of gold and red in the well-kept and strictly managed West End estates with the dense blues and blacks of parts of the East End. London's 'unplanned' nature is also evident, as is the extent to which, much like today, the wealthiest classes often lived in close proximity to the poor and the underprivileged.

The Booth maps were reprinted in 1984 by the London Topographical Society in a large-format, colour facsimile edition, *Charles Booth's Descriptive Map of London Poverty*, 1889, (LTS Publication No. 130). Digitized versions of the Booth investigators' later notebooks — known as the 'police notebooks', as they were written whilst following the local 'bobby' on his beat — are available online at http://booth.lse.ac.uk/ and give a vivid picture of the London streets of the 1890s.

Local and parish maps
Most local history libraries and archives will have a collection of historic maps for their own area. Many of these will be of private estates or property in the district, or perhaps of local improvements. Some local libraries, such as Kensington & Chelsea, have published booklets listing and illustrating their map collections.[1] These offer a useful guide to the development of a local area in a handy format. There are also many local and parish maps among the London-wide collections of the Guildhall Library (Department of Prints, Maps and Draw-

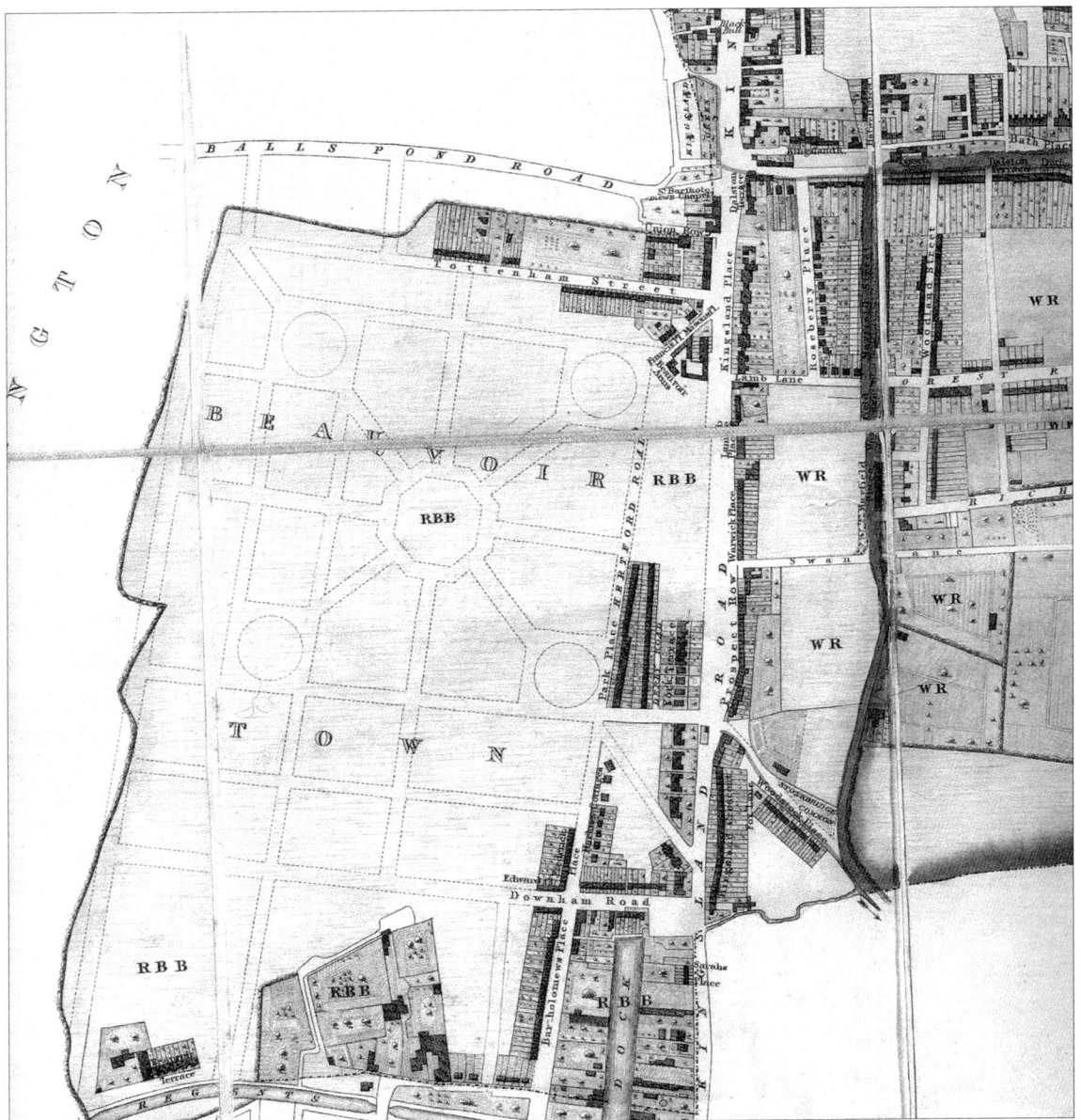

41. An early-19th-century local map: an extract from Thomas Starling's map of the parish of Hackney, 1831, showing the area around Kingsland Road, including an intended layout of De Beauvoir Town, not as eventually carried out.

ings) and the London Metropolitan Archives.

Among the many functions of the local parish was the responsibility for maintaining important public services (such as roads, bridges and watercourses), and for securing the parish boundaries. 18th-century parish surveys include an excellent survey of the parish of Stepney by Joel Gascoyne. Strype's

edition of Stow's *Survey of London* has good 18th-century maps of City wards and parishes. A large number of parish maps date from the early years of the 19th century. Some were drawn up to accompany the publication of parish histories, such as Thomas Faulkner's *History and Antiquities of the Parish of Kensington* (1820), or Thomas Cromwell's *History and*

Description of the Parish of Clerkenwell (1828). Others seem to have been prompted by the reorganization in the 1830s of the tithe system of taxation (see Chapter 5, page 103). In both cases the principal purpose was the accurate definition of ecclesiastical and parochial boundaries and divisions; these often differ from modern administrative boundaries such as London boroughs, electoral wards and postal districts. Maps of this period also show the rural character of much of London before the transport revolution of the mid-19th century and the spread of suburban housing.

In addition, parochial maps often yield other useful information. Streets and houses are usually indicated, and there are sometimes notes on field sizes, names of landowners, the location of sewers and other details. For example, Illustration 41, an extract from Thomas Starling's map of Hackney of 1831, shows an early proposal for the layout of the then un-developed De Beauvoir Town, which differs in many respects from that eventually carried out.

Metropolitan improvements: local government maps and plans

Metropolitan improvements. The steady and continuous expansion of the capital in the late 18th and early 19th centuries prompted much-needed improvements in transport, public health and other utilities. New roads, such as New Oxford Street and Victoria Street, were provided at first by the Crown and central government, until the establishment in 1855 of London's first municipal authority, the Metropolitan Board of Works (MBW). Thereafter the MBW and its successor bodies — the London County Council (LCC) and Greater London Council (GLC) — were responsible for numerous major street improvements across London.

Accurate surveys had to be made of lands through which each new road would pass, showing the proposed route and the houses and other properties that were to be swept away. Victorian street improvements were generally planned to run through overcrowded, insanitary districts, and such plans often show old streets of slum houses which were rarely recorded elsewhere. Information on owners and lessees sometimes survives in associated books of reference. A brief general history of mid- and late-Victorian street improvements was published by the LCC in 1898 as the *History of London Street Improvements 1855–1897*, edited by Percy J. Edwards *(ill. 42)* In addition to the plans and descriptions of the various works carried out between those dates, the volume includes useful comparative maps of London in 1855 and 1897. More detailed information can be found in the records of the relevant metropolitan body at the London Metropolitan Archives. Similar improvements (for example

42. *MBW improvement plan of c.1877, showing intended line of the southern stretch of Charing Cross Road.*

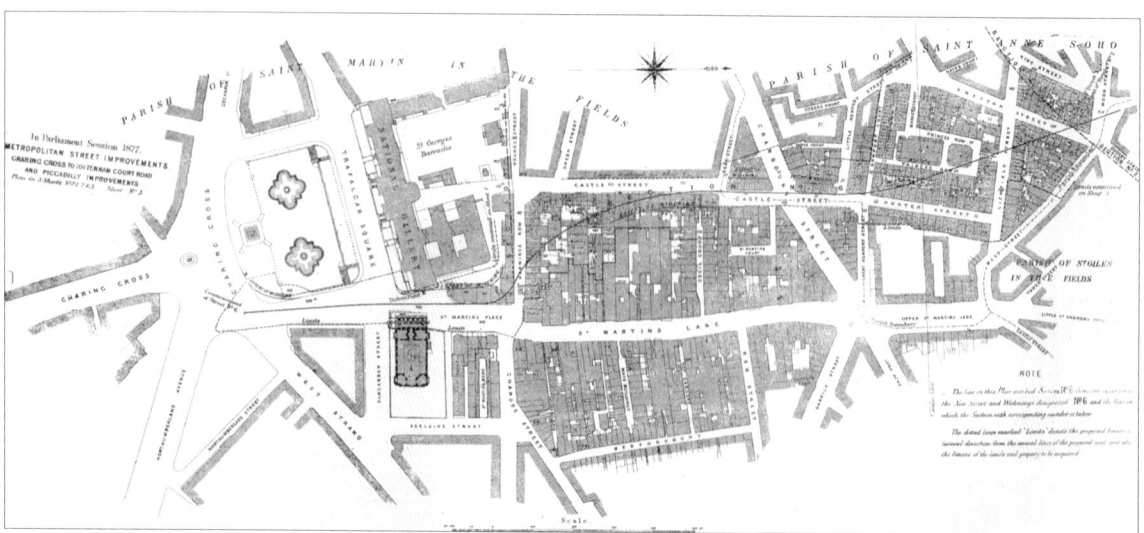

Holborn Viaduct) were made in the City by the Corporation of London, whose records are held by the Corporation of London Record Office (CLRO), now co-administered with the LMA as part of the Corporation's Joint Archive Service (JAS).

Other public works carried out by the metropolitan authorities, district boards and vestries and others included new bridges, tunnels, the embanking of the river, new drains and sewers; the records of many of these schemes also record housing to be demolished or in the vicinity of the improvement. The Victorian transport explosion saw London covered by a web of railway and tube lines. Deposited plans and books of reference for such schemes, similar to those of the metropolitan authorities, can be found in the House of Lords Record Office or in local or county archives.

Local authority plans. A number of London's local history collections and local authorities retain copies of plans which from 1856 were required to accompany applications for new buildings, and conversions of or additions to existing buildings. Where these survive and are accessible they can be of immense value: in addition to useful ground- and floor-plans, and sometimes elevations, the plans or the accompanying correspondence can provide the names of owners and contractors, and an approximate date of construction or alteration, which can be checked against other sources.

Drainage plans and town planning applications can be found among the records of the local borough council in the appropriate archive, although many are still stored (usually on microfilm) and used by the local planning or district surveyors department. The City of Westminster Planning Department has a self-service 'One Stop Shop' where current planning applications may be consulted without appointment, and where some earlier applications can be ordered for viewing on microfiche. An excellent set of older drainage plans for the Westminster area are part of the collections of the City of Westminster Archives Centre. Islington Borough Council Planning Department has a good microfilm collection of applications, which includes many early 20th-century and

occasionally Victorian plans. (See also Chapter 2, pages 69, 71.)

Building Act Cases. House plans can be found amongst the surviving files of records made by the Building Regulation Division of the LCC and GLC Architects' Departments as part of their administration of the various London Building Acts *(ills 43 & 44)*. Like the local authority records discussed above, the material in these Building Act Case files is usually concerned with the applications for new buildings (or alterations and extensions to existing buildings), which were required by legislation governing the size of buildings, their structural stability and other safety matters such as fire prevention. Domestic properties feature among the surviving files, many of which record now demolished buildings. Following the abolition of the GLC in 1986 about 40% of their files (some 2,500) were selected for retention; the rest were destroyed. An alphabetical index by street name is on the open shelves at the London Metropolitan Archives, where the documents are now held. Only a few local archives, such as Hackney and Camden, retain collections of the copies of Building Act case files that were passed to them by the central authorities. Other files may be with local borough libraries, or may still be in use by the local borough council. (See also page 64)

43. BA Case plans: elevation of Queen Alexandra Mansions, Judd Street, 1912.

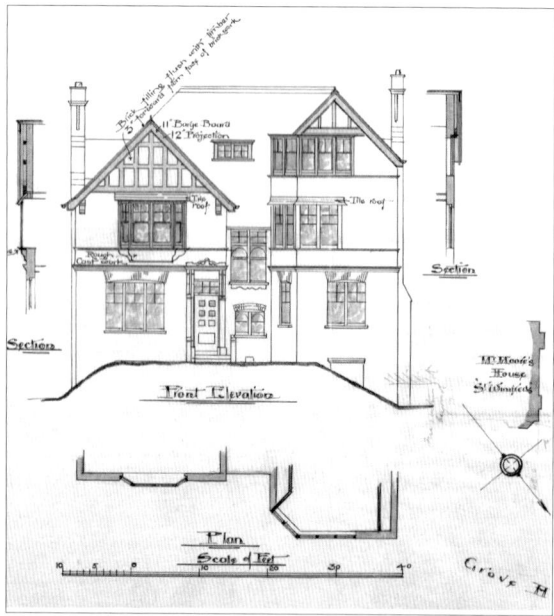

44. BA Case plans: Elevation and part plan of a house in Grove Hill, Lordship Lane, Dulwich, for William Webb Esq., showing timber-work to façade, 1895.

Commissioners of Sewers plans. From the 16th century until early Victorian times, London's increasingly complicated but defective network of sewers and drains was administered by various commissions of sewers, each representing a different geographical district. These were replaced in 1848, at the time of a major cholera outbreak, by a single Metropolitan Commission of Sewers, which itself was superseded in 1855 by the new Metropolitan Board of Works, one of the first tasks of which was the maintenance of main sewers and the prevention of sewage entering the Thames (see also page 59).

Maps and plans drawn up for these bodies to assist with the design and maintenance of drainage systems are now held at London Metropolitan Archives, and many of these are of benefit to the house historian. General plans, such as a Westminster Commissioners of Sewers map of 1817 showing watercourses under its jurisdiction between the City and Fulham, can give a good idea of general building development in an area.[2] Plans of new buildings and streets, showing the proposed connection of

houses to existing drains and sewers, were presented to the authorities, although it must be remembered that these may not always show the layout as eventually built (see *ill. 50*). Other plans record the insanitary conditions in some areas before improvement, including slum housing which was later demolished. Two detailed maps of 1849, carried out for the Metropolitan Commissioners of Sewers, record the long-gone 'Potteries' district of Notting Hill, with its crowded groups of hovels, many with pig-sties in the back yards, and unhealthy pools of stagnant water (a consequence of local brickmaking and clay digging).[3]

Architects' plans and other house plans
The largest collection of architects' drawings and plans in this country is that of the Royal Institute of British Architects (RIBA) Drawings Collection, now held at the Victoria & Albert Museum. Although most of these items relate to churches, public buildings and large town mansions or country houses, plans of the more modest types of domestic property can be found in the collection. An index has been published in a multi-volume set. Other valuable collections of architects' drawings and plans are held at the V&A, and at the British Museum and the Guildhall Library.

Plans of houses are frequently to be found amongst the records of London's local authorities and landed estates (see above and pages 91–2). Many documents of title — such as mortgages, leases and deeds — include plans of the property in question. Some of the entries of registered deeds in the late-18th- and early-19th-century volumes of the Middlesex Deeds Registry contain informative house-plans (see pages 84–6).

The various bodies established to manage, record and investigate historic buildings, such as the Society for the Protection of Ancient Buildings (SPAB), the Survey of London, the Royal Commission on the Historical Monuments of England (RCHME) and, more recently, English Heritage, have created many maps and plans of houses as part of their work. In London, the LCC and GLC's Historic Buildings Division recorded numerous buildings under threat in the capital. Their series of some 11,000

*45. Historic Buildings Division elevation, No. 47
West Hill, Wandsworth.*

drawings is now part of the National Monuments Record (NMR), and stored in English Heritage's NMR Centre at Swindon. Illustration 45 shows a typical example from the collection, an elevation of 47 West Hill, Wandsworth.

Other types of maps and plans

For information about estate maps and plans, please see the relevant section in Chapter 4, on estate records (pages 91–2). Similarly, tithe surveys are dealt with alongside rates and taxes in Chapter 5 (page 103), and war damage maps under bomb damage records in Chapter 10 (page 149).

NOTES AND REFERENCES

1. Kensington & Chelsea Public Library, *An Historical Atlas of Kensington & Chelsea*, 1971; and *Kensington and Chelsea maps: a select list*, 2nd edn, 1971.

2. LMA, WCS/PR/57.

3. LMA, MCS/P1/10–11.

FURTHER READING

Peter J. Aspinall, 'Sources for Urban History (11): The Use of Nineteenth Century Fire Insurance Plans for the Urban Historian', in *Local Historian*, vol. 11, no. 6, May 1975, pp. 343–9

Felix Barker and Peter Jackson, *The History of London in Maps* (Barrie & Jenkins), 1990

Geraldine Beech and Rose Mitchell, *Maps for Family and Local History* (National Archives), 2004

Charles Booth (ed.), *Survey of the Life and Labour of the People in London* (1st edn, 2 vols, 1889–91); (2nd edn, 9 vols, 1892–7); (3rd edn, 17 vols, 1902–3)

Ida Darlington, 'The London Commissions of Sewers and their Records', in *Journal of the Society of Archivists*, No. 5, April 1962, pp. 196–210

Percy J. Edwards (ed.), *History of London Street Improvements 1855–1897* (LCC), 1898

Philippa Glanville, *London in Maps* (The Connoisseur), 1972

J. B. Harley, *Ordnance Survey maps: a descriptive manual* (Ordnance Survey), 1975

J. B. Harley and C. W. Phillips, *The Historian's Guide to Ordnance Survey Maps* (published for the Standing Conference for Local History by the National Council of Social Service), 1964

B. P. Hindle, *Maps for Local History* (Batsford), 1988

John Howgego and Ida Darlington, *Printed Maps of London circa 1553–1850* (Dawson), 1st edn, 1964; 2nd edn (Howgego only), 1978

Ralph Hyde, *Printed Maps of Victorian London, 1851–1900* (Dawson), 1975

Ralph Hyde, 'Mapping London's Landlords: The Ground Plan of London: 1892–1915', in *Guildhall Studies in London History*, vol. 1, No. 1, Oct 1973, pp. 28–35

London Topographical Society, *The A to Z of Regency London* (LTS Publication No. 131, Harry Margary), 1985

London Topographical Society, *The A to Z of Georgian London* (LTS Publication No. 126, Harry Margary), 1982

London Topographical Society, *The A to Z of Restoration London* (LTS Publication No. 145), 1992

Richard Oliver, *Ordnance Survey Maps: a concise guide for historians* (Charles Close Society), 1993

Public Record Office, *Maps and Plans in the Public Record Office: vol. 1 British Isles*, 1967

Gwyn Rowley, *British Fire Insurance Plans* (Charles E. Goad), 1984

Gwyn Rowley, 'British Fire Insurance Plans. The Goad Productions c.1885–c.1970', in *Archives*, vol. XVII, no. 74, Oct 1985, pp. 67–78

W. A. Seymour (ed.), *A History of the Ordnance Survey* (Dawson), 1980

John Schofield (ed.), *The London Surveys of Ralph Treswell* (London Topographical Society Publication No. 135), 1987

David Smith, *Maps and Plans for the Local Historian and Collector* (Batsford), 1988

CHAPTER TWO

Records of Local Government

Metropolitan government has long been a contentious issue. Its beginnings lie amid the cholera outbreaks and 'Great Stinks' of early Victorian times, when new London-wide bodies were created to deal with the increasing demands on the capital's infrastructure brought about by its rapid expansion and urbanization. To central government ministers in Whitehall, an effective upper tier of government for London was a double-edged sword: a prerequisite for a well-run capital city, perhaps, yet potentially a powerful centralized political opponent. In the recent past we have witnessed metropolitan government's controversial end in the demise of the much-maligned Greater London Council (successor to the much-lamented London County Council), dismantled by the Conservative government between 1984 and 1986; yet we have also witnessed something of a rebirth (albeit in a much slimmer form), with the creation in 1999–2000 under a Labour government of the Greater London Authority and appointment of a directly-elected mayor for London.

Municipal records can tell us much about the form and fabric of London, as well as about the processes and regulations which helped shape it. Some of these sources have been covered already by Alan Cox in relation to public housing,[1] and much of the documentary material considered below can be used in the study of buildings other than houses. London government records are divided between those of capital-wide and local authorities, and so the sources below are grouped in two such sections. These are preceded by a short historical guide to London government and its various bodies. Today some types of records – even

those within the same London borough collection – are still arranged by former parishes or metropolitan boroughs, and so some knowledge of the changes to local government structures over time is helpful.

LONDON GOVERNMENT: A BRIEF GUIDE AND CHRONOLOGY

When considering the numerous bodies that have been involved in running London, it is as well to begin with the City of London. The City's independence is a recurring oddity in the history of London government. A city in its own right, acknowledged by Royal charter, governed by its own corporation, with its own mayor, sheriffs and courts, and even its own police force, the City of London remained largely untouched by 19th- and 20th-century local government re-organizations, preserving most of its ancient rights and privileges. These have included a monopoly of markets within a seven-mile radius, and – until the creation of the Thames Conservancy in 1857–8 – the governance of the River Thames for the 80-mile stretch from Staines to the Medway.

Outside the City, before the introduction of metropolitan government in the 1850s (and indeed for some time after), local government was still nominally in the hands of the church, through about 200 local parish vestries, which had responsibility *inter alia* for paving, lighting and cleaning the streets, though by this time some duties had been taken over by secular boards of trustees, established by special Acts of Parliament. Without a single supreme authority for the capital, administration at a higher and wider level was still the responsibility of the county magistrates for Middlesex, Surrey and Kent, who met at regular Quarter Sessions to discuss and implement county business. (There was also a fourth bench of magistrates covering Westminster.) Although the county magistrates exercised supremacy, by the early 19th century they were interfering less and less in local affairs, which as a result were largely discharged by the vestries. In addition, there were also some 50 or so turnpike trusts, which built and maintained many of London's roads through tolls paid by travellers; and also eight independent metropolitan commissions of sewers, whose job it was to ensure that their sewers discharged successfully into the Thames (though strictly this requirement was confined to surface water only, not underground drainage).

The first London-wide body (if we exclude the City) was the Metropolitan Police, introduced in 1829, though fundamentally this remained under the control of central government. What prompted the dramatic re-organization of London government in the mid-19th century were fears for public health, and the gradual realization after some terrible outbreaks of cholera and typhus in the 1830s and early 1840s that the biggest threats came from insanitary housing, inadequate drainage and sewerage, and contaminated drinking water. First came the Metropolitan Buildings Office (MBO), in 1844, the first statutory body with responsibility for controlling all building development in a wider London area, similar in size to the pre-1965 County of London. This was followed in 1847 by the Metropolitan Commission of Sewers (MCS), formed to provide an adequate drainage system for the capital, replacing the old independent sewers commissions with a single unified body (though this still excluded the City). However, the Sewers Commission was discredited by further cholera outbreaks in 1849 and 1854, and a modern and effective drainage system for London was delayed until the establishment in 1855 of the **Metropolitan Board of Works** (MBW).

London-wide government proper begins with the MBW. In addition to the drainage responsibilities inherited from the Sewers Commission, the new board was given the task of coordinating the administrative work done at a local level, where the parish vestries were re-organized – the 23 largest retaining their independence, the rest being merged into 15 new district boards of works. Subsequently the MBW inherited the MBO's role of building regulation, with its network of district surveyors; and it also had the power to make, widen and improve streets, and to regulate street-naming and house-numbering. In later years, further Acts extended the board's powers to cover such London-wide issues as river embanking, the fire service, commons and open spaces.

The MBW's area of responsibility, which defined London's geographical limits, was based on the London regional districts used for the census of 1851, and included some outer parishes which were still largely rural in character. This became, with minor modifications, the County of London administered by the MBW's successor body, the **London County Council** (LCC), established in 1888–9. The LCC was the first such body to be elected directly by Londoners, and was later given extra powers in fields such as education, transport, and, subsequently, health (until 1948), to add to those inherited from the MBW. Its greatest success, however, was in its pioneering policies in providing and designing local-authority housing.

In 1899–1900 the shape of local government changed when a London Government Act replaced the old district boards and vestries with 28 new metropolitan borough councils (ill. 47). This change was essentially an attempt by the Conservative central government to check the power of the LCC, then in the control of the left-wing Progressives. But the outer boundary of the LCC County of London remained unchanged for another 60 years, despite the fact that many built-up parts of the capital extended beyond this, and were administered by the adjacent counties and county boroughs, and a network of rural and urban district councils.

Only in the early 1960s did the LCC become obsolescent, and it was replaced in 1965 by the **Greater London Council** (GLC) as part of a radical re-organization of metropolitan and local government. In addition to the former LCC county, the GLC administered a Greater

46. The Metropolitan administrative areas post-1965, when old Metropolitan boroughs (see Ill. 47) were merged and large parts of the surrounding counties were incorporated into Greater London.

London which included the entire former county of Middlesex, as well as adjacent parts of Essex, Hertfordshire, Kent and Surrey, an area of over 600 square miles, with a population of about 7 million people. This was divided into 32 larger London boroughs, forming the new second tier of local government, those in the inner, former LCC area being created by merging the former metropolitan boroughs *(ill. 46)*: for example, the London Borough of Camden comprises the old boroughs of Hampstead, St Pancras and Holborn. Until its demise in the mid-1980s, the GLC had responsibilities for strategic planning, traffic, public transport and housing for Greater London.

LONDON-WIDE CIVIC ADMINISTRATION: THE RECORDS OF COUNTY AND METROPOLITAN GOVERNMENT

County records

For the average London house historian there is little to be gained by wading through the voluminous records of the county authorities for Middlesex, or for Essex, Hertfordshire or Surrey. Most of these records are concerned with law and order and the judicial proceedings administered by the various courts of sessions – for Middlesex alone there are some 6,000 sessions rolls covering the period 1549-1889. The dedicated researcher may be interested in the cleansing and paving of streets (for Middlesex these are to be found in the Surveys of Street Presentiments);[2] but the best source of information on house construction, although limited to certain central areas (i.e. Westminster, St Marylebone, Paddington, St Pancras and Chelsea) are the building surveys and registers connected with the Building Acts of 1764 and 1774. These Acts prescribed, among other things, the types of materials and the thickness of external and party walls, and the later Act divided all buildings into seven rates or classes, determined by their value and floor area at ground level. Their relative success, compared to earlier Acts, was due to their proper enforcement by a network of district surveyors, who were to be given 24 hours notice of any new work, and who surveyed all new

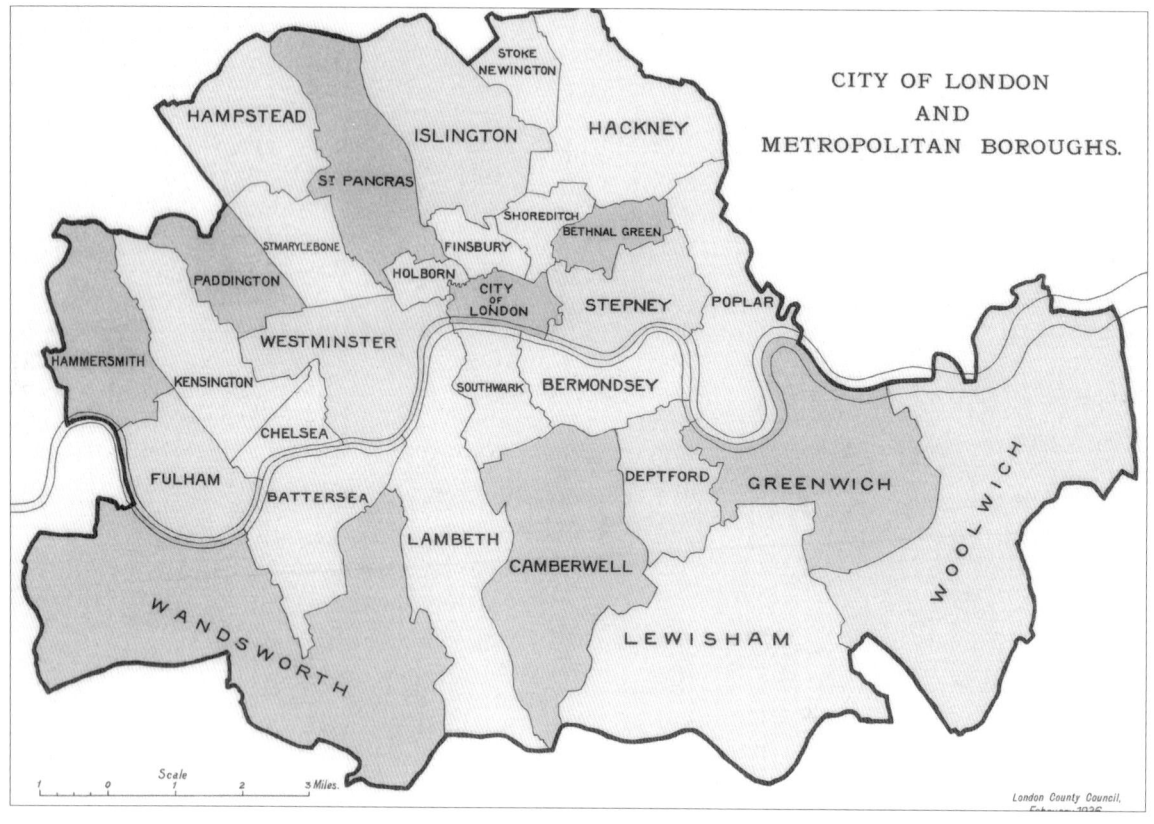

47. The Metropolitan administrative areas pre-1965.

buildings once they were covered in. Among the Middlesex County Council records are: surveyors' certificates as to the state of repair of party walls, and surveyors' affidavits confirming that new or altered buildings complied with the Act's requirements.[3] Although the amount of information given varies from document to document, these surveyors' records usually identify the street and give the name of the occupier, owner or builder. For example, a typical affidavit of May 1782, signed by William Stokes, a Limehouse surveyor, confirms that a 4th-rate house built by John Hudson at No. 2 Godart's Rents, Spitalfields, met the requirements of the Act *(ill. 48).*[4]

Records of the early metropolitan authorities: the Metropolitan Buildings Office (1845–55) and Metropolitan Commission of Sewers (1848–55)

Metropolitan Buildings Office. The 1844 Act which established the MBO regulated the safety and soundness of construction. Buildings were divided into three classes (dwelling houses, warehouses and factories, and public buildings such as churches and schools); and, in the case of the first and second classes, into four rates, each with its own rules as to height, number of storeys, floor area, and thickness of party walls. (For a detailed guide to the class and rate of buildings under the 1844 Building Act see Roger H. Harper, *Victorian Building Regulations*, 1985, pp. 22–3.) All new buildings and alterations were monitored by the district surveyors, whose monthly 'returns' form the principal MBO source.

District surveyors' returns survive for the

Middlesex, to wit. THESE are to certify, that WILLIAM STOKES, Surveyor of Saint Ann's, Limehouse, for the Parishes of Christ-Church, Spital-fields, and Saint Paul's, Shadwell, and the Hamlet of Mile-End New Town, appointed by the Court of Quarter Sessions of the said County of Middlesex, pursuant to the Statute in such Case made and provided, maketh Oath, (and saith)that he did on the *10th* Day of *May* 178*2* survey *a new house of the 4th Rate n° 2 belonging to Mr John Hudson situated in Godart's Rents Spitalfields* and that upon such Survey, this Deponent found the same, to the best of his Judgment and Belief,

agreeable to the several Directions contained in an Act of Parliament passed in the Fourteenth Year of his present Majesty King George the Third, intituled,
" An Act for the further and better Regulation of Buildings and Party-Walls,
" and for the more effectually preventing Mischiefs by Fire, within the Cities
" of London and Westminster, and the Liberties thereof ; within the Weekly
" Bills of Mortality, and other Places and Precincts therein-mentioned ; and
" for indemnifying, under certain Conditions, Builders and other Persons,
" against the Penalties to which they are, or may be liable, for erecting Buildings
" within the Limits aforesaid, contrary to Law."

William Stokes

Sworn before me, one of His Majesty's Justices of the Peace, on the *11* Day of *May* 178*2*

John Staples

48. *A typical 18th-century Middlesex County Surveyor's affidavit, for No. 2 Godart's Rents, Spitalfields, 1782.*

period 1845–52, under the MBO, and for the years 1871–1939, under its successors the MBW and LCC, and are available for consultation at the LMA.[5] The returns for 1853–1870 have not survived. (Duplicate returns for the London districts within the Middlesex County area exist for the period 1845–55 among the records of Middlesex County Council.)[6]

The individual districts policed by the surveyors do not always correspond with old parish or recent borough boundaries, and it may be advisable to check neighbouring districts if the property in question is close to a boundary. Given the large number of entries for each year it is very difficult to find a reference to a particular property without a rough idea of when and where the house was built. However the information given is very precise, and for those investigating a street or larger area, will prove invaluable, providing exact dates of construction, and names and addresses

of some of the individuals involved.

Although pre-1852 and post-1871 returns differ in some respects, the information they contain is fairly uniform. Each month's returns comprise three parts. In Part 1 each entry for that month is given its own identifying number, and includes: the date when notice was received that work was to commence (or the 'discovery' date, i.e. when the surveyor discovered that un-notified building work had already begun); who sent the notice (usually the builder or owner); the names and addresses of the builder and, occasionally, the owner; the address and some idea of the building work (e.g. 'erect a house', or 'add a storey', etc.); and a brief indication of the size and type of building. Pre-1856 returns under the 1844 Building Act give the class and rate (1st class referring to houses); those after 1870, which operated under a different Building Act of 1855, give the height and number of storeys (including the basement). In Part 2 the serial numbers from previous months are given with the date of 'covering in' or completion 'in carcase' (i.e. when a house's roof was put on and the fees became due). The fees due are also listed, and occasionally other notes are made, such as 'suspended' or 'abandoned'. Part 3 is simply an account of fees received, and therefore of little use to house historians. A great number of Victorian returns are for alterations such as new party walls, the insertion of shop-fronts, or new chimneys.

As an example, a Part 1 entry for 25 October 1849 in the Lewisham district tells us that William Neale, a builder of South Street, Greenwich, was then erecting a greenhouse (2nd class, 4th rate, i.e. not above 22ft in height) for Samuel Prior, Esq., at his house in South Row, Blackheath (which is described as 1st class, 1st rate, and therefore rather grand). Neale's work is entered as completed in the Part 2 on 21 November, and the fees (£2 10s.) paid on 12 December.[7]

MBO plans. The LMA has plans of proposed building work submitted to the MBO during its lifetime. There are some 600, but the majority are of large or public buildings, such as churches. An index is available, arranged by pre-1965 metropolitan borough and within that alphabetically by street-name. Those that do relate to domestic property can be very informative. For instance, a plan of large, detached houses being built on ground belonging to Robert Harrild, on the south-west side of Sydenham Park Road, shows which plots had been developed (with outline plans of 1st-class houses and dates of construction), and which were still vacant.[8]

Metropolitan Commission of Sewers. The Metropolitan Commission of Sewers' records at the LMA include general minutes, papers and reports, contracts, ratebooks and plans. Of most interest for house historians are the many drainage applications for the period 1848–55.[9] These give names of applicants and addresses of properties, and are generally accompanied by a sketched plan of the house or street in question. They cover a wide range of building work, from minor alterations at a single house, to proposals for entire estates, such as the application of June 1854 by the builders J. & C. W. Todd to drain 128 detached houses being built on a new estate north-east of Lee High Road (Belmont Park and Blessington Road).[10] Two volumes of street indexes are available.[11]

Metropolitan government records, 1855–1986: the Metropolitan Board of Works, London County Council and Greater London Council

Building Act (BA) case files. This is the major local government housing source, already mentioned in Chapter 1 because of the plans contained in the files (see page 55). These files were compiled by the Building Regulation Division of the LCC and GLC Architect's Department, as part of their work in administering the London Building Acts and ensuring that new buildings, and alterations to existing structures, met the required standards of construction and safety.

The restrictions which attracted most attention (and therefore created the most files) were those governing the construction of new streets and height of new buildings, and projections beyond the general building line, such as bay windows. Applicants, usually the architect or builder but sometimes the owner, sought confirmation that their designs were acceptable, or asked for an exemption from the relevant clause.

Shortly before the abolition of the GLC in 1984–6, some BA case files for important or demolished buildings were transferred to the Greater London Record Office (now the London Metropolitan Archives). On abolition the remainder were examined and about 40% of them (some 2,500) selected for retention; the rest were destroyed. All the surviving BA case files can be examined at the LMA, and indexes are available on open shelves in the catalogue room. As applications were usually referred by the MBW and LCC to the local vestry or board, duplicate records have, on occasion, survived in local libraries and archives (e.g. Hackney and Camden).

Each file should contain correspondence between the applicant and the council regarding the intended works, as well as drawings or plans; where the latter were large in number they were often separated into a second file. The files also contain any documentation from subsequent applications under the Building Acts for the same property. Reflecting the variety of building work regulated by municipal government, they range from large, unwieldy files stuffed full of plans and correspondence for big 20th-century developments (such as Michael Rosenaur's extensive estate of 1930s flats, Kingston House, on Kensington Road); through plans of large blocks of late-Victorian and Edwardian flats (like those of Queen Alexandra Mansions, Judd Street, 1912, for the London Housing Society Ltd, *ill. 43*); to the minutiae of suburban decoration (as in details of timber-work on the façade of a house in Grove Hill, Dulwich, designed in 1895 by the architect Henry G. Bruce for W. Webb, Esquire, *ill. 44*).[12]

District surveyors' returns. See above under Metropolitan Buildings Office.

Board and Council minutes. Matters discussed and decisions taken by the municipal bodies are recorded in the printed volumes of MBW, LCC and GLC *Minutes*, all of which are available on open shelves at the LMA. Each volume is indexed, and references to local housing can usually be found under headings such as Local Improvements, or under matters relating to the various local vestries, boards or borough councils. Any items of particular interest can then be followed in greater detail in the relevant departmental or committee minutes and papers (see below). The richest seam of information, however, particularly for the MBW and earlier LCC volumes, is the list of applications under the Building Acts; these record any applications for new works and alterations to buildings required by the legislation, including those for which no record survives in the BA case files collection (see above). Helpfully, in the earlier volumes the Building Act applications are grouped separately, either at the beginning or end of the general index, and they are listed twice: once by applicant's surname, once by address.

Committee minutes and papers. The work of the MBW and its successors was devolved to special departments, committees and sub-committees, e.g. for Main Drainage, Sewers, Streets and Works & General Purposes. Minutes and papers relating to these committees contain much more detail on any given topic than the abstracted accounts printed in the board or council minutes. They are particularly informative on Metropolitan Improvements – the provision of new roads, tunnels or bridges, etc – or indeed on any other public works such as parks or open spaces, council housing or road-widening, which necessitated the purchase of land. Details can be found of the acquisition of property, including claims for compensation from owners; and surveys of the intended route showing houses to be removed can sometimes be found among the authority's collection of plans. Clerkenwell Road, constructed in the 1870s to connect Oxford Street with Old Street, smashed through densely populated parts of Holborn and Clerkenwell. A plan of the area before the improvement identifies each building thought to require demolition, and an accompanying book of reference lists the properties and gives the names of freeholders, leaseholders and occupants.[13] Brief accounts of public works of this kind can also be found in the MBW's and LCC's printed *Annual Reports*, and in Percy Edward's volume on London street improvements (see *Further Reading*, below).

Of particular interest for the period 1930 to 1965 are the minutes and papers of the LCC's Town Planning Committee and its various sub-committees (listed together in the catalogues at the LMA). The Presented Papers and sub-committee minutes especially contain a great deal of information about planning inquiries which might not be available elsewhere, such as applications, correspondence and decision letters. Although the records are poorly indexed, specific enquiries can be found without too much trouble if the date is know from other sources.

Drainage applications. There are bound MBW volumes of individual applications to lay drains into existing sewers, and these usually relate to the building of new housing. Although they are not indexed, these volumes may be worth consulting if you have an approximate date of construction and have had no success looking for drainage records at local authority level. For instance the volume covering 1879–80 has an application concerning Mansfield Road, in Gospel Oak. The streets thereabouts were planned originally in the 1850s as a prestigious estate of semi-detached villas, but the arrival of the Midland Railway in the 1860s delayed development, and ensured that the houses which were built were aimed at a lower class of occupant. The MBW application is for nine new drainpipes from Nos 108–124 (even) Mansfield Road, and provides the builder's name (James Head) and an approximate construction date (January 1879).[14] This appears to be confirmed by a quick search through the suburban directories.

Street-naming and house-numbering. It is essential when tracing the history of any building in London to ensure that one has the correct street-name and house-number at any given date. Street-names in London have changed with a surprising frequency, and house-numbers (first introduced in London in the second half of the 18th century) did not always follow a logical progression.

Things become a bit easier from Victorian times. Following suggestions made by the Post Office, the MBW began renaming streets in an attempt to reduce duplication, and also began renumbering on an 'odds and evens' principle. The LCC and GLC carried on this work, through the street-naming section of their Buildings Regulations Division (part of the Architects Department), which kept up-to-date records of building numbers and street-names on a card index (later computerized) and on specially drawn maps. On the abolition of the GLC in the mid-1980s the naming and numbering function was transferred to the various local borough councils, but the LCC and GLC records were given to the London Metropolitan Archives.

The GLC database is available for consultation in magnetic form at the LMA. More user-friendly for the average researcher are the several volumes of *Names of Streets and Places in the Administrative County of London*, published by the LCC in 1901, 1912, 1929, 1955 and 1965 (the LMA has a special interleaved copy of the 1955 edition, up-dated with manuscript additions and alterations to 1985).[15] These record any alterations to street-names and house-numbers, and also give the reference for the relevant street-naming or street-numbering plan. There are some 47 volumes of plans, which

49. A typical LCC street-naming or -numbering plan: for the renaming and renumbering of Church Street, Spitalfields, as Fournier Street, 1893.

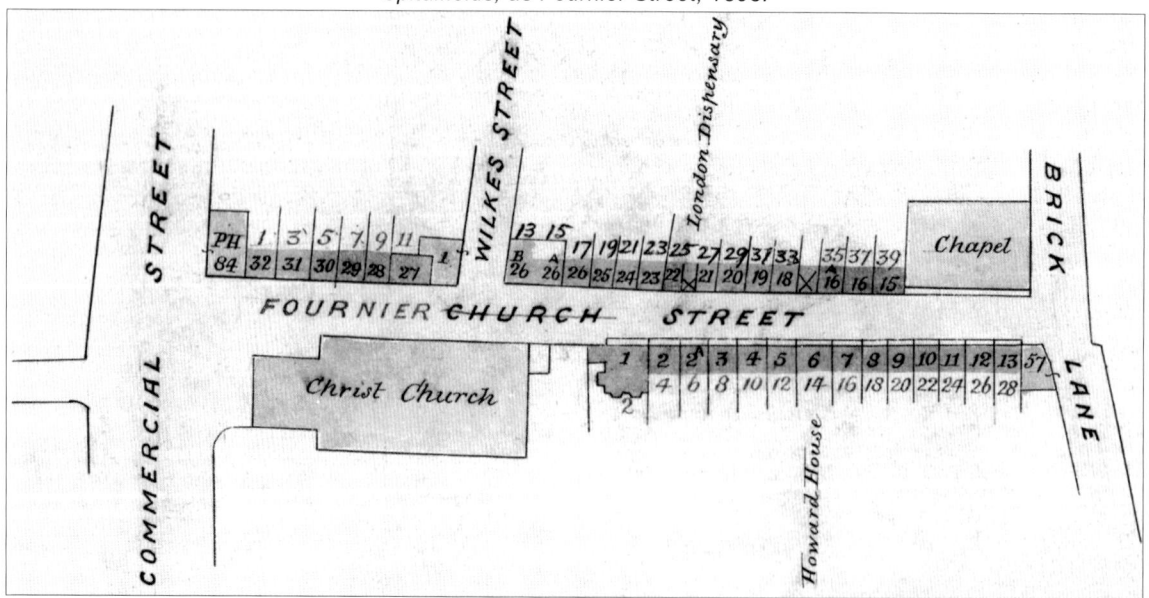

clearly show in colour the various changes that took place (most of these have been micro-filmed and are available for consultation at the LMA). For example, Illustration 49 shows a plan of November 1893, recording the renaming of Church Street, Spitalfields, as Fournier Street (named after George Fournier, a wealthy local benefactor, of Huguenot extraction), and the renumbering of its houses with a logical 'odds and evens' sequence (removing such oddities as a No. 2 and No. 2A).[16] In addition to the books and plans, there are also various typescript files on the origin of London street-names.

Corporation of the City of London (and its Liberties)

Only recently has redevelopment reintroduced the concept of the City of London as a residential district. From the mid-19th century onwards residents moved out with the help of cheap railway travel to the growing suburbs, and their former homes were replaced by offices, warehouses and banks. Those wishing to delve into the pre-1870s world of City housing in local authority records should consult the indexes to the archives of the Corporation of London Records Office, and the records of the various City wards and parishes.

Some areas on the fringes of the City had for a long time an autonomous or semi-autonomous status. For instance the various City 'Liberties' – such as the Liberties of the Fleet (around the Fleet Prison), and the Liberty of the Rolls (in the vicinity of Chancery Lane) – had special privileges, many enjoying exemption from certain ecclesiastical or municipal responsibilities. For instance, as the Liberties of the Tower were neither in the City nor in the county of Middlesex, their residents were free from jury service at assizes or county sessions. The Liberties' independence was gradually chipped away by 19th-century local government re-organizations, and today they have been absorbed into the relevant London boroughs. There are still a few remaining administrative oddities in the capital: for example the Inner and Middle Temples are not formally part of any borough, though most of their services are arranged for by the neighbouring authorities.

LOCAL CIVIC ADMINISTRATION: THE RECORDS OF PARISH VESTRIES, DISTRICT BOARDS OF WORKS, METROPOLITAN BOROUGHS, LONDON BOROUGHS AND OTHER BODIES

Parish records

Most visitors to local history libraries and record offices are familiar with parish records such as the registers of baptisms, marriages and burials which form the backbone to genealogical research. But from the 16th century onwards the parish dealt increasingly with municipal as well as ecclesiastical matters: overseers managed poor relief; surveyors supervised the maintenance of local highways; and parish constables maintained law and order. These and other duties were funded by parishioners through various local rates (e.g., for scavenging, paving, or poor relief). Ratebooks form the principal parish source for house historians, and their contents and use are described in detail in Chapter 5.

Domestic property did not concern the parish unless it was part of its holdings, or in some way affected or encroached upon its territory. Of parish records which may contain data relating to houses and house-building, perhaps the most likely source is the vestry minutes. The vestry was the body which, in effect, governed the parish, meeting regularly as a group or in special sub-committees, to discuss and implement decisions relating to road maintenance, street-lighting, watch-houses, complaints and nuisances, the precise location of parish boundaries and other matters which, on occasion, refer to local housing. They sometimes undertook surveys of the local population (a sort of mini-census), of local property (such as a valuation of all the houses in the area), and 'perambulations' of the route of the parish boundaries, descriptions of which occasionally include adjoining properties. Sometimes the parish authorities made local improvements, such as re-building the parish church, and these usually record the acquisition and demolition of nearby properties. It is always worth asking at the local history library what sorts of parish records have survived and how fruitful a study of them might prove.

For example, records of the Middlesex

Division of the Parish of St Sepulchres include a survey of all the real estate in the division, dated 1653, giving the names of landlords and tenants, and descriptions of all the houses.[17] As for the kind of information that can be found in vestry minutes, those for the Parish of St James, Clerkenwell, for May 1696 record that three houses near the turnpike at the west end of Clerkenwell Green, given to the parish by Leonard Wiglesworth for the benefit of the poor, had 'fallen into decay'. The parish then granted a 51-year building lease to Robert Bellfour, who demolished the old houses and spent £150 erecting two new and substantial brick tenements.[18]

In addition to the records of the vestry, it is worth looking for any surviving documents relating to the other parish bodies connected with local administration, such as paving commissions (which had the power to make and maintain parish pavements), and turnpike trusts. The turnpike trusts were in essence private companies, which raised money by charging tolls for people using the roads, using some of the profits to pay for maintenance. An excellent example of how to use such records is provided by Francis Sheppard's study of *Local Government in St Marylebone 1688–1835* (see *Further reading*, below).

Commissions of Sewers records (pre-1847)

During the 16th and 17th centuries seven independent commissions of sewers were appointed for central riverside districts of London, to be joined after the Fire of 1666 by an eighth representing the City Corporation.

Among the records of these commissions are minute books, contracts for new sewers,

ratebooks (residents likely to benefit from work on particular sewers were charged rates), maps and plans. The minutes can be instructive, recording applications by builders or developers to connect new houses to sewers, and sometimes also listing owners or builders who had connected their properties to the main sewers without permission. The minutes are best used in conjunction with the often very good collections of maps and plans, particularly those for the more built-up central areas such as Westminster or Holborn & Finsbury. Maps of the main drainage for the various parishes within the Holborn & Finsbury district, drawn up *c.*1840, offer a rare picture of the extent of building development there at this time, 30-odd years before the first large-scale OS maps.[19] Plans of proposed new buildings, submitted to the commissions for approval, show the layout of new streets and terraces, and often give the name of the builder or architect. These range from small, sketchy outlines of proposals, to detailed coloured plans of large developments. For instance a rough plan of January 1845 presented to Westminster Commission of Sewers by the Kensington builder Edward Nangle shows the proposed layout of a new street of lower-class but respectable houses, north of Brompton Road, called Raphael Street. As well as providing an approximate date of construction, it is interesting to compare this outline plan with the first large-scale OS map of the area (of 1862–7), which shows the street as built.[20] More polished and detailed is a plan of 1846, by John Dowley, of an intended new sewer to serve Hill Street, in St John's Wood, then in course of construction; note the 'houses being built' on one side, and the names of some

50. Plan of a new sewer in Hill Street, St John's Wood, 1846, by John Dowley, consulting surveyor.

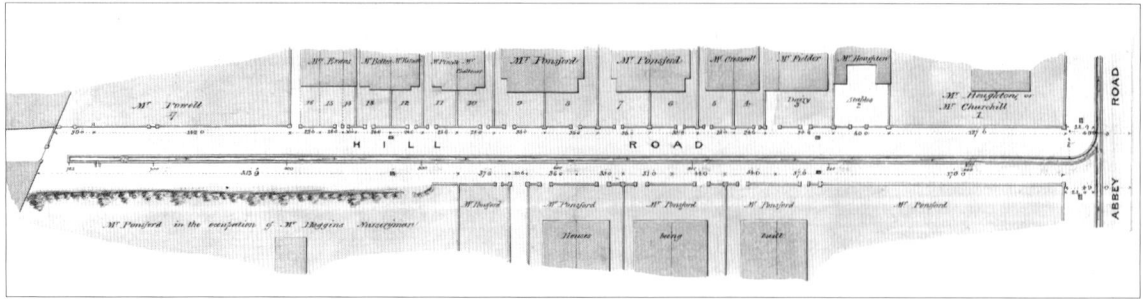

of the builders and lessees *(ill. 50)*.[21] An index to these maps and plans is available at the LMA.

Records of the Commissioners of Sewers for the City are held by the Corporation of London Records Office.

Records of post-1855 vestries, district boards, metropolitan boroughs and London boroughs for inner London

The Act which introduced the Metropolitan Board of Works transferred the municipal powers formally vested in the parishes to 23 vestries and 15 local boards.[22] These bodies were concerned principally with the maintenance and repair of drains and sewers, and no houses could be built or rebuilt without an adequate form of drainage being approved by them. Other powers related to paving, the cleansing and lighting of streets, and the compulsory appointment of Medical Officers of Health to report regularly on the sanitary condition of each area. These powers (with some additions) continued under the London County Council from 1889, and were passed in 1899–1900 to the 28 new metropolitan boroughs created by local government re-organization. Therefore, despite the various changes in central London's government during the period 1855 to 1965, at a local level the principal sources relating to domestic property – ratebooks (in Chapter 5), minute books, drainage applications, and reports of the Medical Officers of Health – remain pretty much the same.

Minutes. Most local history libraries will have manuscript or printed minutes for the vestry or district board, and metropolitan borough council which covered their area. Sometimes these are indexed. Minutes of the Holborn District Board of Works for the late 1880s are fairly typical, referring frequently to cleansing the streets, slum improvements, sewers and other sanitary works, and even (during the winter of 1886–7) to problems with extremely heavy snowfalls in the area, and arrangements to collect and dump the snow in the Thames. There are occasional, more detailed references

to individual properties. For instance, in February and April 1886 the board's surveyor (the architect Lewis Henry Isaacs) reported on terrible housing conditions at No. 58 Red Lion Street, and Nos 27 and 29 Laystall Street, providing a detailed list of defects and necessary remedial works. A later report, of February 1886, refers to illegal underground dwellings at Nos 5, 6 and 8 Elm Street. There are also reports on requests for projections beyond the existing street-frontage, such as that of October 1886 to construct bay windows in part of St George's Mansions, in Red Lion Square.[23]

Informative reports such as these occur less frequently by the time of the First World War: minutes of the 20th-century metropolitan borough councils tend to be more condensed, and generally speaking will probably offer more to the student of council housing; but private residential property does maintain a presence. To return to Raphael Street (see above), the printed minutes of Westminster City Council for the period *c*.1900–1920 (in Westminster City Archives), reveal the physical deterioration of houses in the street, and increasing problems with prostitution.[24] Public access to recent council minutes may be restricted or prohibited to preserve confidentiality.

Drainage applications (see also page 55). Either the local history library or records office, or one of the council departments (such as Building Control or Works), is likely to have a collection of local drainage plans and applications, sometimes dating back to the 1850s. Where they survive, these can vary from sketched outline or site plans, with the intended drainage indicated, to detailed elevations, sections and floor plans. In either case they usually provide an approximate but reliable date of construction, and the builder's name. In Tooting, the terrace of five houses at Nos 70–78 (even) Alston Road differs from the obviously Victorian houses in the immediate vicinity; drainage plans among the collection at Wandsworth Local History Service reveal they were erected *c*.1924 for the City & South London Railway (predecessor of the Northern Line), which owned this strip of land, to designs by Matthew J. Dawson, FRIBA.[25]

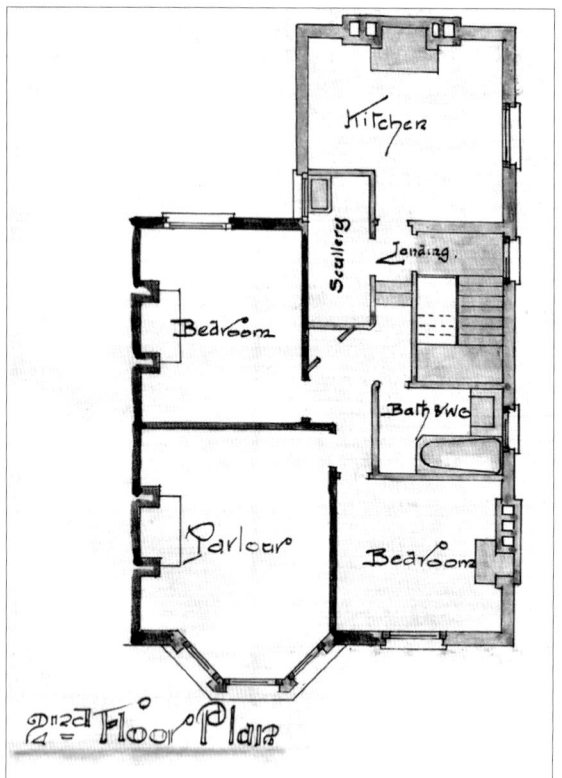
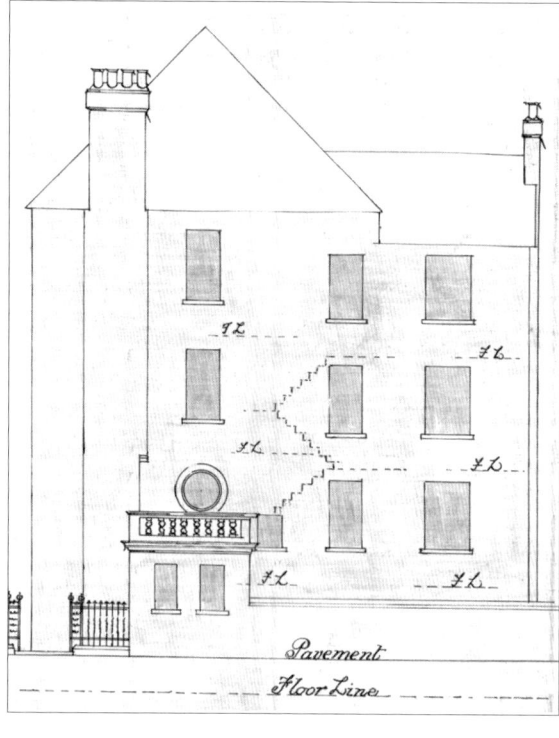

51. Drainage plans of 1897 for the conversion of 55 Queen's Drive into flats, from the records of South Hornsey UDC at Hackney Archives.

Medical Officer of Health reports. As part of their work, the local Medical Officers of Health identified and inspected overcrowded and insanitary districts, recording defects and structural problems, the number and class of occupants, and the incidence of particular diseases. Notes of these inspections can still be found in some local authority collections and can be a great help to students of slum housing. The officers also produced printed *Annual Reports* (usually included as part of the relevant local authority's Annual Report); these are particularly useful in locating poor and insalubrious areas, and following the progress of slum clearance schemes. *Annual Reports* of Poplar District Board of Works for the period 1879–87 (in the collection of Tower Hamlets Local History Library), chart the demolition of dilapidated early-19th-century housing in the Wells Street district of Poplar, and the construction in its place of new model dwellings. The Medical Officer's

reports characterize the type of local occupant ('the habitual pauper – the drunkard and the disturber of our nights'), and describe the wretched living conditions in some detail: for example, a mother, an invalided father, teenage son and four young daughters (one of whom was deaf and dumb) crowded together in a single room.[26]

Outer London local government records since the 1850s: parish vestries, local boards of health, and rural and urban district councils

In outer London, beyond the MBW area, some local boards of health were established in the 1850s, '60s and '70s to augment the work of the parish vestries, but their activities related largely to drainage, water supply and road maintenance, rather than matters of house construction or building regulation. Under the Local Government Act of 1894, the various outer parish vestries and local boards were replaced by urban and rural district councils (UDCs and RDCs). These gradually took on more powers, for example relating to street-lighting and education (from 1903), and inherited any building regulation bye-laws established under the old local authorities.

Records of the outer London bodies tend to be less voluminous and consistent than those for the inner districts. Regulation was more *ad hoc* than in central London, and staff were fewer in number (and often part-time or semi-professional), and so surviving documentation can be patchy. However, the types of records are generally similar to those for central London, and most local history archives should have minutes of the relevant board or vestry, and rural or urban district council, and some boroughs have drainage records, too. The minutes are perhaps more useful in giving a general picture of building development in the area, rather than providing detailed information about individual properties. Records of the RDCs and UDCs really come into their own during the inter-war period, when many outer areas were transformed from rural hinterlands into sprawling suburban dormitories by the capital's rapid outward expansion. In this book, Case History Three makes use of the minutes of the Ruislip–Northwood UDC to flesh out the story of the construction of the Manor Homes estate at Ruislip Manor by George Ball Ltd (see pages 180–186).

Post-war and later changes: today's London boroughs and the growth of planning

Although the London County Council had become a planning authority in 1925, it was not until after the Second World War that the LCC and its neighbouring county councils, along with the metropolitan boroughs and district authorities under their delegation, began to take a much greater interest in town planning. War-damage and post-war reconstruction brought the need for better strategic planning to the fore, but the problem was never tackled fully until the creation of the Greater London Council in 1965. Under the GLC the area covered by London government was greatly wid-

ened, bringing in parts of the adjoining counties and creating the 32 large London boroughs that we have today. The boroughs themselves became planning authorities, taking on responsibility for housing, health and local roads (among other things), with the GLC providing the strategic guidance. This two-tier system produced records at both upper and lower levels, but it is the local planning applications that will be of most use to those studying a particular street or district.

Some local history archives retain copies of planning applications, but a more comprehensive set will be found at the borough council's planning department. For the inner, former London County Council area, these files often contain pre-1965 material, sometimes dating back to the 1920s and '30s, when the LCC was the planning authority for the whole County of London. These planning records are publicly accessible, but you may have to make an appointment to see them. Some of the bigger London councils, such as Westminster and Islington, now offer up-to-date public-access facilities, with material available on microfilm or microfiche, and on application will provide files for specific sites, often containing maps, plans and correspondence, as well as any recent applications and the council's decisions.

NOTES AND REFERENCES

1. See Alan Cox, *Sources for the Study of Public Housing* (LAUF & Guildhall Library), 1993.
2. LMA, MJ/SS, WJ/SS.
3. LMA, MR/B, WR/B.
4. LMA, MR/B/C/1782/009.
5. LMA, MBO/DS/1–52; MBW/1616–1771; LCC/AR/BA/4.
6. LMA, MR/B/SR.
7. LMA, MBO/DS/49/E, no. 279.
8. LMA, MBO/PLANS/371.
9. LMA, MCS/244–304.
10. LMA, MCS/270, application no. 1202.
11. LMA, MCS/305–6.
12. LMA, GLC/AR/BR/23/160468–9; GLC/AR/BR/22/038150; GLC/AR/BR/22/008109.
13. LMA, LCC/MISC.P/114, sheet 5, part 1; MBW/2612.
14. LMA, MBW/1792, no. 1200.
15. LMA, GLC/AR/BR/SN/5.
16. LMA, AR/BA/5/264/4871.

17. Guildhall Library MSS Dept., MS 9081.

18. Islington Local History Centre, Vestry Minutes for the Parish of St James, Clerkenwell, 6, 26 May 1696.

19. LMA, HFCS/PR/7, HFCS/PR/36.

20. LMA, WCS/P44/1457.

21. LMA, WCS/P47/1574.

22. Metropolis Local Management Act, 1855 (18 & 19 Vict., c.120).

23. Camden Local Studies Centre, Minutes of Holborn District Board of Works.

24. Westminster City Council *Minutes*, 28 May 1903, p. 623; 29 Jan 1903, p. 128; 17 May 1906, p. 373; 9 July 1908, p. 443; 24 Nov 1910, p. 652; 8 Dec 1910, p. 666; 27 July 1911, p. 459; 21 May 1914, p. 284; 16 July 1914, p. 411; 15 Oct 1914, p. 525; 5 June 1919, p. 229; 24 July 1919, p. 331.

25. Wandsworth Local History Service, Drainage Plan no. 2171.

26. Poplar District Board of Works, *Annual report for year ending March 1881*, p. 27; *...for year ending March 1884*, p. 22.

FURTHER READING

Ida Darlington, 'The Metropolitan Buildings Office', in *The Builder*, 12 Oct 1956, pp. 628–32

Ida Darlington, 'The London Commissions of Sewers and their Records', in *Journal of the Society of Archivists*, No. 5, April 1962, pp. 196–210

John Davis, *Reforming London: The London Government Problem 1855–1900* (Clarendon Press), 1988

Percy J. Edwards (ed.), *History of London Street Improvements 1855–1897* (LCC), 1898

F. G. Emmison, *County Records* (Historical Association *Helps for the Student of History* no. 62), revised edn, 1961

Martin Gaskell, *Building Bye-Laws and Urban Development* (Historical Association), 1982

Martin Gaskell, *Building Control: National Legislation and the Introduction of Local Bye-Laws in Victorian England* (British Association for Local Housing), 1983

Sir I. G. Gibbon and R. W. Bell, *History of the London County Council 1889–1939* (Macmillan), 1939

Roger H. Harper, *Victorian Building Regulations* (Mansell), 1985

C. C. Knowles and P. H. Pitt, *The History of Building Regulation in London 1189–1972* (Architectural Press), 1972

David Owen, *The Government of Victorian London 1855–1889: The Metropolitan Board of Works, the Vestries, and the City Corporation* (Harvard University Press), 1982, ed. Roy MacLeod

Stephen Porter, 'London Government: A Brief Historical Guide', in *London Town Halls* (English Heritage/RCHME), 1999, pp. 9–13

Gerald Rhodes and S. K. Ruck, *The Government of Greater London* (George Allen & Unwin), 1970

Andrew Saint (ed.), *Politics and the People of London: the London County Council, 1889–1965* (The Hambledon Press), 1989

Francis Sheppard, *Local Government in St. Marylebone 1688–1835. A Study of the Vestry and the Turnpike Trust* (Athlone Press), 1958

Francis Sheppard, *London 1808–1870: The Infernal Wen* (Secker & Warburg), 1971

Elizabeth Silvestre (ed.), *London Local Authority Archives: A Directory of Local Authority Record Offices and Libraries* (Guildhall Library & Greater London Archives Network), 3rd edn, 1994

W. E. Tate, *The Parish Chest* (Cambridge University Press), 3rd edn, 1969

Ken Young and Patricia L. Garside, *Metropolitan London: Politics and Urban Change 1837–1981* (Edward Arnold *Studies in Urban History 6*), 1982

CHAPTER THREE

Title Deeds

In 1925 the Law of Property Act limited the requirement for evidence of title to 30 years, thus rendering obsolete the need to retain older deeds. Since then, recent changes in land registration have removed the legal requirement for title deeds, and many such documents – redundant to the modern house-buyer but of great interest to local historians – have been passed by solicitors, banks and council departments to local record offices; the British Records Association has done much valuable work in this field. Other collections can be found amongst family or estate papers (see Chapter 4); and there are many references to old deeds, and extracts from them, in disputes recorded in the Proceedings of Chancery (at the National Archives, see Chapter 10). Most borough archives have a series of local deeds, usually with some form of catalogue (even if simply a card index), and the London Metropolitan Archives has an extensive set of deeds, including those of ex-council property for all London boroughs and metropolitan bodies. In addition, there are two series of enrolled deeds which are of interest to London historians: the Close Rolls (also at the National Archives), and, for London north of the Thames, the Middlesex Deeds Registry (at the LMA), one of the best sources for property transactions.

If you are studying the history of a house which you have purchased, any surviving deeds will have been passed by your solicitor on completion to your mortgage lender. You have the right to inspect these (most banks and building societies will charge a fee for the privilege, or for providing a copy), but these may refer back only to a comparatively recent date. Since the introduction of compulsory land registration, house-purchasers are less likely to find much of historical interest among the deeds lodged with their mortgage lender. Today the Land Registry guarantees title to all the registered properties in England and Wales, and can provide online enquirers with copies of title plans and basic property and ownership information from the register for a small fee.

Originally there was no need for deeds or documents of title, as land was not 'owned' in the modern sense, but belonged ultimately to the Crown, and was given by the monarch to subjects in return for service or some payment in kind. Tenants could sub-let parts of the land granted by the Crown to others in a like manner (a process called *subinfeudation*). Any change of ownership was made official by a public ceremony known as the *Livery of Seisin*, which marked the physical entry of the new owner or tenant on to the property, at which part of the land or building in question, such as a sod or brick, was handed over symbolically in the presence of witnesses. The transaction's public nature ensured that the new owner or tenant could not escape his duties, and defaulting gave the lord the right to take back the property and grant it to another. Eventually such transactions were written down, to assist memory. The crucial part of the earliest conveyances, known as *feoffments*, was the endorsement written on the back, which recorded that livery of seisin had take place – without this the deed was meaningless. The feoffment was not an agreement between two parties, like later deeds, but was more of a statement of what had already occurred; hence, it is in the past tense – 'have given granted and... confirmed to'. Conveyancing history thereafter is

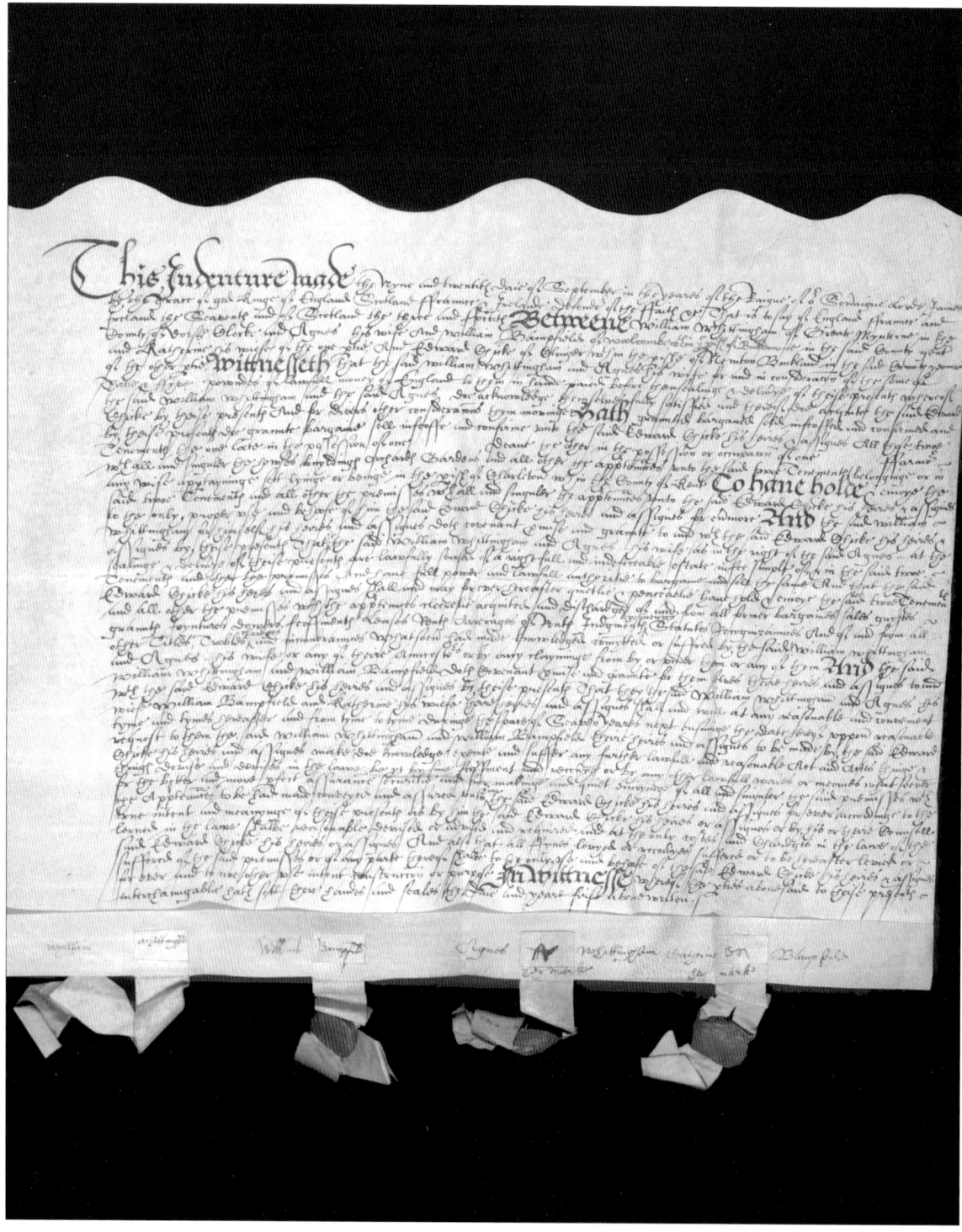

52. *Deed recording the bargain and sale of two 'tenements' at Charlton, 1609.*

dominated by the new types of deed devised by lawyers to avoid livery of seisin and make such transfers a private business. London house researchers are more likely to come across 18th- and 19th-century deeds than medieval ones, but their use demands some knowledge of how the various forms of conveyance evolved.

Using old deeds

Old title deeds are a heterogenous group of documents (ills 52 & 53). Differences in size and format are many, and occasionally unnerving: be prepared for a short scrap of paper, or a cumbersome many-paged document, such as the leases and releases of the 18th and 19th centuries. Before studying some of the various types, and examining their characteristics, it is well to consider some basic advice on reading and interpretation. The information deeds contain is fundamental to those involved in researching the history of houses – dates of sales, terms of tenancies, purchase prices, rents, names and addresses of owners, tenants, occupants, sellers, purchasers or mortgagees – but this is often embedded in a long and repetitive document, littered with legal jargon. The lack of punctuation can be a little off-putting at first (it is unnecessary in a legal document, where there can be no misinterpretation), but, luckily, most of the legal phrases are formulaic and can be disregarded. Indeed, with practice, as the structure of deeds becomes familiar, it is possible to pick out the sections where the useful information is given, without having to read the whole document.

Helpfully, the first words of these sections are usually emphasized by being capitalized or written boldly, making them easy to identify. First come the *Premises*, which give the date of the deed and the names of the parties to it, beginning: 'THIS INDENTURE MADE....' and 'BETWEEN'. Next is the *Testatum*, introduced by the word 'WITNESSETH...', which states the purpose of the deed, e.g. a lease, explaining which party is selling or leasing the property, and to whom. This section also includes a reference to money changing hands – the 'consideration' – a purchase sum if a freehold sale, or a 'fine' or lump sum used to buy the term if a lease. There is also a description of the property (beginning 'ALL THAT...') which is usually reasonably accurate, often with some idea of its size or construction, or internal fittings, and giving a precise identification by its relation-

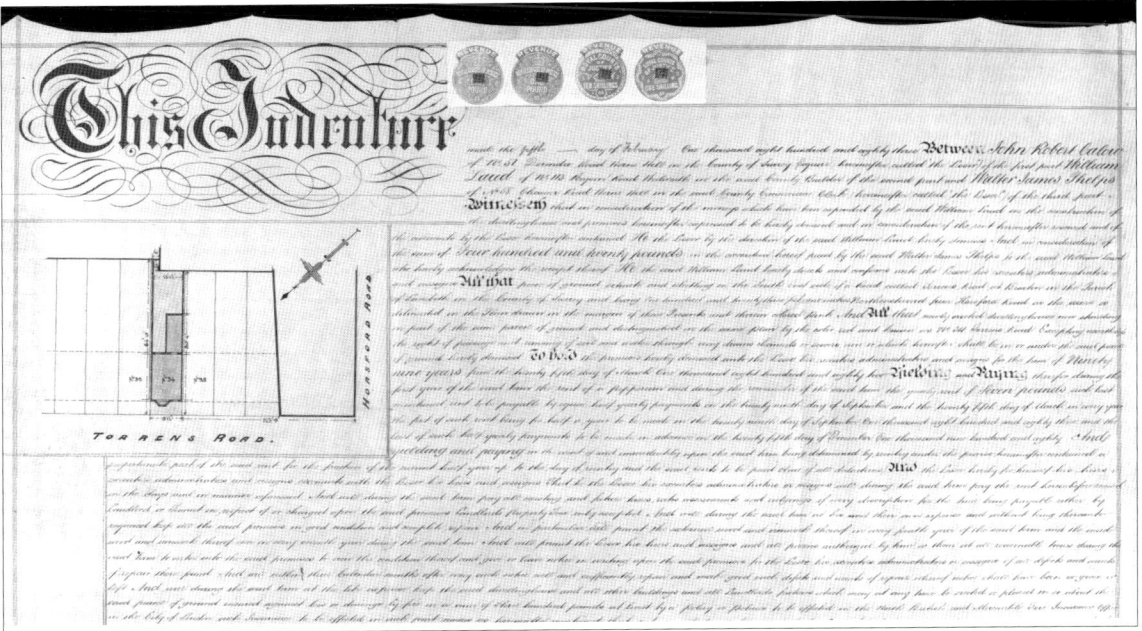

53. *Typical deed: Building lease (with plan attached), 5 February 1883, of No. 34 Torrens Road, Brixton Rise.*

ship to adjoining roads, buildings or other local landmarks. A house is usually referred to as a tenement or *messuage* (a legal term for a dwelling). Sometimes a handy site- or ground-plan will have been included in the margin for clarity. The *Testatum* is followed by the *Habendum*, which begins 'TO HAVE AND TO HOLD...', and which also defines the tenure: a freehold sale will be 'for ever', a lease or assignment will state a term of years. In the case of leases the *Habendum* is followed by an additional clause, the *Reddendum*, 'YIELDING AND PAYING...', which outlines the rent or services due. Finally comes the *Testimonium*, concluding the deed, declaring that it was signed by all the parties in the presence of witnesses.

Occasionally a deed may include *Recitals* of previous transactions relating to the property – a valuable source of useful data on the house's earlier history, which may not be found so easily elsewhere. Recitals come after the *Premises*, and are introduced by the word 'WHEREAS...', for the first recital, and 'AND WHEREAS...' for subsequent ones. Where recitals occur the opening phrase of the *Testatum* changes to 'NOW THIS INDENTURE WITNESSETH'.

There are some other, minor points relating to old deeds which may be of use or interest. The word *indenture* refers to any deed with two or more parties; this would have been written out twice (or more if necessary) on a single piece of parchment, and separated by a wavy or 'indented' cut. Each party kept a copy (the buyer or tenant kept the first version, the seller or landlord the other, called the counterpart), and their authenticity could be affirmed at any time by reassembling the pieces. Similarly, any deed which records the acts of a single party is a *deed poll*, so-called because, in contrast to the undulating line of the indenture, it has a straight or 'polled' edge. Remember that a party to a deed can consist of more than one person. Each party will be acting in a different capacity – e.g. sellers, buyers, or mortagees; or, if the conveyance is of a deceased person's estate, one party may consist of executors or beneficiaries of a trust established by the will. A deed without a seal or signature is unlikely to have been executed, and one which has had zigzag cuts made through it has been cancelled.

To conclude this section, a few words about dates and the calendar. Until the introduction of the new-style calendar in 1752, the new year began on 25 March and ended on 24 March following: e.g., December 1720 was followed by January 1720, February 1720 and 1-24 March 1720 (1721 beginning the next day, on 25 March 1721). To avoid confusion, it is common practice in modern works to give both old- and new-style calendar dates when referring to the period January-24 March, e.g. 15 February 1720/1.

Tenure: freeholds, leaseholds and copyholds

In most cases old deeds will refer to one or more of the three principal types of land tenure – freehold, leasehold and copyhold.

Freehold land is land held absolutely and indefinitely, 'for ever', without any date of termination (as in a lease). There were two forms of freehold: *fee simple*, the most common, applied to estates of inheritance, which could be passed to heirs or sold to purchasers and their heirs, unconditionally; and *fee tail* (originally called fee simple conditional), which usually limited ownership to specified heirs (e.g. the eldest heirs male, or occasionally, female) – this land was said to be 'entailed' and could not be sold.

Leasehold tenure applies to land or buildings leased by the owner to a lessee or tenant for a limited period, usually a stated number of years, in return for which the tenant agrees to pay rent and obey certain conditions. A lease direct from the landlord or freeholder is a *head lease*, and the holder of this could then issue a *sub-lease* or *under-lease* to another, and so on, until there were several layers of concurrent leases, but only one occupier, at the bottom of the chain.

Copyhold – also called customary tenure – covered properties originally granted by the lord of the manor to tenants who held them at his will according to the particular customs of that manor. Copyhold land could be leased, bought and sold, entailed or left in a will. Each change of ownership took place in the manorial court, where the exiting owner (or vendor) would 'surrender' his holding to the steward of the manor, in order for it to be 'regranted' to the new owner (or purchaser). The lord of the manor was entitled to a payment or 'fine' from each new copyholder. Such transactions were entered on the manorial court roll, and a copy kept as evidence of title by the new owner – hence the name 'copyhold'. From the 17th century onwards some copyholders had their land converted to freehold by the lord of the manor in a deed called a deed of enfranchisement. This was increasingly important during the speculative-building booms of the 18th and 19th centuries, as building leases were rarely issued for copyhold land (though there were exceptions).[1] Copyhold or customary tenure was finally abolished in the 1920s. (See also *Manorial Records*, below.)

Some types of deed: a short guide to the most common forms of agreement

Uses and the **Bargain and Sale**. One of the tactics dreamt up by medieval lawyers to avoid feudal duties and restrictions was the *Use*, by which property was transferred from one party (seller) to a second party (the nominal purchaser, often a number of people), to hold for the use of a third party (buyer). Legally, the second party was the owner of the estate, and liable to render service, although the effective owner was the third party, who thus escaped paying their feudal dues. The Statute of Uses was passed in 1536 to counter this, by recognizing the third party as the legal owner in such cases. The legal profession's answer was the *bargain and sale*, a deed formerly used to transfer personal property, but here employed to convey uses. In its basic form, the seller bargains and sells a property to the purchaser for the purchaser's use. As the Statute of Uses recognized the holder of the use to be the legal owner, the purchaser became the legal owner without the need of a public ceremony of livery of seisin. The official response to this was the Statute of Enrolments of 1536, which sought to defeat secrecy by insisting that all bargains and sales of freehold property must be enrolled in a court within six months; many will therefore have an enrolment in formal handwriting. The bargain and sale is a common form for conveying both freeholds and leaseholds, easily recognizable from the phrase 'Granted Bargained and Sold.'

Lease and Release. The lease and release first appeared in the early 17th century as a means of selling freehold property without the unwanted publicity of livery of seisin or the inconvenience of statutory enrolment. Such was its simplicity and success that it remained the most common form of freehold conveyance until the 1840s, when new legislation introduced a simple deed of grant and finally rendered obsolete both livery of seisin and the conveyances which had been introduced to circumvent it.

As the name suggests, the lease and release consists of two documents. On one day the seller bargains and sells a lease of a property for one year to the use of the purchaser at a token rent (usually a peppercorn). By the Statute of Uses this rendered the lessee (the purchaser) possessed of the property without need for livery of seisin and, as this was only a lease, the deed was not subject to enrolment. On the day following, the lessor, for a price, releases to the lessee the freehold reversion of the property – this is not the land or building itself, but the owner's intangible future right to recover it on the termination of the lease (legally defined as an *incorporeal hereditament*), and, as such, transferable by written deed.

This type of deed is easy to recognize, consisting as it does of two documents dated consecutively, the smaller lease usually tucked inside the longer and more complicated release. The lease is purely a legal ploy, not a genuine lease, from which it can be differentiated by a phrase saying that this is 'to the interest and purpose that...[the lessor]...may be in actual possession'. Usually the lease, the simpler of the two documents, concerns only the two main parties, even if other parties are involved; all parties are named in the release. The latter states that the property has been 'Granted Bargained Sold Aliened Released' etc, and has the tell-tale phrase that the purchaser is already in possession of a lease bearing the date 'the day next before the day of the date of these presents', or something similar. In this way, if only one of the two documents survives, it should be possible to work out what is happening.

Leases. In a standard lease the owner of a property (the *lessor*, who can be the freeholder or a leaseholder) conveys a property to another (the *lessee*) for a defined period, usually a number of years but occasionally for a certain number of lives (see *lease for life*, below). In return the lessee agrees to pay rent and obey certain conditions. In earlier leases it was customary for the annual rent to be quite a small sum, the true value of the lease being indicated by the 'fine' or lump sum which the lessee paid to purchase the term; this will be mentioned as the 'consideration'. By the 18th century, however, this system was giving way to the more familiar modern version with no fine but a substantial rent. Frequently, previous occupiers are mentioned. At the end of leases are numerous clauses regarding the payment of taxes, the landlord's or lessor's right of re-entry should rent be unpaid, and covenants about the upkeep of the property, the tending of the soil (if appropriate), and often restricting noisome or offensive trades. These are (for the most part) formal in nature, and can usually be disregarded, though any clause forbidding sub-letting without the landlord's consent would be entered here, and those studying rural or semi-rural areas may be interested in the arrangements made for agriculture. Remember that the leaseholder of a house may not have been the person residing there; most London houses were sub-let by leaseholders to occupants on short-term tenancies.

Leases could be sold (or *assigned*), for a fee, to another person, who then became the landlord's tenant. Such a deed will involve at least three parties (the two parties to the original lease and the new tenant), and should recite the previous lease. The operative phrase here will be something akin to 'hath given granted bargained sold *assigned and set over*'. It was common practice for a builder, once he had completed his houses, to sell or 'assign' his building leases to an investor, or perhaps not take the lease at all, and participate in its being granted directly to a third party.

Occasionally, one may encounter a *lease for life* (or *lives*), a form of demise sometimes adopted by corporate landlords (such as colleges and churches), and also found among manorial records. In this type of deed the term of the lease, rather than a number of years, is defined as the lifetimes of certain named persons (usually relatives of the lessee, but sometimes including a well-known person, such as the King), the lease expiring at the death of the last survivor. Given the indeterminate duration of the lease, payment was usually by a substantial fine, with a small rent. In practice, however, it was not uncommon on the death of a 'life' for the lease to be surrendered and a new lease issued, with a new 'life' added, allowing the property to remain almost indefinitely in the same family.

Sometimes the duration of a lease will be noticeably long – say 500 or 1,000 years – with a substantial fine but a small rent. This form of tenure was, in effect, a sort of freehold. Frequently in these cases the original owner of the freehold was not known, even though they were entitled, under the terms of the lease, to receive rent. Holders of such long leases could sell the property simply by assigning the lease.

One especially important type of lease to the house historian is the *building lease*, a particular form of long lease granted by a landowner or his immediate undertenant to a developer or builder, who, as part of the terms of the lease, is required to build a house or houses. The size, number and appearance of the houses, and the amount of time allowed for their construction, would have been settled beforehand in a building agreement or contract (known as 'articles of agreement'), which rarely survive outside the records of estates.[2] In building leases the identifying factors are the term (usually between 61 and 99 years), and the rent, which was a token one (a peppercorn) for the first year or two, giving the builder time to get the house finished before having to pay out money. For instance, Macclesfield Street in Soho, originally developed in the 1680s, was partially rebuilt in 1729–30 under building leases issued by John Jeffreys, copies of which can be found in the Middlesex Deeds Registry. No. 9 (since demolished with other houses on the north side for the formation of Shaftesbury Avenue) was leased to John

Ladyman, a local glazier, on a 61-year building lease, at a rent of a peppercorn for one year, and £9 per annum thereafter.[3] Much of 17th- and 18th-century London was developed under such building leases; illustration 53 shows a late-Victorian example, a building lease of a terrace-house in Torrens Road, Brixton. (See also the section on the leasehold system, pages 13–15, and Chapter 4 on estate records.)

Abstract of title. An abstract of title is a list of all deeds relating to a property or estate, drawn up at the time of sale and passed to the new owner with the relevant deeds. They are often found among estate and personal papers, and are much easier for the researcher to use than having to locate and read every deed. For example, in the LMA's collection of estate records is a 19th-century abstract of title for No. 54 Upper Berkeley Street which gives the full history of its changes in ownership from its construction *c.*1792 until 1863.[4]

Mortgages. As most householders are painfully aware, a mortgage is a deed in which the owner of a property (mortgagor) borrows money from another (mortgagee), with the property as security for the repayment of the loan. Should the mortgagor fail to repay, the property defaults to the mortgagee, who is entitled to sell it to recover his money. Old deeds recording this are (confusingly) very similar to a standard conveyance or lease, as the owner either 'sold' the property to the mortgagee for the amount of the loan (a *Mortgage in Fee*, usually in the form of a lease and release), or leased it to him for a very long term, e.g. 500 or 1,000 years, with the loan serving as the fine (*Mortgage by Demise*). Usually, if the mortgage takes the form of a lease, this is made clear by the insertion after the *Reddendum* of a special clause, the *Proviso*, beginning 'PROVIDED ALWAYS...', which states that the deed becomes void and the property is re-conveyed to the mortgagor on repayment of the principal plus interest. (This right of the mortgagor to retain his property provided he pays off the mortgage and interest is often referred to as the 'Equity of Redemption'.) A date for repayment may be given (usually one

year after the execution of the deed), but this was not binding and in practice can be ignored.[5] However, if a mortgage was effected by lease and release, there is no *Reddendum* and often no *Proviso*, making identification impossible without information from other deeds or sources. Similar problems can occur if the only record is in an abstracted or registered form, such as an entry in the Middlesex Deeds Registry.

If the mortgagee required repayment before the mortgagor was able to do so, the mortgage could be transferred or 'assigned' to a third party, in the same manner as a lease. *Assignments of mortgages* are often 'endorsed', i.e. written on the back of the original agreement, and are therefore also referred to as *endorsements*. Sometimes the borrower took advantage of the assignment to borrow an additional sum from the new lender, increasing the total amount to be repaid.

Feet of fines. A fine or final concord was a settlement to a fictitious legal action relating to land, originally introduced as an alternative to the feoffment. As a court record it was evidence of title, subsequently used to bar an entail and convey entailed land. The purchaser (usually referred to as the *plaintiff* or *querent*) alleged that the seller (or *deforciant*) had previously agreed to sell him the land but had failed to honour this. However, before judgement was made by the court the two parties fictitiously agreed that the property did actually belong to the querent. This final agreement was recorded in a tripartite indenture: two parts were kept by the two parties to the agreement, and the third part, a copy at the bottom, known as 'The Foot', was kept as a record by the court. The document was cut through the word CYROGRAPHUM, written across the top of the foot and between the other two copies – in this way the three pieces could be reassembled at any time to check their authenticity.

Feet of fines can be found amongst most collections of deeds, and many local record societies have published printed calendars of fines for particular counties. At the National Archives they are filed under the law term in

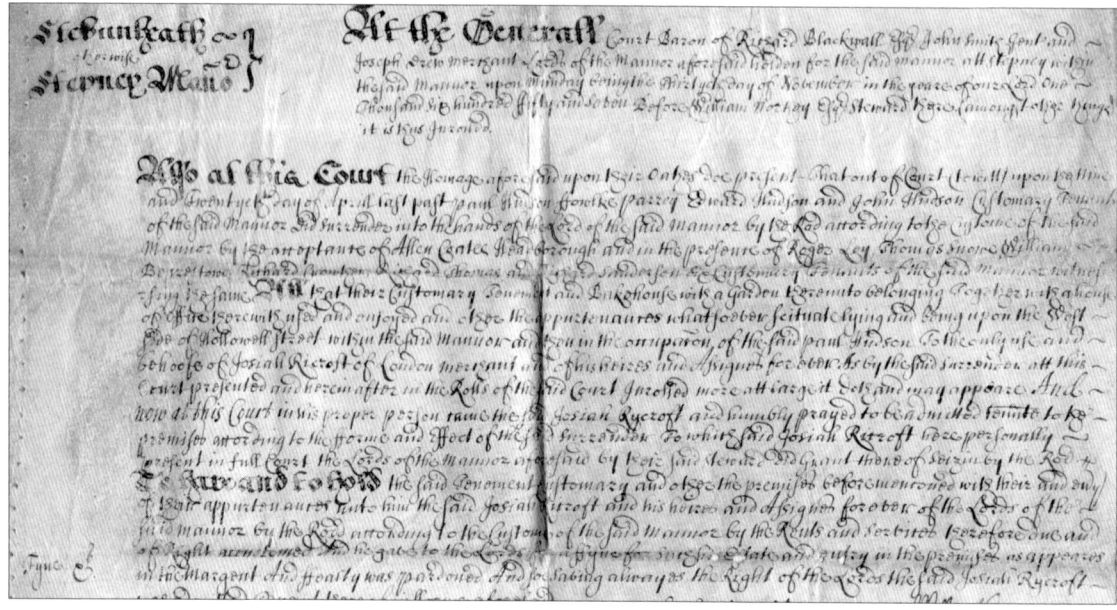

54. *Typical manorial admission and surrender of a house, bakehouse and garden on the west side of Holywell Street, in Stepney manor, 1657.*

which they were recorded, and grouped by county. Like other common law records, they are in Latin to 1733 (except for the Commonwealth). The use of fines was abolished in 1833. A fine is instantly recognizable from its opening sentence: *Hec est finalis concordia* – 'This is the final agreement'.

Common Recovery. This was another fictitious action dreamt up to bar entail, though in this instance carried to a conclusion in court. The purchaser (or *demandant*) brings an action against the seller (or *tenant in tail*) to 'recover' the property, claiming fictitiously that it is his, but that he had been illegally ejected by an equally fictitious third party (for some reason often called Hugh Hunt). The tenant calls on a fourth party (the *vouchee*) to warrant or vouch for his title; but when the demandant withdraws to 'imparl' or talk with this vouchee as to the title, the vouchee fails to appear, and is held in contempt of court. Therefore, the tenant, unable to support his case, loses the action and the demandant is awarded the property in fee simple. As with feet of fines, as a record of court the recovery is in Latin until 1733. Both were abolished in 1833 by an Act which substituted a simple deed of disentailment.

Manorial records

As we have seen, copyhold was an important form of land tenure in and around London until the later 19th century. Any changes in tenancy or ownership were recorded in the court rolls or minute books of the manor. If these have survived, they are most likely to be found in the LMA or, for outer areas, the relevant county record office, or at the National Archives. The Historical Manuscripts Commission has a useful 'Manorial Documents Register' which lists by county and name the holdings of known manorial records; this is now accessible via the Internet.

Some manors, for example those covering Westminster, have records from the fourteenth to the 20th centuries, but most others will have gaps among their collections. If you are lucky enough to know the name of a copyhold owner from another source, in a manor with a good run of records, you should be able to trace the property back through time, as each change of ownership (called *admission*), when the incomer 'swore fealty' to the lord of the manor, also recorded the name of the previous owner and his date of admission. Early records, before 1733, will be in Latin, but there are many good guides to manorial records, most of them with advice on how to spot the stock phrases in Latin and glean from them the essential information (see *Further Reading*, below).

As with owners of leases, the copyholder was not necessarily the occupant. If he wished to let his property to a tenant, a licence was required from the manorial authorities, unless general permission had already been given for leases of similar, or longer, duration. These can be found among manorial records, and will furnish the names of the interested parties. Manorial documents may also contain: applications for permission to build on the 'waste' (vacant) land of the manor; lists of manorial property and tenants (often called an *extent*); and, as the manorial business was carried on by a court, enrolments or registers of deeds, mortgages and recoveries.

Close Rolls

Although the counties of Yorkshire and Middlesex had a policy of registering deeds of title (see below), there was no central English registry of conveyances until the introduction of the Land Registry in the late 19th century. However, some individuals did take the opportunity of having their transactions made 'official' by endorsement or enrolment in one of the 'courts of record'. Of these, the most useful and accessible collection is that of the many private deeds enrolled in the Court of Chancery, in legal documents known as the Close Rolls (National Archives, class C54).

These comprise sheets of parchment which have been sewn together end-to-end into large rolls. The rolls were made up by regnal year, and divided into different 'parts', the number of parts depending upon the amount of legal work generated that year. Enrolment of private deeds had been common since the 13th century (originally on the backs of the rolls), but the Statute of Enrolments of 1536 (by which all bargains and sales of freehold property had to be enrolled by one of the law courts or a clerk of the peace) made enrolment of deeds thereafter a large part of the Chancery clerks' business.

Various indexes to deeds in the Close Rolls are available on open shelves at the National Archives (C275): by grantor (i.e. seller or lessor) and county; and, unusually, for the period 1509–1837, a very useful series of indexes by grantee (i.e. buyer or lessee). Once you have found a likely index entry, it is important to note the part number of the roll for that regnal year. Once you have ordered the relevant part, you will probably have to search through it to find the entry; the names of the parties are given in the left-hand margin. Before 1733 the enrolled deeds and indexes are likely to be in Latin, except for the Interregnum, but after 1733 both the rolls and indexes are always in English. Consulting the Close Rolls for the first time can be a complicated business, but the National Archives has some good information sheets giving guidelines for their use, and explaining their history.

The Middlesex Deeds Registry

Without doubt one of the most valuable sources – probably the most valuable – for those researching the changing ownership of houses and other property in London north of the Thames, in the former County of Middlesex, is the Middlesex Deeds Registry (MDR), held at London Metropolitan Archives. (Middlesex included all of pre-1965 London north of the river, including Westminster, but excluding the City of London.)

The MDR was a public register of deeds, established by Act of Parliament in 1708 and begun the following year, in which all sales, leases of more than 21 years, mortgages and wills affecting land in the county of Middlesex had to be registered before any subsequent transfer could be valid in law. Short-term leases and furnished tenancies were excluded, as were deeds relating to copyhold land. Similar deeds registries also existed in Yorkshire.

The register began in 1709 and continued until 1936, generating some 12,000 volumes of memorials and indexes. However its comprehensiveness (and therefore usefulness) diminishes for inner London after 1899, when registration in the Land Registry of title to property in the County of London north of the Thames became compulsory, exempting parties from registering in the MDR. However, for those parts of outer London outside the LCC area (e.g. places like Acton, Ealing, Harrow,

1875　　　G

	Name	Reference	No.	Place
	Goodwyn	Maria Anne			
	Goodwyn	Elizabeth	} & Midland R⁴ C°	24 427	Hendon
	Goodwyn	Julius Edm⁴			
	Goodwyn	Henry W^m			
	Goodwyn	Maria Anne			
	Goodwyn	Arthur Ino. Bowdler	} & Eley Henry	24 519	d°
	Goodwyn	Elizabeth			
	Goodwyn	Julius Edm⁴			
	Goodwyn	Thomas Wildman			
	Goodwyn	Arthur Ino. Bowdler & Evans Ino	26 835	d°
	Goodwyn	Arthur Ino: Bowdler & Bishop H⁴			
		Mannin & anor	}	27 154	d°
	Goodwyn	Arthur Ino: Bowdler & Heisch			
		Sophia Antoinette	}	27 536	—
	Goodwyn	Arthur Ino: Bowdler & Macandrew Ja⁵	28 110	Hendon
	Goodyear	Frederick J⁴ & Martyn W^m	15 644	Finchley
	Goolden	Richard H⁴			
	Goolden	Katherine	} & Goolden Rich⁴ Edw⁴ & an⁴	18 543	—
	Goolden	Richard H⁴			
	Goolden	Katherine	} & Goolden Wm Hugh		
	Goolden	William Hugh	} & anor	18 544	—
	Goolden	Richard Edw⁴			
Vac⁴	Goosey	William Philip & Young Allen W^m			
		& another DISCH⁴ 21. April 1876	}	19 160	—
	Goosey	William Philip & Cooke Benjn	19 552	Pancras
	Goosey	William Philip & Haine Ino: Weeks	19 553	d°
	Goosey	William & Goosey Wm Philip	21 44	d°
	Goosey	William Philip & Whitbread Wm Jan⁴	21 46	d°
	Gordon	Edwin & Brown Edw⁴ H⁴ & anor	18 316	S⁴ Martin in fields
	Gordon	Henry & Crowder Aug⁴ Geo	18 457	Whitechapel
	Gordon	Sir Henry Percy Bar⁴ & Metropolitan			
		Board of Works		18 908	Chelsea Jan⁴
Vac⁴	Gordon	Thomas & Nicholson W^m & ors DISCH⁴ 30: June 1876	19 201	—
	Gordon	Charles W^m & Barclay Tho⁵ Geo & ors	19 965	—
	Gordon	Thomas & City of London Brew⁴ C° lim⁴	23 211	Pancras
	Gordon	John Glenny & Mooyaart Edw⁴	23 752	Marybone
Vac⁴	Gordon	William Geo: & Sewell & Blackie DISCH⁴ 22. July 1878	27 684	Blackwall
	Gordon	Paul Joshua & Patterson Wm Geo	28 503	Marybone
	Gordon	Henry Wobridge & Burton Wm Sam⁴ & ors	29 784	Islington
	Goring	Maria Arabella			
	Goring	Georgiana Louisa	} & Fearon Jessy		
	Goring	Frances Eliz^th	} Tyndale	15 765	Kensington

55. *Typical page of MDR index.*

Barnet, Enfield etc), the MDR remained a comprehensive register until 1937, when compulsory registration in the Land Registry was extended to take in the rest of Middlesex, rendering the MDR redundant. Sometimes, though rarely, during this last period of its operation, deeds for these outer areas were copied in full in the register, rather than being abbreviated versions. Even for inner London, some deeds – mostly mortgages and leases for little more than 21 years – continued to be registered in the MDR until registration ceased in 1938.

In order to register a deed, an abbreviated copy or 'memorial' on parchment would be presented to the Middlesex authorities with the original by one of the parties involved. On payment of a fee (proportionate to the length of the document) the original deed was endorsed with the date of registration and a registry serial number, and returned. The memorial, having been checked against the original deed, would be copied into the register volume; the serial number, names of principal parties and the date were written in the margin.

With so many volumes of registered deeds, the sheer bulk of the MDR is the greatest obstacle to its use. Separate index volumes do exist for each year, arranged by the capital letter of the surname of the first party (the vendor or grantor); the names of other parties are usually given too (ill. 55). The indexes become truly alphabetical from 1828. From 1718 a final column lists the parish where the property was located; topographical indexes are available for the period 1709–17. Thus in order to trace a particular transaction it is necessary to know the vendor or grantor's name and an approximate date. This will not always guarantee success: title deeds were sometimes not registered until the property changed hands again, when registration of the first transaction was essential for the second sale to be legitimate. For those historians working on the history of a large area or parish where building development began in the 18th or 19th century, it is theoretically possible, if laborious, to trace most of the original building leases by working through the index volumes and noting all transactions for that area.

Much more difficult is tracing the history of ownership or development for a single site or building. As you have to know the names of owners or grantors and dates, standard practice – working backwards from the known to the unknown – is almost impossible. However, if the builder is known from another source, such as the district surveyors' returns, it may be possible to find the property in the MDR, as he is likely to have mortgaged the house.

To give a typical example, as part of the research for the *Survey of London* volume on Knightsbridge, it was possible, by looking through the MDR over a 100-year period, to reconstruct much of the history and changes in ownership of a long-demolished house, latterly known as Grosvenor House, situated on the west side of Knightsbridge Green, just north of the Brompton Road. Other sources indicated that this house had been built around 1630 as part of the estate of Sir William Blake, and had later been owned or occupied by Katherine, Dowager Viscountess Ranelagh, sister of Robert Boyle, the eminent scientist. A rather grand 'capital mansion', with wainscotting in the hall and parlour, and a fine garden with elm and other trees, it was purchased in February 1704/5 by Philip Moreau (d.1733), of a wealthy family of Huguenot merchants. The house became the family home and centre of a small estate, which was broken up and sold at auction in May 1759 by Charles Frederick Moreau.[6]

Looking in the MDR indexes under 'Moreau' for 1759, 1760 and 1761, numerous references relate to the sale. However, the sequence in the registers does not always reflect the chronology of events. An entry for 1761 records that the Moreaus' house was purchased by one of the family, David Moreau, at the end of March 1760; and an entry under his name for 1760 shows that in the following October he sold the house to the Hon. Colonel Mordaunt Cracherode of Queen's Square, for £880.[7] These deeds provide a lot of useful information: the property had been 'new built' by Philip Moreau's son and heir, Captain James Philip Moreau, who died in 1748 (it is this rebuilt house that is illustrated in Salway's plan of the Brompton Road area of 1811, *ill. 56*); and after the death of Captain Moreau's wife, Esther, the house had been let by the family

56. *Illustration of Moreau house from Salway's survey of Kensington and Brompton roads, 1811.*

57. *MDR illustration of houses in Theberton Street, Islington, 1837.*

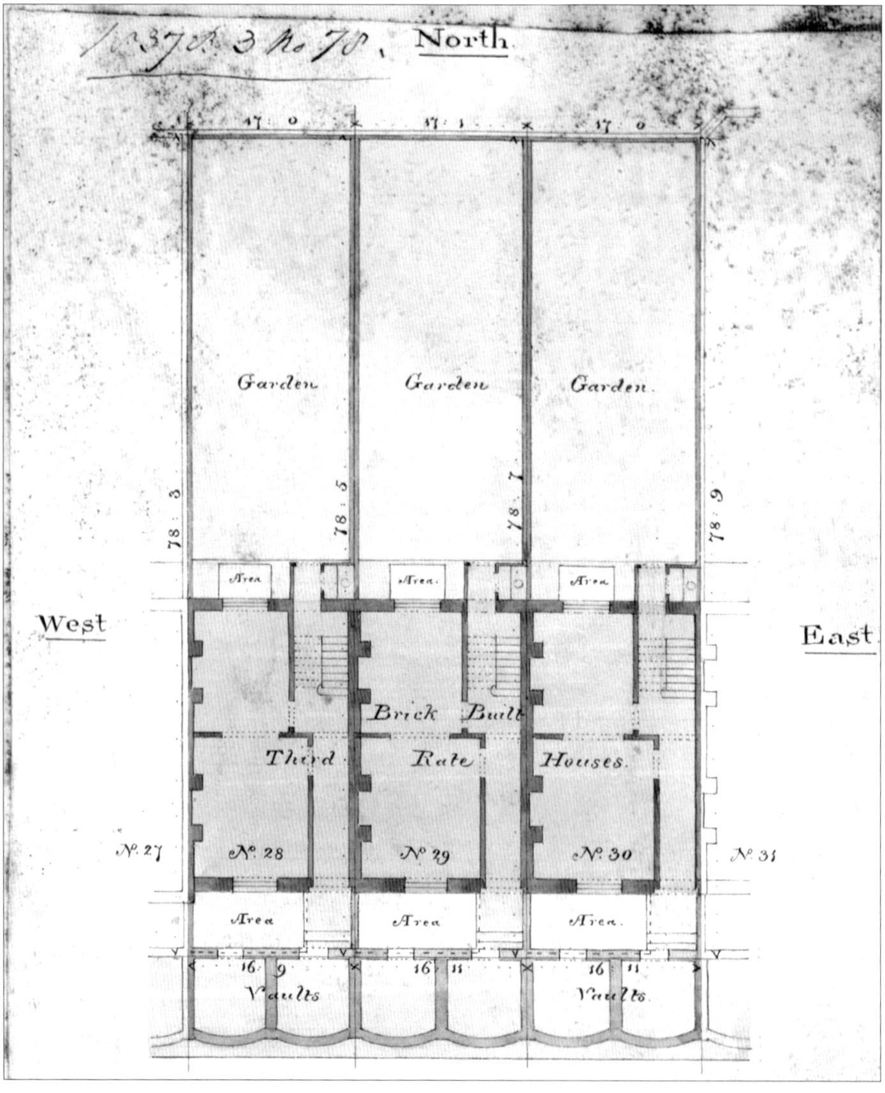

to Alexander Thistlewayte, Esquire.

Carrying on the search, Cracherode's name occurs in the MDR index of 1761 for a Knightsbridge property, as in September of that year he registered a sale of the house to Thomas Broderick, Vice-Admiral of the Blue. His tenure was also short, for in the following May he sold the house to the Reverend Martin Madan.[8] Madan was an interesting character, chaplain of the nearby Lock Hospital (for venereal disease), and the author of a work in favour of polygamy (*Thelyphora*, 1780), which caused a minor furore when published. Madan died in 1790, and the MDR for 1798 records excerpts from his will. All his property – including his estates in Britain, a lease of a plantation in America, and 'all his Negroes and stock' – was left to his wife, Jane. She, too, died in 1790, and in her will left the Knightsbridge house to her son, also Martin, who in 1798 sold it to Nathaniel Gosling, a member of a prominent banking family. Note that the two wills recording the bequest of the house were registered some years later, when the property was sold. From Gosling the former Moreau house passed in 1812 to William Wood Watson of Camberwell. It is not until 1857 that the final sale is registered. In that year George Watson Wood, a descendant of William Wood Watson, sold Grosvenor House to Richard Tattersall the younger. The deed lists many former occupants, the most recent being Alfred Josias Rogers, on a 21-year lease from Watson Wood.[9] This brings to an end the history of the house. It was demolished shortly after the sale to make way for Tattersalls' new horse and carriage mart at Knightsbridge Green (opened 1863), which remained in business until badly damaged during the Second World War. The site is currently occupied by a 1950s office block, Caltex House.

From the late 18th century the registers also contain some useful and often attractive maps and plans. These range from roughly sketched site plans to detailed house-plans (with room layouts, as in illustration 57), street plans, and elaborate coloured maps of entire estates. Occasionally an elevation finds its way in amongst the registers. Those of the early 19th century are particularly good: for example, a wash el-

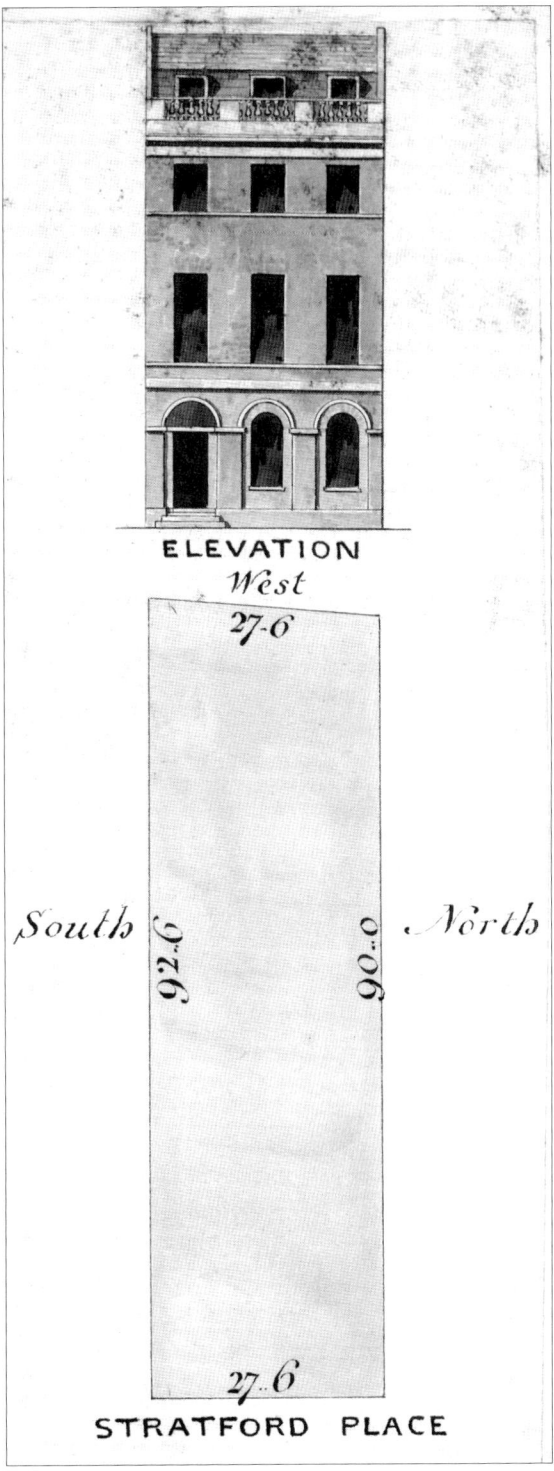

58. *MDR illustration and plan of house on east side of Stratford Place, St Marylebone, 1814.*

evation and block plan accompanies the registered lease in 1814 of a house on the east side of Stratford Place in St Marylebone *(ill. 58)*.[10] After 1892 a separate series of traced plans was kept in bound volumes; the register will state if such a plan exists for the deed you are studying.

Should anything be hard to read or interpret in the register entries, it may be worthwhile consulting the original memorials, as mistakes or omissions were sometimes made at the transcription stage. Memorials for the years up to 1837 are also available at the LMA; those from 1838 on were destroyed in 1940.

For those trying to trace the architect or designer of a house or houses, it is often worth checking the names of witnesses to transactions such as building leases, mortgages and assignments, as occasionally one of these may be an architect or surveyor involved in the development.

NOTES AND REFERENCES

1. For example, three sides of Ennismore Gardens, an elegant Victorian square tucked behind Princes Gate in the Knightsbridge/Brompton/South Kensington borders, was built on a field which for some 70 years had been held on copyhold and leased to the occupants of Kingston House, the Kensington Road mansion behind which it was situated. The 3rd Earl of Listowel, whose family had owned the Kingston House estate from 1813, secured the field's enfranchisement from manorial control in 1867, and development began the following year. See Westminster City Archives, Acc. 943/2.

2. The records of the Grosvenor Estate in Mayfair include 90 such pre-lease agreements for houses in the Grosvenor Square area, by which Sir Richard Grosvenor and his successors agreed to grant leases to various builders within 40 days of tiling-in, or of the first and second floors being laid. Some agreements had stipulations concerning the right to use stable-yards, etc., and all had clauses specifying the term of years and ground-rent. Agreements such as these could be bought, sold, assigned or mortgaged. For building agreements and building leases on the Grosvenor Estate, see *Survey of London*, vol. XXXIX, 1977, pp. 13–17.

3. LMA, MDR 1729/6/194.

4. LMA, Q/DEW/29.

5. See A. A. Dibben, *Title Deeds 13th–19th Centuries*, 1968, p. 13.

6. Kensington Local Studies Library, deed 3799: TNA, C6/171/115: Westminster City Archives, Acc. 1188, bundle II

7. LMA, MDR 1760/4/160–1; 1761/3/452.

8. LMA, MDR 1761/3/453–4

9. LMA, MDR 1798/4/650–2; 1812/9/81–2; 1857/5/527.

10. LMA, MDR 1814/4/547. The same period is rich in elevations and plans for new houses on the Eyre estate in St John's Wood. For the use of the deeds registry in piecing together the early building history of this estate, see Malcolm Brown, 'St John's Wood: The Eyre Estate Before 1830', in *London Topographical Record*, vol. XXVII, 1995, pp. 49–68.

FURTHER READING

N. W. Alcock, *Old Title Deeds* (Phillimore), 1986

A. D. Carr, 'Deeds of Title', in *History*, vol. L, no. 170, Oct 1965, pp. 323–8

Julian Cornwall, *How To Read Old Title Deeds* (Birmingham University Department of Extra-Mural Studies), 1964

Ida Darlington, 'The Middlesex Deeds Registry', in *Transactions of the London & Middlesex Archaeological Society*, vol. 19, part 1, 1956, pp. 52–6

A. A. Dibben, *Title Deeds 13th–19th Centuries* (Historical Association), 1968

G. Green, 'Title Deeds: A Key to Local Housing Markets', in *Urban History Yearbook*, 1980, pp. 84–91

P. D. A. Harvey, *Manorial Records* (British Records Association: Archives and the User No. 5), 1999 edn

W. Branch Johnson, 'Notes Before Reading Court Rolls', in *Amateur Historian*, vol. 4, no. 3, Spring 1959, pp. 98–100

R. E. Latham, 'The Feet of Fines', in *Amateur Historian*, vol. 1, no. 1, Aug–Sept 1952, pp. 5–9

E. Legg, 'Title Deeds', in *Amateur Historian*, vol. 6, no. 3, Spring 1964, pp. 86–90

J. Kissock, 'Medieval feet of fines: a study of their uses with a catalogue of published sources', in *Local Historian*, vol. XXIV, no. 2, 1994, pp. 66–82

Eve McLaughlin, *Manorial Records* (McLaughlin Guides), 1996

B. P. Park, *My ancestors were manorial tenants* (Society of Genealogists), 1990

Hugh Peskett, 'Leases for Lives', in *Genealogist's Magazine*, vol. 17, no. 6, June 1973, pp. 327–9

Francis Sheppard and Victor Belcher, 'The Deeds Registries of Yorkshire and Middlesex', in *Journal of the Society of Archivists*, vol. 6, no. 5, April 1980, pp. 274–86

Francis Sheppard, Victor Belcher and Peter Kelsey, 'The Middlesex and Yorkshire Deeds Registries and the Study of Building Fluctuations', in *London Journal*, vol. 5, no. 2, 1979, pp. 176–217

Denis Stuart, *Manorial Records, an introduction to their transcription and translation* (Phillimore), 1992

CHAPTER FOUR

Estate Records

For much of its history London outside the City has been divided into estates owned by a variety of private landlords, religious institutions and corporate or charitable bodies. Best-known among these are the fashionable West End estates developed under aristocratic families such as the Russells, Grosvenors, and Cavendish-Harleys, but these represent only a small percentage of built-up London. Many other districts owe their character and appearance to very different types of proprietor. Alongside the aristocrats stand the royal family and the church, both big landowners in the capital: there are the Crown estates in the West End, those of the Duchy of Cornwall in Kennington, the Bishop of London in Paddington, and the Archbishop of Canterbury in Lambeth. Next in this estate hierarchy come the corporate bodies, guilds and livery companies, schools and colleges: the Corporation of the City of London; the Mercers' Company (Stepney); the Skinners' Company (St Pancras and Clerkenwell); the Brewers' Company (St Pancras and Clerkenwell); Eton College (Primrose Hill); and Dulwich College (Dulwich), to name but a few. But the remainder of the land in and around London belonged to a kaleidoscopic range of private individuals from all walks of life and social backgrounds. The reasons for this fragmentation are manifold, but it was partly a consequence of the redistribution of monastic property after the Dissolution, and partly a consequence of the individual's unquenchable desire for improvement through acquisition and investment. A large-scale ground-plan showing the ownership of land and property in London was prepared in 1892–1910 by the London County Council, using OS 25-inch sheets as a base. This *Ground Plan of London*, now held at the London Metropolitan Archives, covers an area of over 114 square miles and records the ownership of some 35,000 separate estates (although over 8,000 of these consisted of single houses).[1]

Regardless of the social standing of an estate owner, building development was the most popular and effective way of making money from his or her landholdings (see section on the leasehold system, page 13). Speculative building on estates on London's fringes began in earnest with the Earl of Bedford's Covent Garden development of the 1630s. Thereafter, a number of other great aristocratic estates followed suit: Bloomsbury Square (the Earl of Southampton), St James's Square (the Earl of St Albans), Hanover Square (the Earl of Scarborough), and Grosvenor Square. But this type of large estate was almost exclusively a west-London phenomenon; there was nothing comparable in scale or wealth towards or east of the City, or south of the Thames. However, the high standards of construction and management which characterized the best of the big West End estates did provide an ideal model – if a difficult one to replicate in practice – for those laying out ground for building on smaller and poorer estates. And the success of this pattern of land-ownership and estate development ensured its survival into the Victorian era and beyond.

Where to find estate records

The biggest problem facing the researcher looking for London estate records is a fundamental one of access to the material. Many estates which owned land in present-day Greater

59. *The estates of London (from Francis Sheppard's* London 1808-1870: The Infernal Wen, *1971)*

1	Adelphi	18	Choumat	30	Crooke	47	French School
2	Angell	19	Christ Church College,	31	Crown	48	Gascoigne
3	Audley		Oxford	32	Cubitt (Kensington)	49	Gibson
4	Battle Bridge	20	Christie	33	Curzon	50	Girdlers' Company
5	Bedford, Duke of	21	Church Commissioners	34	Dartmouth, Lord	51	Graham
6	Berkeley (Samuel)		(various estates)	35	Day	52	Grand Junction Canal
7	Berners	22	Church Commissioners	36	De Beauvoir		(formerly Bishop of
8	Brett		(former Bishop of	37	De Crespigny		London's)
9	Brewers' Company		London's)	38	Doughty	53	Grosvenor (Duke of
10	Brompton Hospital	23	City Lands	39	Drapers' Company		Westminster)
11	Cadogan	24	Cleaver	40	Duchy of Cornwall	54	Grosvenor (Duke of
12	Calthorpe	25	Clothworkers' Company	41	East		Westminster) -
13	Camden Charities	26	Conduit Mead	42	Edwards (Lord Kensington)		Cubitt
14	Camden, Earl of	27	Corporation of London	43	Eton College	55	Gunter
15	Campbell-Cole		(Bridge House)	44	Eyre	56	Haberdashers'
16	Charterhouse	28	Craven	45	Foundling Hospital		Company
17	Chelsea Hospital	29	Cromer-Lucas	46	Freake	57	Hall

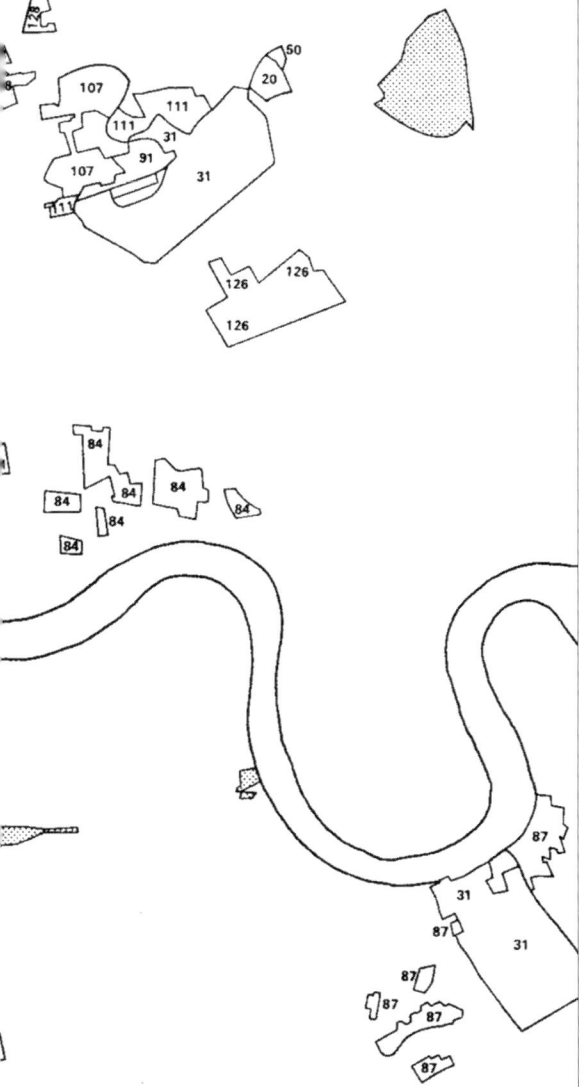

90 Norland
91 Norris
92 Northampton
93 Paxton
94 Penton
95 Penton (McWilliam)
96 Phillimore
97 Pickering
98 Portland-Soho
99 Portland (Cavendish Harley),
    Howard de Walden
100 Portman
101 Powell
102 Rugby School
103 St Bartholomew's Hospital
104 St John's College,
    Cambridge
105 St Leonard's, Shoreditch
106 St Quintin
107 St Thomas's Hospital
108 Salisbury
109 Sanders
110 Sekforde
111 Sir John Cass Charity
112 Skinners' Company
113 Slade
114 Sloane-Stanley
115 Smith's Charity
116 Somers
117 Southampton
118 Spurstow's Charity
119 Stonefield (Richard Cloudesley)
120 Sutton
121 Swinton
122 Talbot
123 Thornhill
124 Thurloe
125 Torriano, Kentish Town
126 Tredegar, Lord (incloses part of Coborn)
127 Trinity House
128 Tyssen-Amhurst
129 Vallotten
130 Vaughan
131 Vauxhall, Manor of (various developers)
132 Von Zanat
133 Walcott
134 Wenlock
135 West End House
136 Williams
137 Wright

58 Harlar
59 Harpur Trust (Bedford
    Charity)
60 Harrison
61 Harrow School
62 Holland (Ilchester)
63 Hoof
64 Hope
65 Hutchins
66 Inderwick
67 Ironmongers
68 Jesus College, Oxford
69 Kensington Gore
70 Kilburn Priory
71 Ladbroke
72 Lambeth Wick
73 Lambs Farm

74 Leicester
75 Leman
76 Listowel, Earl of
77 Lloyd-Baker
78 Lloyd-Lisson
79 Maddox-Pollen
80 Maddox-Pollen (Burlington)
81 Maitland Park
82 Maryon-Wilson
83 Mawby
84 Mercers' Company
85 Mildmay (Newington
    Green)
86 Minet
87 Morden College
88 Newport
89 New River

London no longer exist, and their records – like their freeholds – have been dispersed. A good starting-point in such cases is the local archive for the area in question, or the London Metropolitan Archives (LMA); if neither of these holds the collection, they may know who does. Alternatively, the National Register of Archives (NRA) has lists and catalogues of family papers and former estate archives held in record offices and private collections throughout the country. It is now possible to search these NRA lists electronically, via the World Wide Web, either by family name or London area. By typing in 'Southwark', for example, a whole string of entries appears, one of which refers to the title deeds and estate papers of the Hussey family of Scotney Castle, Lamberhurst, held at Kent Archives. The NRA's copy of the catalogue gives further details, listing deeds of houses in Stoney Lane, Tooley Street and elsewhere in the area, owned by the family.[2]

For those estates which still own and manage housing in London, it is worth enquiring if they have an archive or archivist attached to the estate office. On occasion, students and specialist historians have been allowed access to documentary material which is normally unavailable to the public. The *Survey of London*, for example, made extensive use of the records of the Grosvenor and Bedford estates in its studies of Mayfair and Covent Garden. However, even the bigger estates may not have the facilities or inclination to accept personal visits from members of the public. It is worth checking, therefore, if your estate's history has already been examined by an historian or the *Survey*. For instance, Donald Olsen's account of the development, maintenance and rebuilding of Bloomsbury and Covent Garden is founded largely on his investigation of the records of the Foundling Hospital and Bedford estates.[3]

In some cases, even though the estate may still function, some of its records may have been lost. The Cadogan family, owners of a large amount of lucrative land and property in the Sloane Square and Sloane Street areas of Chelsea, lost many of their family papers (including documents relating to building work on the estate in the 18th and 19th centuries)

when the family moved in the 1890s from its town-house in Cadogan Place to a new country residence, Culford Hall in Suffolk. There was a fire in the removal van in which the records were stored overnight in London.[4]

However, even if the original papers are inaccessible or missing, all is not lost if the estate in question was located north of the Thames. Between 1709 and 1938, any sales, mortgages or leases of over 21 years of property in Middlesex had to be registered in the Middlesex Deeds Registry (MDR), now kept at the London Metropolitan Archives. With a little patience and perseverance, it should be possible to piece together the development of an estate by trawling through the MDR indexes for building leases for the relevant years under the landowner's surname (see *Middlesex Deeds Registry,* page 81).

What the records contain

Estate records embrace a great diversity of documentary material recording the everyday activities involved in the administration of an estate. Naturally, the amount and complexity of the records will vary with the size and age of the estate, although serendipity also plays its part: the survival or otherwise of the records, as with the Cadogans, is often dependent upon quirks of fate. *Deeds* and other *conveyances*, such as assignments and mortgages, will record the purchase, transfer or disposal of all or part of an estate, and often provide a detailed description of the estate at the time of the sale. To quickly gain an impression of changes in ownership, it is often worthwhile consulting the lists and catalogues of record offices such as the LMA, as these will give the salient points of each deed. If an entire estate was offered for sale, there could be a printed *sale catalogue*, almost a complete survey in itself.

Building agreements and *building leases* can be used to reconstruct the pattern and pace of estate development. Jean Imray used such documents from the Mercers' Company Archives to chart the building over of the company's estate in Stepney in the first half of the 19th century. Between 1817 and 1850, some 90 acres of formerly arable land was lined with streets and houses. The agreements and leases reveal that, although three builders between them erected about 700 of the 1,100 houses, the majority of builders involved on the estate operated on a relatively modest scale: for instance, no less than 16 builders were responsible for the construction of Bromley Street. Her study of the documents also revealed the fluctuations in the demand for houses over the period, the financial difficulties of some builders, and the long genesis of some parts of the development, such as the Arbour Square area.[5] Agreements and leases also say much about an estate's attitude to management. In Mayfair, the Grosvenor family helped ensure the good progress of building development on its estate in the 18th century by paying for the construction of vaults beneath the new streets and the making-up of the roadways, and then recouping the expenses from their lessees. The Grosvenors also advanced money to builders, purchased improved ground rents, provided mortgages, and even allowed arrears of ground rent to accumulate – all to support economic stability among the builders on their estate.

But they kept very tight control of the architectural appearance of the buildings erected, and of the types of trades carried on within, through clauses and covenants in the building agreements and leases.[6]

A large number of unpublished *maps and plans* recording London's estates is accessible to the researcher. These were drawn up usually as part of the day-to-day management, and can vary in scope from individual house-plans to extensive maps showing proposals for laying out entire estates for development. Most are to be found at the appropriate record office, alongside the other estate records, but over the years some have found their way into other collections. The British Library Manuscripts Department holds many manuscript maps of British estates: London examples, such as those of the Althorp estate in Battersea, are indexed by both estate name and London district. The British Library Map Library also holds a series of 19th- and 20th-century sale catalogues for large properties, many of which contain printed estate maps.

Large-scale estate maps can provide the

60. An extract from the Bedford estate's plan of Tooting Bec manor, 1729, showing the area centred on St Leonard's church, Streatham High Road.

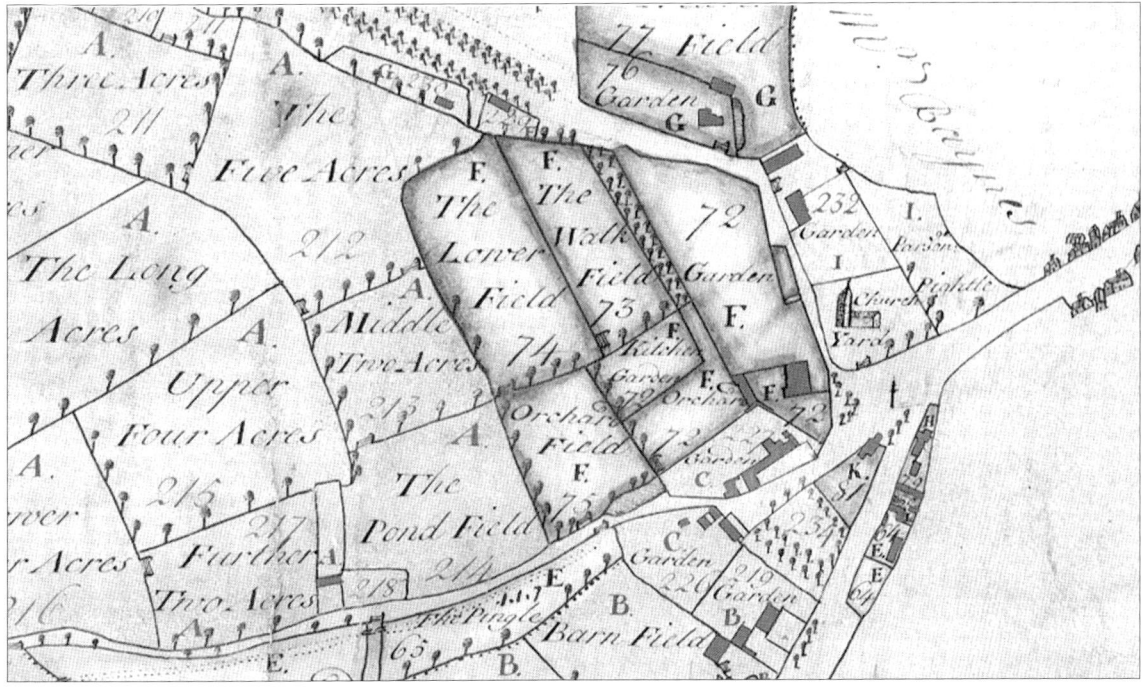

quickest and most accessible overall view of an estate at a particular date, showing field boundaries, the names and acreages of fields, roads and lanes, streams, ponds and greens, and some indication of building development, usually with an accompanying written schedule (or *terrier*) listing the names of purchasers and lessees. For example, in the LMA's collection of Bedford estate records is an attractive coloured map of 1729 showing the family's holdings in the manor of Tooting Bec, now part of Tooting and Streatham, in south London *(ill. 60)*. This has the fields coloured to indicate differences of ownership, little elevations of buildings in and around Streatham High Road (including the church), and a table of tenants' and copyholders' names.[7]

For the student of London's medieval and early modern housing stock, some fine estate plans survive among the records of property-owning institutions such as Christ's Hospital or the City livery companies, many of which are in the Guildhall Library (Manuscripts Department). Of these, the best-known are those compiled for Christ's Hospital by the surveyor Ralph Treswell. His drawings are a picturesque hybrid of plan and elevation, showing the typical appearance of London's early 17th-century houses. Similar later-17th-century City estate plans were commissioned to establish some order amid the chaos which followed the Great Fire. Other examples include those in the archives of St Bartholomew's Hospital, which owned property outside the hospital precinct, for example in the Chick Lane area. A number of City estate plans have been reproduced by the London Topographical Society, and there are good collections among the records of the City Livery companies at the Guildhall Library (see *ill. 61*).

Two or more maps of different date can be compared to follow the development of an

61. *Typical 19th-century estate map: plan of an estate in Old Street, belonging to the Worshipful Company of Ironmongers, by Robert Sibley, 1843.*

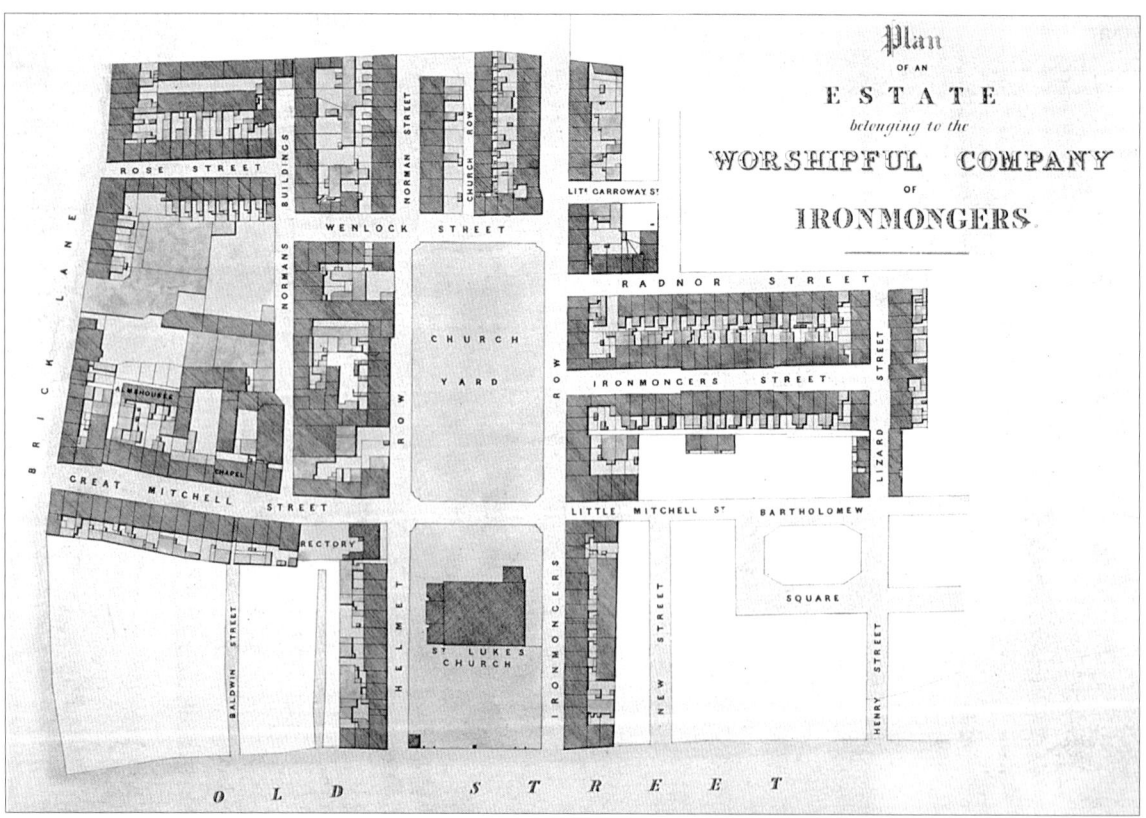

estate over time. Particularly useful in the case of estates which have undergone considerable change are the plans drawn up by surveyors or architects at the time of the first development, showing the original layout and arrangement of building plots or houses. Records of Eton College's estate at Chalcots, Hampstead, include successive layout and house plans, which show how builders responded to the collapse of the great building boom of the 1820s by scaling down the early, ambitious plans for big detached villas to something less costly, but still respectable.[8] For those studying Victorian houses, maps and plans such as these can be used in conjunction with information gleaned from deeds, leases, *Directories* and census enumerations to build up a very detailed picture of the appearance and social character of an estate.

Rentals and surveys – or 'terriers' – occur usually in the form of a list of tenants, with the terms of their tenancies, amount of rent paid, and sometimes other details. Among the papers of the Clitherow family of Boston Manor, near Brentford in Middlesex, is a rental book for the period 1784–1805, during the lifetime of James Clitherow III (d.1805). This bound volume covers all the estates and lands owned by the family at the time – in London, Middlesex, Northamptonshire, Huntingdonshire and elsewhere – and gives annual abstracts of all the rents received, estate by estate, year by year, including information on the numbers of empty houses. Such care and attention in keeping up-to-date records typifies James Clitherow III's active approach to estate management, engendered by his discovery on succeeding to the family estates that his income was to be less than expected, owing to the large provision made by his parents for his younger brethren. In the rental are details for each tenant about the type of property, term of lease, and rent paid, with useful notes on any changes during the period. For instance, one of the entries relating to the family's small estate near Broad Street in the City of London reads: 'Thomas Clarke holds a piece of ground in Pinners Court Broadstreet in London adjoining Pinners Hall, whereon he has built three Houses on a building Lease, which expires M[s.]

1839 at 162£ a yr'. A further note adds that Clarke died around Christmas 1792 and bequeathed his lease to his son-in-law, Thomas Stowers of No. 22 Charterhouse Square.[9]

Certain estates, particularly the bigger ones, will have *minute books*, which can provide a further insight into the general policy of estate management; and *accounts*, if they survive, will record in detail the annual income and expenditure. Either or both of these should also furnish contracts with or bills from developers and contractors. In his study of Victorian Camberwell, Professor H. J. Dyos made use of the minute books, journals and contracts of the Corporation of London's Bridge House estates to piece together the protracted development between 1844 and 1875 of the Trafalgar Avenue estate, a small run of residential streets to the south of the Old Kent Road. The Bridge House records provided the chronology of development for the different terraces and streets on the estate, the names of the many builders involved, and details of the leases and building agreements. One of the features of the estate, evident to Dyos from the records, was the way in which a slowly built-up, modestly-sized estate, involving a large number of speculative builders and lessees, was carefully managed throughout by 'a wary landowner'.[10]

Many estate papers will include bundles of *correspondence*. Private letters can reveal much about family relationships, or about the relationships and working practices of an estate's officers or employees, such as the surveyor or solicitor. Returning briefly to the Clitherow estate: among the correspondence of Lt-Col. John Bourchier Stracey-Clitherow of Hotham Hall, East Yorkshire, are letters of 1913–14 from his solicitors (Gadsden & Pennefather of Bedford Row, Holborn) relating to new houses being erected on the family estate at Brentford, in Clitherow Avenue. From only a few letters it is possible to date these houses accurately. The builder's name is given – a Mr Hidden (presumably Francis Dew Hidden & Co Ltd of Boston Road, listed in the 1914 Middlesex *Directory*), and there is also a brief insight into the process of development and sale on the estate. Stracey-Clitherow is informed by his solicitors that a Mrs Steel has acquired No. 25

Clitherow Avenue, and has repaid the mortgage he lent her. Another letter explains that Hidden has made arrangements with a Mrs Richardson to build her a house on the avenue 'of a somewhat larger size than those he has previously erected' – of 38ft frontage, the plot to be sold to Hidden at the 'usual' price of £4 per foot of frontage, i.e. £152, and sold on by him for £157; as Mrs Richardson was 'finding all the money', there was no need for Stracey-Clitherow to 'make the usual advances'.[11]

Estate Acts of Parliament

Of the various types of private legislation which survive among the records of Parliament, the largest by far is that relating to the settlement of estates. Until the late 19th century it was common for family estates to pass from father to son by 'strict settlement', i.e. to an heir for the remainder of his life (as tenant-for-life), then to his eldest son for his life, and so on, each generation protecting the interests of the next. In this way a family's wealth through its property was made safe from dissipation by any 'black sheep'. By 1848 an astonishing two-thirds of the land in England was held in this way.[12] However, such a restrictive system of inheritance did create problems: landowners were unable to liquefy assets in times of need, for instance to repay debts incurred by their predecessors, unless the tenant-for-life and his heir agreed to bar the entail; and estate development in the traditional, speculative manner was impossible, as strict settlement prevented freeholders from granting leases of more than 21 years duration. Furthermore, it was nigh on impossible for those outside the landowning elite to bring new money into the system by 'buying their way in' to the ranks of the gentry.

For those owning an entailed estate the solution to such problems was to obtain at personal expense a special Private Act of Parliament – an Estate Act (also known as a Settlement Act). This entitled the owner to sell his estate or grant leases for longer than 21 years for building development. These Acts, and other material relating to them, such as the initial Private Bill and evidence to the House of Lords, are filled with details about families

62. *Sales particulars from Hackney Archives Department: mid-19th-century details of nine houses in Clarence Terrace, Haggerston (note the reference to the window tax, which ceased in 1851).*

and their estates. Such an Act of December 1699 enabled Joseph Gardner, a merchant, and his wife Sarah (née Ridges) to dispose of three 'Old and ruinous' houses in St John's Lane and St John Street, Clerkenwell, in order to repay outstanding mortgage debts. The property had been left by Sarah's father to one of her brothers, but the bequest was on condition that all outstanding debts be repaid, which did not happen. She gained possession, but on marriage to Gardner her estate was entailed on their male issue (they had three daughters) – hence the Estate Act.[13] The wide social range of those petitioning for an Estate Act is noteworthy; private legislation of this nature was as desirable to the wife of a local merchant like Gardner, with two or three houses, as it was to the aristocracy.

Estate agents' and auctioneers' records

Many record offices have been presented with business records of firms of auctioneers, surveyors and estate agents. Of these the greatest

BY ORDER OF THE MORTGAGEE.

PIMLICO, S.W.

Situate just off the Vauxhall Bridge Road, within a few minutes' walk of Victoria Station.

Particulars and Conditions of Sale

OF

No. 3, CHURTON PLACE,

Vauxhall Bridge Road.

A SUBSTANTIALLY-BUILT 9 ROOMED HOUSE.

Let on a quarterly tenancy at

£48 PER ANNUM.

Held upon Lease for an unexpired term of 18 years, at a Ground Rent of £6 10s. per annum.

Which will be Sold by Auction,

BY

MESSRS. FURBER

AT THE MART, TOKENHOUSE YARD, LOTHBURY, E.C.,

On WEDNESDAY, 7th FEBRUARY, 1912

At TWO o'clock precisely.

Particulars and Conditions of Sale may be obtained at the Mart, E.C.; from PERCY K. LANGDALE, Esq., Solicitor, 50, Holborn Viaduct, E.C.; Messrs. SINGLETON, FABIAN AND Co., Chartered Accountants, 8, Staple Inn, W.C., and from the Auctioneers,

Telephone HOLBORN 1086.   3, Warwick Court, Gray's Inn, W.C.

63. *Sales particulars in 1912 of 3 Churton Place, Vauxhall Bridge Road.*

proportion usually relate to sales of property: sale and valuation books, registers of property, sales particulars and catalogues *(ills 62 & 63)*, account books and files of correspondence. Where agents were closely involved in estate management, their records may also include leases, applications from tenants, valuations made for estate duty, probate or enfranchisement, and estate maps and photographs. These can be very useful in determining the extent and condition of an estate and its housing at a given time, and can help piece together the history of building development in the area.

Several of today's firms have a long pedigree, and may retain important historical records relating to sales and estate management in the past. It is always worthwhile writing to agents you know to have been involved with house-sales in your area, as they may be willing to make records available. Chesterton & Sons, for example, have volumes of plans and photographs showing houses of the 1860s, some newly built and some still under construction,

on the Phillimore estate in west London, in addition to leases and other records relating to the estate.[14] The firm's founder, Charles Chesterton, originally a poulterer, became a prominent figure in local administration, and acted as agent for the Phillimore estate. His grandson, the architect Frank Sydney Chesterton, designed some buildings on the estate before his death in action during the First World War.

NOTES AND REFERENCES

1. LMA, LCC/VA/GP/01. Between 1911 and 1914 a second edition of the *Ground Plan* was begun on larger 5-foot Ordnance sheets, but this was never completed (these are at LCC/VA/GP/02).

2. Historical Manuscripts Commission, NRA 4540: Kent Archives, Hussey MSS, T79–T82.

3. Donald J. Olsen, *Town Planning in London. The Eighteenth and Nineteenth Centuries*, 1964

4. R. Pearman, *The Cadogan Estate*, 1986, pp. 96–7.

5. Jean Imray, 'The Mercers' Company and East London, 1750–1850: an exercise in urban development', in *East London Papers*, vol. 9, no. 1, Summer 1966, pp. 3–25.

6. See *Survey of London*, vol. XXXIX, 1977.

7. LMA, E/BER/S/E/5/3/1.

8. Donald J. Olsen, 'House upon House: Estate development in London and Sheffield', in H. J. Dyos and Michael Wolff (eds), *The Victorian City: Images and Realities*, vol. 1, 1973, pp. 333–57.

9. LMA, Acc/1360/168, p. 91.

10. H. J. Dyos, *Victorian Suburb. A Study of the Growth of Camberwell*, 1966, pp. 91–6.

11. LMA, Acc/1360/523/1–51.

12. M. Bond, 'Estate Acts of Parliament', in *Short Guides to Records*, 1st series (Historical Association), 1994, pp. 54–8

13. House of Lords RO, House of Lords Papers, 22 Dec 1699, no. 1477; *The Manuscripts of the House of Lords, vol. IV (New Series), 1699–1702*, 1965, p. 58.

14. Information supplied to the Survey of London by Victor Belcher. See also *Survey of London*, vol. XXXVII, 1973, Chapter 4.

FURTHER READING

Maurice Bond, *The Records of Parliament. A Guide for Genealogists and Local Historians* (Phillimore), 1964

Maurice Bond, 'Estate Acts of Parliament', in *Short Guides to Records*, 1st series (Historical Association), 1994, pp. 54–8

Philip Booth, 'Speculative Housing and the Land

Market in London 1660–1730: Four Case Studies', in *Town Planning Review*, vol. 51, no. 4, Oct 1980, pp. 379–98

David Cannadine, *Lords and Landlords: the Aristocracy and the Towns 1774–1967* (Leicester University Press), 1980

Henry S. Cobb and Ann Saunders (eds), 'Handlist of the Hampstead Garden Suburb Archive: a Users' Guide' (Hampstead Garden Suburb Trust/LMA), 2001

H. J. Dyos, *Victorian Suburb. A Study of the Growth of Camberwell* (Leicester University Press), 1966

Jean Imray, 'The Mercers' Company and East London: the first two hundred years', in *East London Papers*, vol. 6, no. 2, Dec 1963, pp. 89–104

Jean Imray, 'The Mercers' Company and East London, 1750–1850: an exercise in urban development', in *East London Papers*, vol. 9, no. 1, Summer 1966, pp. 3–25

Simon Jenkins, *Landlords to London: The story of a Capital and its growth* (Constable), 1975

Donald J. Olsen, *Town Planning in London. The Eighteenth and Nineteenth Centuries* (Yale University Press), 1964

Donald J. Olsen, 'House upon House: Estate development in London and Sheffield', in H. J. Dyos and Michael Wolff (eds), *The Victorian City: Images and Realities*, vol. 1, 1973, pp. 333–57

Robert Pearman, *The Cadogan Estate* (Haggerston Press), 1986

S. E. Rasmussen, *London: The unique city*, 1948 (especially Chapter 9)

John Schofield (ed.), *The London Surveys of Ralph Treswell* (London Topographical Society Publication No. 135), 1987

Francis Sheppard, *London 1808–1870: The Infernal Wen* (Secker & Warburg), 1970

Brian S. Smith, 'The Business Archives of Estate Agents', in *Journal of the Society of Archivists*, vol. III, no. 6, Oct 1967, pp. 298–300

H. Victor Smith, 'The Origin & History of the Bridge House Estate' (typescript in Guildhall Library), 2 vols, 1932–8

Sir John Summerson, *Georgian London* (Penguin), 1991 edn (use recent Yale edn)

Survey of London, vol. XXXVI, 1970; vol. XXXVII, 1973; vol. XXXIX, 1977; vol. XL, 1980

CHAPTER FIVE

Rates and Taxes

In this world nothing can be said to be certain, Benjamin Franklin tells us, except death and taxes. Throughout history the Crown, the church and the state have levied money from the citizenry, both in peacetime and in war. Taxes which we now accept as inevitable, such as income tax, were often introduced as short-term expediencies in times of need, or to fund foreign campaigns. As few people are fortunate or poor enough to escape the taxman, records of taxation offer a wealth of historical information about a large proportion of society and its property. However, it would be mistaken to credit even the taxman with infallibility: under-assessment and evasion were not uncommon, nor were corruption and bribery, and some sections of society, such as paupers, were exempt. But, by and large, the various sources described below can be regarded as reliable. Only those tax records which are of particular use to the London house historian are listed and explained. Other taxes or assessments (such as those on hair-powder or carriages) which may be of interest to the dedicated researcher can be pursued via the recommended *Further Reading* at the end of this chapter.

Ratebooks

In recent decades local ratebooks have emerged as a significant historical source on a par with census returns, and they are especially valuable for the period before the introduction of comprehensive street directories and census enumeration in the 1840s. For house historians the ratebooks offer an accurate record of the occupation and value (and therefore size) of property. They can be used to trace the history of individual buildings, or used in bulk to analyse changing social and economic factors of streets or larger areas.

A rate was a local charge or tax, levied primarily on the occupiers of property (rather

64. *Ratebook for Black Horse Yard and Rathbone Place, St Marylebone, 1758. The columns show the annual value of each hereditament and the rates payable for six months.*

65. *A 20th-century ratebook extract: ratepayers in Queen's Grove and St John's Wood Park, St John's Wood, in April 1939 with names of owners as well as occupiers, a brief description of the properties, and their gross and rateable values; note also the number of houses emptying at the time ('late Connaught, late Fullerton', etc).*

than owners) by the local authorities to help fund the provision of public services. The amount charged was calculated from a notional annual rental value for the property – not the actual rent paid by tenants – though the figures were based on periodic valuations of buildings in the parish (see below and *ill. 67*). There were various purposes to which the money raised could be put, included scavenging, the repair of roads or sewers, and the patrols of watchmen; each rate may have its own series of records. However, the majority of surviving ratebooks are those relating to the relief of the poor, a rate which was made compulsory in England from 1601.

As the rates were generally levied by and for the parish or local government, surviving books are usually to be found in local borough record offices and libraries. The frequency of survival varies from district to district.

Ratebooks can be bulky items, often in poor condition, and increasing pressures on local archive storage space and conservation facilities have meant that many have been microfilmed, or simply destroyed. But a number of local collections do have a good run of 18th- and 19th-century ratebooks; and where poor-rate records are not continuous, other types, such as watch and highway rates, are sometimes available to fill the gaps. Some historic areas, such as Southwark and the Cities of Westminster and London, have ratebooks dating back to the sixteenth century.

Ratebooks customarily take the form of bound volumes, and the basic information recorded therein consists of columns of names of ratepayers (usually, but not exclusively, the occupants); gross and rateable valuations of the house; and the amount of rate charged and payments made *(ills 64, 65)*. Owners are sometimes also given, and occasionally there is a note on a building's use. Entries are arranged street by street within each ward of the parish, often simply following the routes taken by rate-collectors on their rounds. This order, though it should relate to the contemporary street-plan, may seem irrational to present-day readers.

The simplest use of these books is as a source for the names of the various ratepayers for the particular house, street or area under study. Ratebooks for St Paul Covent Garden record the filling up of Inigo Jones's famous 'Great Piazza' in 1635–40 with men of title and eminent public figures, and further study reveals the social decline of the area by the mid-18th century.[1] To find the earliest occupant of a house it is best to work backwards from a date when the occupant is known, say from the census or directories, using Ordnance Survey or other maps to check local government or parish boundaries. Work back every five years or so, rather than through every single year. Note the names of occupants and the gross and/or rateable assessments for the

house in question, listing also five or six of the occupants on either side; this well help identify the house even if some occupants and the street name or house numbers should change or disappear. To save writing all the names each time, a simple line, tick or 'ditto', can signify where there is no change of occupant (see example below).

A similar technique can be used to identify the date when a house or group of houses was first rated, giving an approximate date of construction. For example, take Nos 46, 48 and 56–66 (even) Brixton Water Lane, near Brockwell Park in south London (ill. 66). Stylistically, these small, two-storey houses appear to date from the early decades of the 19th century, but there is a noticeable difference between the semi-detached cottages of Nos 46 and 48, and the terrace of Nos 56–66. By working backwards through surviving poor ratebooks for the area in Lambeth Archives, it is possible to determine reasonably accurate construction dates for both types of house.[2]

The table below shows clearly that the pair of cottages, Nos 46 and 48, must date from

[House No.]	1850		1840		1830–1	
	Water Lane					
	Moreau		Moreau	60+24	Moreau	55
[46]	H.Christian	36	J.F.Wulff	36	[- no gap -]	
[48]	C.Fauclope	36	------	36	'Empty'	50
[56]	A.W.Gray	28	Cochrane	28	Attwood	30
[58]	G.Blundell	28+3	H.Weston	28+3	Smith	35
[60]	G.Hayward	50	------	50	-----	30
[62]	Woollaton	40	------	40	-----	30
[64]	A.Slack	30	------	32	James	30
[66]	R.Williams	35	Elderton	35	Catherwood	28
			E.Burrow	28	R.Lyle	80
			T.Boot	28	Elderton	28
	1829–30		1824		1815	
	Water Lane					
	Moreau	55	Winter	55	Winter	45
	'Empty'	50	do. (factory)	50	Hall (_ac)	2
[56]	Bacquet	30	------	30	Edward (150ac)	450
[58]	Parsons	35	Lovegrove	28	Dixon (6ac)	30
[60]	Hayward	30	------	30	Dixon	40
[62]	Woolaton	30	------	30	Dixon (9ac)	45
[64]	[illegible]	30	Stanley	30	[- no gap -]	
[66]	Catherwood	28	------	28	[- no gap -]	
	R.Lyle	60	------	16+84	[- no gap -]	
	Elderton	28	Soloway	28	Soloway	15+14

66. *Nos 56 and 58 Brixton Water Lane, Brixton Hill, photographed in 1973, dateable to 1815–24 from a study of 19th-century ratebooks in Lambeth Archives.*

1831–9, and seem to have been built on the site of a disused manufactory. The terrace of Nos 56–66 is of some 15 to 20 years earlier. The names and acreages recorded in the 1815 ratebook between Winter and Soloway may well refer to other land near by (as has been stated, the collectors' routes were not always regular); but there is nothing comparable to the distinctive group of entries for the six houses which have been noted for 1824–50. An approximate date of construction for Nos 56–66 can therefore be given as 1815–24, which corresponds well with the stylistic evidence. Unfortunately these date spans cannot be narrowed down further, as no ratebooks survive for the intervening years.

Noting the amounts of the assessments not only helps identify particular properties over a period of some years, but can give an idea of the relative value (and therefore size) of one house to another in the same area. Occasional revaluations would account for an increased assessment for all the properties in the same district. But significant changes to the rate charged for one house in relation to the other buildings around it could indicate additions or alterations, or even total rebuilding. However, as always, proceed with caution: if such changes coincide with a change of occupants, the rate-collector may simply have altered his route.

Other useful information sometimes found amongst the ratebook entries include notes on the occupation of the ratepayer, or on the use of the property, such as 'house', 'shop' (which could signify either a retail shop or workshop), or even 'manufactory', as above. Any recent demolition or redevelopment was often noted by the rate-collector in comments like '6 new houses building', or 'house now gone'.

Interpreting the ratebooks, however, can often be difficult. In the early years, the absence of street names and numbers can make identification problematic, and unfortunately this uncertainty is often greatest when houses or a street were newly built, and when accurate information is most sought after. It should also be remembered that, frequently, in the early years of a new street, gaps would exist between

1	2	3	4	5	6	7	8	9	10	11	12
112	Gilbert Taylor	Lt.Col.Sir J.Kean	Garage & Rooms		46A HAMILTON TERRACE	80			64	80	64
113	Dr.Reginald Henry Miller	Harrow School	House		47	150			121	150	121
114	Joseph Hexman Harty	Watson Estate	House		48	160			130	160	130
115	Charles Abraham Mocatta	Mrs.M.C.Cripps	House		49	160			130	160	130
116	Samuel Baird	Harrow School	House		50	300			246	300	246
117	William Henry Ash J.P.	do.	House		51	160			130	160	130
118	Mrs.Amelia Elkan	Self	House		52	180			146	180	146
119	Dr.Ronald Montague Handfield Jones	Harrow School	House		53	180			146	180	146
120	Mrs.Elizabeth Mary Wombwell	Self	House		54	180			146	180	146
121	Ernest Montague Marx	Harrow School	House		55	180			146	180	146
122	R.H.C.Thomas	A.H.Cockerton	House		56	220			180	220	180 No 56A House rgarage G.350 R 288 £ 416.
123	Mrs.Edith Isabel Ellsen	A.H.Cockerton	House		57	170			138	170	138 Ho rgarage G.200 R.163 £ 410.
124	Mrs.Beatrice Walton		House		58	200			163	200	163
125	Mrs.Elizabeth W.Caroline Kay	Self	House		59	200			163	200	163
126	Nigel Cohen	Self	House		60	200			163	200	163 G. 245 R.228 £ 434
127	Maurice Henry Barnett	Harrow School	House		61	200			163	200	163
128	Henry Claudine Ash	S.Rogers	House		62	200			163	200	163
129	Charles William Warne	H.Rogers	House		63	200			163	200	163
130	Mrs.Beatrice Walton		House		64	200			163	200	163
131	Edward Phillips	Harrow School	House		64A	200			163	200	163
132	Haman Sado	Self	House		64B	250			205	250	205
133	Dr.Chas.George Drummond Morier	Self	House		65	230			188	230	188 G.245 R.228 £ 393
134	Dr.Chas.George Drummond Morier	Self	Garage		65A	13			9	13	9 absorbed in cottage

67. *A Valuation List of c.1930 for part of Hamilton Terrace, St Marylebone, listing occupiers, owners, and the gross and rateable values of the houses.*

the small clumps of houses put up by different builders; and it was common for occupants to move, often to other new houses near by, after only a few years. And watch out for the subdivision of properties, or the joining together of two houses. Finally, although it might seem strange, a ratebook entry does not necessarily confirm that the house in question was occupied at the time: a vacant furnished house would be regarded by the authorities as 'occupied', and its owner liable to pay rates, as would one where only a servant had been left in charge. As always, it is best to check with other sources, such as deeds and maps, or for later years, directories and the census.

As mentioned above, the periodic Valuation Lists, where they survive, are also worth consulting *(ill. 67)*. These are often very precise in the information they give (sometimes more so than the ratebooks).

IR58: the Board of Inland Revenue Valuation Office survey for the Finance (1909–10) Act, 1910

The Finance (1909–10) Act,[3] one of Lloyd George's new measures during his momentous budget year of 1909–10, introduced a short-lived tax on landownership, requiring private owners to pay a proportion of the increase in value to their property attributable to public improvements such as new roads or drains. Known by the catchy title 'increment value duty', the tax necessitated an exhaustive new survey of land and buildings in England and Wales – hence its nickname, 'the new Domesday'. The Valuation Office was established to carry out the original survey, and its records, now preserved in the National Archives (formerly PRO), provide an incredibly detailed 'snapshot' of property in England and Wales at the beginning of the 20th century. The tax was abolished in 1920.

The country was divided into separate income tax divisions, districts and parishes, and surveyed between 1910 and 1915. The final records were entered into small bound volumes, called field books (class IR58), which today constitute a major historical source. The information recorded in the books can vary from district to district (and from book to book), but will usually include the names of the owner and occupier, the owner's interest (whether freehold or leasehold), and details of occupiers' tenancies (such as term and rent). Recent sales are sometimes noted. Particularly useful are the physical descriptions of the buildings, which often include a list of rooms (with details of fittings and décor), a note on the state of repair, and occasionally sketch site or ground plans. An indication of the building's age and some useful informal notes are also common.

A good example is provided by the IR58 entries for Nos 67–69 Ennismore Gardens. These three large, double-fronted houses were constructed in the early 1880s by the Kensington builder William Radford as part of a small-scale, speculative development on the Listowel family's Kingston House estate at Knightsbridge; they have since been demolished. Estate records suggest that Radford had misjudged his market in building these old-fashioned, Italianate houses. He had difficulty finding buyers and had to ask Lord Listowel for more time to finish the development. The IR58 field books are particularly instructive, giving the sort of 'on-the-spot' information that would be difficult to find elsewhere. By 1913, when the notes were made, No. 69 had become a block of residential flats, described as 'substantially built...and originally a private house (never occupied) and...converted about 1900'. The house at No. 67 is described as never completed 'or occupied other than by a caretaker'. An expenditure of about £2,000 would have to be made to complete & modernize fit for letting'. Another note states: 'planning not very good and rooms badly lighted'.[4]

Finding individual properties in the IR58 class of records for the first time can be daunting but becomes relatively easy with experience. Each property within an income tax parish was given a unique number – called an assessment or hereditament number – which can be discovered by consulting the relevant record maps (IR121 for London, IR124–135 for counties – their survival is patchy) and Class lists.

Other surviving documents relating to increment value duty include valuation books (also known as 'Domesday Books'), usually found in local record offices. These are not as informative as the IR58s, with notes confined to ownership and value, but can also be used to ascertain hereditament numbers.

68. *Extract of a marked-up IR121 map, showing Sterndale Road and other streets near Brook Green.*

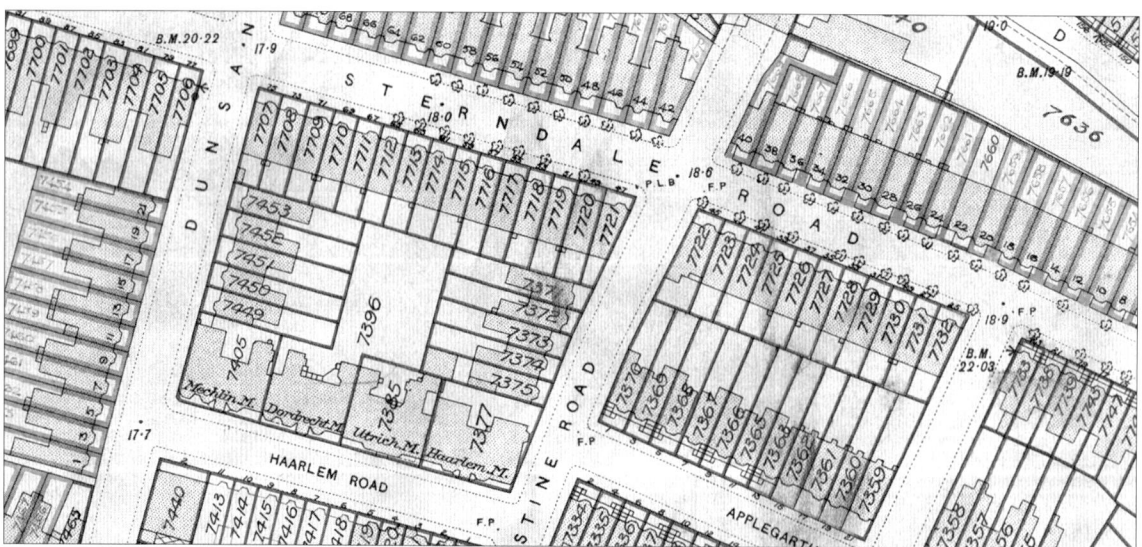

Tithe surveys

The tithe was a tax paid by farmers towards the maintenance of the church and clergy, equivalent to one-tenth of the annual proceeds from their land. It was part of state law from the ninth century and persisted until the Tithe Redemption Act of 1936. As recently as the 18th century the tax was frequently paid in kind, with produce or livestock, hence the large medieval tithe barns erected to store crops and animals.

In 1836 the Tithe Commutation Act replaced what had become a complicated and inconsistent method of payment with a fixed rate, known as a rent-charge. The new system was based on a comprehensive survey of land use, ownership and occupation in England and Wales, the most detailed of its kind since Domesday.

Although concerned primarily with agricultural land, tithe surveys are of considerable use to London house historians. Maps were drawn up of all tithable land at scales of between 25in and 50in to 1 mile, and these are an invaluable source for the 20–30 year period before the first large-scale Ordnance Survey maps were produced in the 1860s. Tithe records are particularly useful for those researching the outer areas of Greater London – formerly in the counties of Essex, Kent or Surrey – and also for certain undeveloped inner areas, which were still predominantly rural at the time of the survey.[5] Some parishes and towns previously affected by enclosure were not subject to the new Act: the National Archives has a 'County Diagram index' showing the parishes covered, and a handy county-by-county catalogue was published recently.[6]

Tithe records take the form of 'apportionments' – handwritten or printed lists of landowners, occupiers, the size and nature of their holdings and the amount charged – and local maps showing the various properties affected. The maps are often detailed, and each individual plot was given a unique identifying number *(ill.69)*. The apportionments contain a lot of useful information, such as names and descriptions of properties, and the state of land cultivation. A short extract from the apportionment of 1852 for the parish of Hadley (alias Monken Hadley), in Middlesex, serves as an example below.[7]

Sometimes, as below, there are two columns of charges: one for the clergy, the other for lay 'Impropriators', to whom, over the centuries, a portion of the tithes had been conveyed.

After the initial survey and assessment, subsequent sub-divisions of property were recorded in 'Altered Apportionments', which can tell us much about mid- to late-19th-century building development in certain areas. For instance, an altered apportionment of March 1881 for Hammersmith shows 13 new, detached houses on church land on the north side of the Uxbridge Road, next to the parish boundary at Stamford Brook.[8] The lessee (and presumably builder) is given as William Tubb. On a larger scale is the suburban development shown half-built on the Holland estate at Brixton in an altered apportionment of August 1849. Some 70 or 80 semi-detached and terrace-houses are shown on plots lining new streets in and around Barrington Road; the division of other, as yet undeveloped plots is indicated,

Owners	Occupiers	No. on plan	Name/ Description	State of Cultivation	Quantity	Charges
J. Dart, Esq.	'In Hand' (ie himself)	271	Meadow	Meadow	1a 1r 3p	3s / 1s 6d
		276	ditto.	ditto.	1a 2r 16p	4s / 2s
		272	national school		6p	
		273	Four cottages		11p	
		274	Cottage		3p	
Dr Rev. Proctor	'In Hand'	283	Garden		2r 4p	4s / 2s
		287	Wood		3a — 4p	3s
		277	Meadow	Meadow	2a 2r 25p	7s 6d / 5s

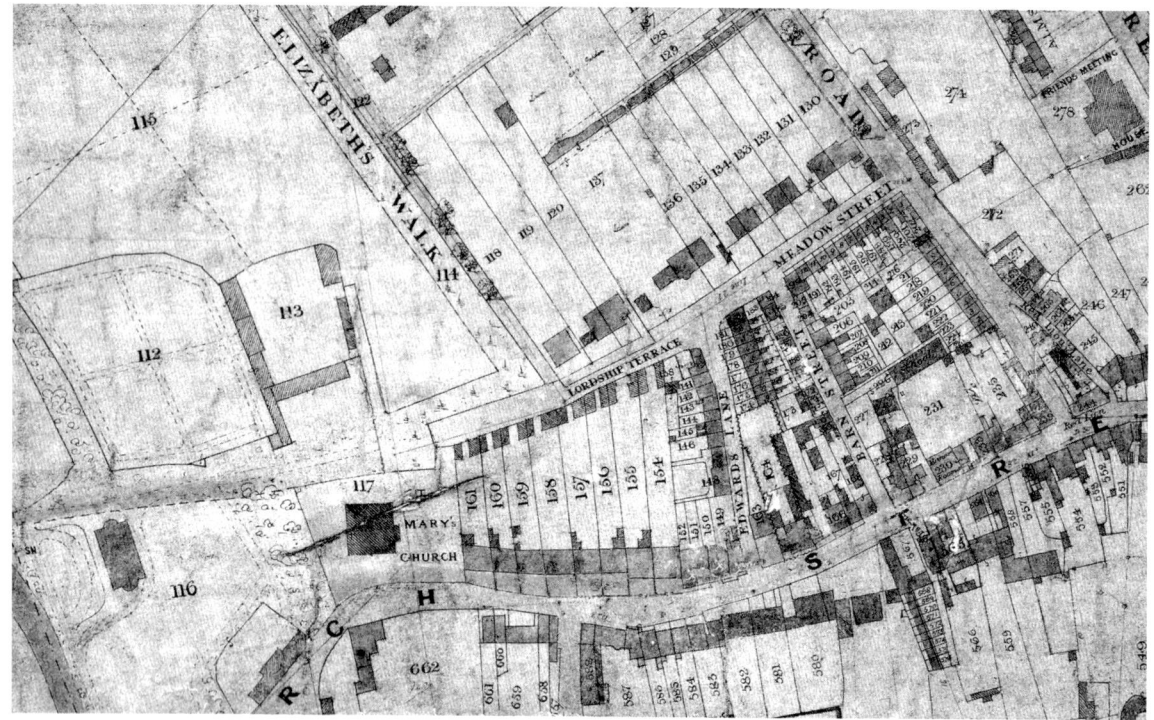

69. *An extract from the tithe map for Stoke Newington, 1826.*

70. *Extract from a land tax collector's book listing tax-payers for houses and land on the north side of Mile End Road, 1744. Some of the houses still exist today. Those listed under Thomas White, Charles Abbott and Joseph Pitt are now Nos 115–119 (odd); they were built in the early 1700s. The 'empty house' and Rebecca Brandon's are Nos 133–139, built in the 1740s by Thomas Andrews, a bricklayer.*

30								31
18	Thomas White	3	12	0	32	John Goodlad	6	8
	Charles Abbott Empty					Empty		
18	Joseph Pitt	3	12		30	Rebecca Brandon	6	0
10	Susanah Ireland	2	0		20	Mary Emmitt 3/4	3	0
160	Robert Westfield	32	0		19	Will Eade	3	16
25	Richard Maddock	5	0		12	John Norriss	2	8
	Ditto Stock 2.0.0	2	0		13	William Connop	2	12
30	Katherine Norriss	6	0			George Cummings		

as are the intended positions of more houses. Six years earlier this area, of some 26 acres, had comprised two meadows occupied by Dr William Ball. The altered apportionment lists over 25 separate leaseholders and the occupants of the houses in their possession. Unoccupied houses are also noted.[9]

All county record offices have copies of some tithe apportionments and maps, and usually these can be consulted in their original form. However, the most comprehensive set are those of the Tithe Commission now held in the National Archives (class IR29 and IR30), but increasingly these must be viewed on microfilm or microfiche.

Land Tax

Introduced in the 1690s, the land tax was originally a tax on both real and personal property. By the mid-18th century it was confined almost entirely to land (the personal element was partially superseded in 1798 by the supposedly temporary introduction of income tax). Land tax was calculated and gathered in county 'quotas': thus each county (and hundred or parish within each county) was assessed largely according to its wealth. These quotas remained unchanged between 1798 and the 1960s, when the tax was finally abolished.

The tax assessments are most useful in listing annually the names of the owners or proprietors of land in each parish. In contrast to most ratebooks, after c.1780 the names of owners and occupiers are both given.

Land tax records were not kept as accurately as those for local rates, and survival is patchy. Other than the City and parts of Westminster, systematic investigation of returns for London is only possible for the period 1780–1832, when copies or 'duplicates' of assessments were kept by clerks of the peace. These are a useful source for changes in property ownership and occupation in the period before the introduction of civil registration. The land tax ceases to be of much use after c.1840, when, in any case, some of this information can be found in directories or census returns.

The records consist of various columns of data: the names of proprietors or copyholders (not necessarily the freehold owners); the names of tenants or occupiers; the name or description of properties (often simply 'house and land'); and the amount of tax assessed. Below is an extract from an assessment of 1790, again using Monken Hadley as an example.[10]

As with the ratebooks, the land tax records can be used to discover an approximate construction date for some buildings, by working back through a series of returns. For instance, Mr Hall's 'new cottage' does not appear in the 1789 return, and no mention is made of Mr Elemont's '4 new small cottages' before 1786. Some care should be taken interpreting land tax assessments: the columns are not always drawn up in the same order or filled in consistently, and it can be difficult to ascertain if any 'dittos' refer to the entry above or that adjoining. Some historians have used the amount charged to an individual as an indication of the amount of land owned, but cau-

Rental value	Owner	occupiers	charge
£10	Wm. Elemont	himself & Widow Wise	£1 3s 4d
£12	do.	J. Cox	£1 9s
£7	do.	2 cottages	16s 4d
£3	do.	Purrat	7s
£7 10s	do.	3 cottages	17s 6d
£7 10s	do.	'4 new small cottages'	14s
£10	Widow Wise	David Hall	18s 8d
£2 10s	David Hall	'new cottage'	5s 10d
£30	W. Dickinson	'the Manor house'	£1 3s 4d
£13	J. Hill	Mrs King	£1 8s

tion should be exercised here, too: the quota system did not produce consistent charges from county to county, and assessments were sometimes calculated annually and sometimes quarterly. However, a fixed rate from 1798 of 4*s* in the £1 does facilitate tracing back changes in ownership or the sub-division of plots for building, as the total amount should remain roughly the same.

It is rare to find land tax records surviving from the period *c*.1690 to *c*.1770. One notable exception is the City of London and its liberties, which has a good set of returns, available on microfilm in the Guildhall Library's Manuscripts Department. The Guildhall collection also covers some areas outside the City's jurisdiction for the same period, such as Spitalfields and Stepney. Illustration 70 shows returns for houses on the north side of the Mile End Road from the tax collector's book for 1744. Some 18th-century records for Westminster are in the City of Westminster Archives Centre, others are at the LMA. The particularly useful 'clerks of the peace' copies for the period 1780–1832 are now held by the relevant county record offices (e.g. those for Middlesex are at the LMA). An unusual one-off survival is the nationwide set of assessments for 1789 held at the National Archives (class IR23).

Window Tax

Another tax introduced in the late 17th century was the window tax, charged upon householders or occupiers of buildings with more than a certain number of windows (usually between 7 and 10). This tax persisted, with some modifications, until 1851, and many of the 'blind' windows seen on London's houses from before this date are probably related to its imposition *(ill. 71)*. The unfortunate disappearance of decorative Georgian fanlights from over the doors of some terrace-houses may also relate to the window tax: in the sales particulars reproduced in Illustration 62, reference is made to the tax affecting the windows of houses in Clarence Terrace, Haggerston, the sellers stating that these could easily be reduced below the level of taxation by removing the fanlights.

Few returns survive, and where they do the information recorded is often difficult to inter-

71. Window tax: No 12 Theobalds Road, of the 1720s, with blind windows in return front to King's Mews, in 1974.

pret usefully. The name of each householder or other person liable to pay is given, along with the number of 'taxable' windows or the amount to be charged. But not all the windows in a house were liable to the tax – some, such as those in service areas or shop-fronts, were exempt – and unscrupulous owners are known to have disguised windows to evade payment.

However, for those parts of London where window tax returns exist, the number of windows taxed can give a rough indication of relative house sizes. And, in a similar way to ratebooks, sudden changes in the amount charged for an individual property, or in the number of its taxable windows, can be a sign of extension or rebuilding.

Anyone interested in looking at window tax returns should get in touch with their local record office. Alternatively, lists of surviving records have been published (see *Further Reading* under Gibson, Medlycott and Mills).

Hearth Tax

Also of limited use to the average house historian are the records of the late-17th-century hearth tax. This short-lived tax required all householders except the poor to pay a sum for each fireplace or stove in their house. The special value of the returns is the indication they can provide of the relative size of a district or parish, its population density, and the distribution of wealth (by inference from the number of hearths). Unfortunately the lists give no idea of location. Unless the occupants at the time are known, identification of individual buildings is almost impossible, save for large properties such as inns, or smithies and bakeries (where mention is made of a forge or oven). The tax was abolished in 1689.

The National Archives has assessments from the years 1662–6 and 1669–74, when the tax was levied by the King's receivers (class E179/367–8). Some hearth tax returns can also be found in local record offices, among records of the quarter sessions. For the outer parts of London, some county record societies have published useful lists of hearth tax assessments: for example, see C. A. F. Meekings (ed.), *The Surrey Hearth Tax 1664* (Surrey Record Society, vol. VXXVII), 1940. Recently a new series of county transcripts has been begun by the British Record Society in conjunction with local societies, under the supervision of the Roehampton Hearth Tax Project Team, based at the University of Surrey.

NOTES AND REFERENCES

1. City of Westminster Archives Centre, ratebooks for St Paul's, Covent Garden. Such information can also be found in the leases issued by the Bedford Estate. See *Survey of London*, vol. XXXVI, 1970, pp. 77–97.
2. Minet Library, P2/121–138.
3. 10 Edw. VII c.8.
4. The National Archives (TNA), IR58/91020/193,196.
5. In 1836 93% of the land in Surrey and 95% in Essex was subject to the payment of tithes, as opposed to only 49% in the more densely developed county of Middlesex. See R. J. P. Kain and Richard R. Oliver, *The Tithe Maps of England and Wales*, 1995, pp. 174–93, 306–12, 503–12.
6. R. J. P. Kain and Richard R. Oliver, *The Tithe Maps of England and Wales*, 1995.
7. LMA, TA/MHAD/02.
8. TNA, IR29/21/23.
9. TNA, IR29/34/17. The layout of these streets was

apparently the work of the eminent architect Henry Currey, whose father, Benjamin, was the solicitor for Lord Holland's estate. See *Survey of London*, vol. XXVI, 1956, p. 109.
10. LMA, MR/PLT/162.

FURTHER READING

Geraldine Beech and Rose Mitchell, *Maps for Family and Local History* (National Archives), 2004

Edward Cannan, *The History of Local Rates in England*, 2nd edn (King & Son), 1912

Stella Colwell, *Family Roots: Discovering the Past in the Public Record Office* (Weidenfeld & Nicolson), 1991

Ida Darlington, 'Ratebooks' in *History*, vol. XLVII, 1962, pp. 42–5

M. J. Daunton, 'House Ownership from Rate Books', in *Urban History Yearbook*, 1976, pp. 21–7.

Eric J. Evans, *Tithes: maps, apportionments and the 1836 Act*, revised edn (British Association for Local History), 1993

William Foot, *Maps for Family History* (PRO publication), 1994

J. Gibson, *Hearth Tax Returns and other later Stuart Tax Lists and the Association Oath Rolls* (Federation of Family History Societies), 1996

J. Gibson, M. Medlycott and D. Mills, *Land and Window Tax Assessments* (Federation of Family History Societies), 1993

Donald E. Ginter, *A Measure of Wealth: The English Land Tax in Historical Analysis* (Hambledon Press), 1992

David Grigg, 'A Source on Landownership: The Land Tax Returns', in *Amateur Historian*, vol. 6, no. 5, 1964, pp. 152–6

Roger Howell, 'Hearth Tax Returns', in *History*, vol. XLIX, 1964, pp. 42–5

H. G. Hunt, 'Land Tax Assessments', in *History*, vol. LII, 1967, pp. 283–6

M. Jurkowski, C. Smith and D. Crook, *Lay Taxes in England and Wales, 1188–1688* (PRO), 1998

R. J. P. Kain and R. R. Oliver, *The Tithe Maps of England and Wales* (CUP), 1995

R. J. P. Kain and H. C. Prince, *The Tithe Surveys of England and Wales* (CUP), 1985

London Rate Assessments and Inhabitants Lists in Guildhall Library and the Corporation of London Records Office (Guildhall Library handlist), 1960

Brian Short, *The Geography of England and Wales in 1910: An Evaluation of Lloyd George's 'Domesday' of Landownership* (Historical Geography Research Series, No. 22), 1989

Brian Short and M. Reed, 'An Edwardian Land Survey: the Finance (1909–1910) Act 1910 Records', in *Journal of the Society of Archivists*, VIII (1 & 2), 1986

J. E. Smith, *A catalogue of Westminster records*, 1900

W. E. Tate, *The Parish Chest*, 3rd edn (CUP), 1969

M. Turner and D. Mills (eds), *Land and Property: the English Land Tax 1692–1832* (Sutton), 1986

R. W. Unwin, *Search Guide to the English Land Tax* (West Yorkshire County Record Office), 1982

W. R. Ward, *The Administration of the Window and Assessed Taxes, 1696–1798* (Phillimore), 1963

Chapter Six

Records of Occupation

A substantial quantity of records relating to the occupation of London's houses is available to the researcher in the form of lists of names and addresses, particularly for the 19th and 20th centuries. Of these, the most frequently used are: ratebooks (see page 97); directories; census returns; and electoral registers and poll books. Carefully studied and analysed, these can tell the local historian much about ordinary people, their family lives, employment and social status. They can also be used to trace the building date of a particular house, or to follow the development of a street or area, or indeed the entire capital.

The simplest way to discover the previous occupants of a London house is to work backwards through the annual volumes of street directories. In general, these list the main occupiers of London properties for each year during the period c.1841–c.1970, though poorer areas were often neglected. For the period between 1841 and the beginning of the 20th century, comprehensive lists of all London buildings and residents can be found in the census returns. These also give much more background information than directories about the occupants, such as their age, place of birth, relationships, status and employment. For the recent past, since c.1970, when street directories ceased to list occupiers of domestic property, local electoral registers provide a useful if brief list of occupants qualified to vote. Recent ratebooks, too, where these are accessible, can be used for the modern period.

Good collections of directories, registers and poll books can be found in large repositories such as the London Metropolitan Archives and Guildhall Library, though most local borough archives have a good selection for their area. Local archives also keep census returns for their district, but for those researching more than one area it is best to consult the national collection, currently held at the Family Records Centre in Clerkenwell. Increasingly in recent years, librarians and archivists have been removing directories and registers from their shelves, and microfilm copies are now the norm.

Directories

Although the first printed list of London merchants was published in 1677, directories did not begin to appear in large numbers until the 1740s and '50s, when titles such as *Kent's Directory* and the *Universal Pocket Companion* provided a guide to the capital's merchants and retailers; the latter also included information on transport and the postal service. As industry and commerce expanded in the 1760s and '70s, so the market grew with the introduction of new competitors, among them the *London Directory*, the *New Complete Guide* and the *Universal Director*.

All of these early directories were intended primarily for those involved in trade and commerce, for whom efficient communication was essential — hence their concentration on selective lists of prominent residents and businesses, often with additional information about coach services, inns and local banking facilities. Unlike later street directories, the lists they contain are arranged usually by surname in alphabetical order, regardless of address, which makes them of little use in finding the occupant of a particular house or street. A typical excerpt follows, from the *London Directory* of 1798:

Drewry Samuel, *Merchant*, 12, Park-street, Westminster

Dring and Fage, *Hydrometer-makers*, 6, Tooley-street, Southwark

Drinkald John, *Lighterman*, 19, Beer-lane, Great Tower-street

Driver and Eyre, *Imperial and Trunk-makers*, 19, Cockspur-street

Druce J. *Navy Agent*, Navy Office, Somerset Place

Druce Robert, *Packer*, 9, Little St. Thomas Apostles

Druce Thomas, *Stationer*, 23, Chancery-lane, and Holborn Bars

Drummond & Lindsay, *Merchants*, 10, Sackville-street, Piccadilly

Directories like this were often compiled by agents on house-to-house visits, or from advertisements for information in newspapers, and it should be remembered that their prime purpose was to make a profit. From 1800 the Post Office began to publish its own directories, also for profit, but compiled and checked with the aid of their letter carriers, to help ensure efficient mail delivery. This *Post Office London Directory* was to dominate the directory market. After 1837 the production of *Post Office Directories* was managed by Frederic Kelly, hence they are also known as *Kelly's Directories.*

Each of the pre-1841 directories is restricted to the more 'respectable' residents and streets, with little or no mention of the poorer parts of the capital, a common failing with nearly all directories. However, despite such shortcomings, for those interested in social or economic history, early directories will give an indication of the incidence of particular trades or nationalities in certain areas. For example, directories of the 1820s and '30s list some specialist Italian artisans and craftsmen in Holborn and Clerkenwell, particularly in the vicinity of Hatton Garden and Saffron Hill: John Corti, a barometer- and thermometer-maker in Eyre Street Hill, John Mombelli, a carver and gilder, in Charles Street, and F. Pastorelli, a barometer-maker, in Cross Street. Settled migrants such as these formed the nucleus of a community which, by the end of the 19th century, had become the centre of Anglo-Italian culture in London, known as 'Little Italy'.[1]

Street directories. Despite some improvements (including the introduction of a classified trades section in 1840), Kelly's *Post Office London Directory* remained a straightforward alphabetical list of names, occupations and addresses until 1841, when a new street-by-street section was included as part of a multi-directory format. Other publications, such as Court Directories (see below), *Johnstone's* (1817–18), *Robson's* (1823–43) and *Pigot's* (1838–40) had already experimented with this kind of arrangement, but only the *Post Office Directory* was to continue it successfully until as recently as *c.*1970, when, for reasons of security or confidentiality, residential property was excluded.

Post Office London Directories after 1841 follow a standard format which becomes easy to use with experience. Following the official directory comes the street directory, the section of most interest to the house historian. Here streets are given in alphabetical order, with house-numbers (where applicable), names of inhabitants and sometimes their occupation, if it was carried on at that address. Remember that the street-names and house-numbers may have changed and should be checked (see section on street-naming and numbering, page 66). For example, Illustrations 72 & 73 show excerpts from the London *Directories* for 1863 and 1871, listing properties on the east side of Holloway Road: the earlier volume has an old system of naming and numbering in separate rows or 'terraces' of houses; this has been superseded by a consecutive system of even numbers in the later volume.

After the street directory, the remainder of the publication is dominated by the commercial or professional directory (arranged alphabetically by surname), the classified trades directory, and a court directory (of the upper classes, later known as the 'Private Residents Directory'); there are also other lists, of clerics, lawyers, bankers, etc. At the end are advertisements, often illustrated, giving a fascinating insight into the life of the period.

Geographically, the London *Directories* were restricted to the capital's centre, though over the years their coverage expanded as the city spread outwards. Anyone researching houses

Holloway place, *Holloway.* **(N.)**
See Holloway road, West side.

HOLLOWAY ROAD. (N.)
EAST SIDE.
Hanington Chas. & Joseph (Highbury nursery)

Porter's row —
6 Page Samuel, saddler
5 Roper Henry, bootmaker
4 Shephard James, plumber
3 Beeston Joseph Robert, plumber
1 Gurney William, beer retailer

Porter's place —
2 Wright Robert, farrier
3 French James, tinman
7 Preston Samuel, dairyman
8 Mason Wm. earthenware dealer

Wilson Fredk. hairdresser 1 ⎫
Surrey Miss Harriet, milliner 2 ⎪ *Highbury cottages*
TyrrellMissMary,tobacconist 3 ⎪
King Arthur, fancy repository 4 ⎭
East Chas. fly proprtr. (Porter's pl)
Taylor Henry (Highbury brewery)
Pond Wm. Jas. tobacconist (Ivy ldg)
Rouw George, cowkeeper (Hope cot)
Dove Benj. Dixon, esq. (Sunbury ho)
... *here is Highbury crescent west.*..
4 Wickham Edward, surgeon
5 Elliott Thomas, furniture dealer
6 Waghorn Rd. marble paper manfr
9 Fielding William, butcher
10 Briggs John, beer retailer
12 Jones Michael, jun. grocer
13 Brooks Joseph, dairyman
15 Hughes Henry, wheelwright
15 Dyke Robt. & Co. ice safe makers
16 Walton John, baker
17 Griffiths John, ironmonger
18 *Lord Nelson,* Augustus Fisher
19 Goaman John, saddler
...... *here is Aston buildings* ....
21 Kent John, marine store dealer
LarnerAlfd.Thos.watchmakr 3 ⎫
Cooper Thomas Wm. hatter 2 ⎬ *Bell's place*
Grinsted Henry, butcher 1 ⎭
1 Sharwood Robert, boot & shoe ma

Lowndes place —
2 Hubbard John, dyer
3 Bryan Miss Ann, stay warehouse
5 Thorne Stephen, boot & shoe ma
6 Knopf Carl, hairdresser

Nash Geo. marine store dlr 3 ⎫ *Manor place*
Dixon Charles,ironmonger 2 ⎬
Hewes Jesse, baker 1 ⎭
WarrenGeo.cabint.ma.2&3 ⎫ *Flower's buildgs*
Smith Wm. Christopher, 1 ⎬
gasfitter ⎭

Frances place —
1 Lawrence John, cooper
2 Redding Joseph Thos. beer retailer
3 Davis George, zinc worker
5 Wall Jacob, hair cutter
9 Hunnings Edward, plumber
10 Wilkins Thomas, esq
5 Chitty Mrs
4A, Barlow Joseph Thos. auctioneer
1 Oldham Mrs. Elizabeth A. school
2 Malkin Albert, artist & photogrphr
Holloway Institute
1 Crabbe Thomas, corn dealer
2 Good William, tobacconist
3 Chegwidden William, draper
4 Walter John, greengrocer
5 Wittle James, beer retailer
6 Thomas Richard, toy dealer

HealeyHy.Fras.marble sawing mils
Pied Bull, Richard Wooff
James & Ashton, builders
11 Palmer John Stephen, oilman
12 Ewens Thomas, butcher
13 WarrHenryJas.Richard,bricklayer
14 & 16 Close John, grocer

here are Slaney pl. & Pleasant passage

Pleasant place —
8 Kemp Hen. Robt. chemist & drugst
1 Butcher Frederick, glass dealer
2 King George Henry, plumber &c
3 Rimble Richard, trimming seller
4 Ody Richard, carpenter
5 Newcomb Richard, grocer &c
⎧ Stevens William, baker & corn dlr
6 ⎨ POST OFFICE RECEIVING HO.
⎩ & MONEY ORDER OFFICE
7 Tapper Ambrose Wm. butcher
... *here is Hornsey road* ....
ColeyChs.Wm.pawnbrkr.(1James pl)
Hughes James Samuel, beer retailer (2 James place)

Nottingham place —
1 Hegan Mrs. Elzbth. wardrobe dlr
2 SpencerThos.Walter,carver&gildr
4 Bridgland Edwd.Hughes,fruiterer
4 Stokes Emanuel, ironmonger
5 Barton John Sumner, stationer &c
Rickett, Smith & Co. coal office

Wheeler MissAmelia,milliner 1 ⎫ *Phoebe place*
Rose William, poulterer 1 ⎬
Baber Miss Caroline, milliner 2 ⎭

Railway place —
8 Perryman Edward, linendraper
6 Shillingford Richard, printer
7 Burr Edward, tobacconist
5 Mummery Fredk. Hy. upholsterer
4 Pakeman Robert, tailor
3 Wouters Charles, hairdresser
2 Ginder James, stationer
1 King Thomas, auctioneer &c
Prince of Wales, Alfred Browne

Dorset pl —
Cuttill Henry, sculptor
2 Mobbs Mrs. Avice, fruiterer
2 Walkden Mrs. Caroline, milliner
3 Arnold George, boot & shoe maker
4 Welch & Anthony, plumbers &c

3 Richardson Mrs. Sarah, staymaker
Cushee Edward, esq. (Veranda cot)
Phillips John, carpntr. 2 ⎫
Jacob James, carpenter ⎬ *Harriett terrace*
Arnold George, dairy ⎪
Osborne Charles, grocer ⎭
Harrison Jas. esq. (Melville cottg)

Loraine terrace —
1 Taylor Charles, surgeon
2 Sharpe Charles, hosier &c
3 Soley George, grocer
.... *here is Loraine road* ....
4 Cox & Cutler, plumbers &c

John's ter —
1 Davison Robert, milliner
2 White Miss Mary Ann, stationer
3 Cochrane Miss Annie, baby linen warehouse
4 Weller Richard, tailor
5 Wilson Thomas, milliner
6 Suckling Nathaniel, leather seller
7 Gahan Stephen, hosier

Priest John, esq. (Thorne cottage)
Smith, Beck & Beck, opticians & microscope makers(Lister works)
Dodd Jas. silver music string maker (Image cottage)
Welch Henry, auctioneer
.... *here is Tollington road* ....
Wickes Henry Adolphus, linendraper
Jones Geo. jeweller (Camden house)
⎧ Hinton Miss Mary, toy warehouse
⎨ POST OFFICE RECEIVING HOUSE

Geary William, carver & gilder
Harvey James, livery stables
Stuart Alfred, seedsman
Gay Henry Louisa, coffee rooms
King's Head, John Tharratt

1 Pugh Thomas, dairyman
1&2 BurninghamChas.Wm.cheesemg
3 Lovell Robert, straw hat maker

Wellington place —
1 Kenning George, bootmaker
3 Simpson Fredk. Wm. watchmaker
4 Staveley William, plumber &c
4A, PerfectJas.Robt.furniture broker
5 Wilson Thomas, chemist &c
6 Calderara Miss Caroline, milliner
7 Galer Alfred, baby linen warehouse
7 Goode Thomas, esq

Holloway ter —
6 Smith Edward Cullum, stationer
6 Galer Charles, fruiterer
11 Lovell Robert, pianoforte wareho
10 Arthorp Thomas, staymaker
9 Baynes Fredk. James, ironmonger
8 Clarke Mrs. Sarah, dyer
7 Palmer Miles Rook, fancy repository
6 Hambidge Wm. ham & beef dealer
5 Spire George, tailor
4 Taylor Robert Samuel, tobacconist
3 Beazley John, fishmonger
1 2 &*Nag's Head,* Richd. Hollyman
..... *here is Seven Sisters' road* .....

Bowman's pl —
1 Gyllenship Gustavus A. stationer
2 & 3 Fyson George, linendraper
4 Hustwitt Philip, confectioner
5 Hayer John, boot & shoe maker
6 Redding John, cheesemonger
7 Robbins Rowland, fruiterer
8 Samuel & Lane, ironmongers
9 Goslett Alfred, grocer
Morgan Mrs. Eleanor, boarding school (Bowman's lodge)
WhittakerH.Kendle,esq.1 ⎫ Polling-
Hugoe&Tate,dressmkrs. 2 ⎬ ton
Lowther Lockwood,esq. 3 ⎪ villas
Bird Mrs. 4 ⎭
KingGeo.Thos.dairym.(1Princs.cots)

UPPER HOLLOWAY. (N.)
EAST SIDE.
Willsher George, confectioner
PickettJno.stonemsn.(ThreeMile cot)

Hercules terrace —
1 Horsey Henry, butcher
2 Harborow Edward, grocer
3 Kimbell Napoleon, linendraper
4 *Hercules tavern,* Stephen Neate
5 Applegate Edwin, chemist
5 *London District Telegraph*Co. (limited)

Euston place —
1 Elliott Fredk. earthenware dealer
2 Burgess Thomas, greengrocer
3 Richardson Samuel, hairdresser
4 Gates Samuel, butcher
5 Edwards Edward, plumber
6 Collins James, bricklayer
7 Small John, baker
8 Hammon Wm. boot & shoe maker
.... *here is Windsor road* ....
1 Willy Thomas, undertaker
2 Connett John, bootmaker

Clifton pl —
3 Hutchings Miss MaryAnn,tobacnst
5 Wood Richard, carpenter
6 Boyce Joseph, tailor
7 Smith Richard, cooper
Dutton Robt. plumber (Poplar cot)
Gibbs William, esq. (Poplar house)
Oliver Mrs. 1 ⎫ Manor
Greenwood Michael, esq. 2 ⎬ cottages
.... *here is Manor road* ....

Manor pl —
1 James Joseph, cheesemonger
2 ⎧ Rait Mrs. Mary Sophia, hosier
⎨ POST OFFICE RECEIVING HOU
3 Richards William, grocer
5 Ambler Elisha, esq
7 Godwin Frederick, grocer
Cock tavern, George Woodcock
here is Grove road ....

72. Part of the east side of Holloway Road, from the 1863 Directory, still at that date divided into 'places' and 'terraces'.

Hollen st. 10 *Wardour st.*
(**W.**) & 23 *Gt.Chapel st. Soho.*

2 Jennens Edwin Davis, decorator
3 Corby William, bootmaker
4 Barton Edward, music printer
5 Hildersley Henry, chairmaker
8 Vose George, whip mounter
12 Woodham Thomas, plumber
13 Blain Mrs. Sarah, chandler's shop
14 Sitch William, water gilder
16 Jones David, tailor
18 Hildersley Wm. chair manufactur

Holles street, 27 *Cavendish square* (**W.**), to 130 *Oxford st.*

2 Belcher William & Son, grocers
3 Renaux Lucien Theodore
4 Rowell J.Reed, army & navy tailor
5 Graham & Beard, dressmakers
6 Fletcher Miss Mary
7 Kerton George, private hotel
8 Read Thomas, dentist
9 Buckland Miss Amelia, private hotel
10 & 11 Ford & Glover, habit makers
12 Christian, Adams & Co. linendprs
13 Underwood & Colman, solicitors
16 Bull Edwin, architect
Bull Andrew Mensal, surveyor
17 Lloyd Thomas
18 Samson Augustus, lodging house
19 Mayer & Co. church furnitur. ma
Simpson James Tennant
Daniell Frederic William
20 Ayerst William Edward, surgeon
22 Stephens Benjamin, goldsmith
23 Hunt William & Co. publishers
Roberts Miss
24 Boosey & Co. military instrmt.ma
25 & 26 Lemaire Pierre, private hotel
27 Housden Mrs. Jane, brush manfr
28 Boosey & Co. music publishers
29 Headman Mrs. Agnes, preparations for the hair

Holles st. *Clare market*
(**W.C.**), 58 *Stanhope street.*

7 Quantock Thomas, bootmaker
13 *Fishmongers' Arms*, John Leeson
16 Cove Joseph, undertaker
19 Barnett Richard, ginger beer ma
20 Pearce William, bootmaker
25 Curtis James, military sash makr

Hollingworth street (**N.**),
Westbourne road east.

Prince Albert, Wm. J. Beeching
Temporary Home for Lost & Starving Dogs,
James Pevitt, manager
1A, Crofts William, cowkeeper
10 Lee John, shoemaker
38 Oxley Frederick, butcher
39 Guinn William, greengrocer
Pyle Richard, ginger beer maker

Holloway place. (**N.**) *Now numbered in Holloway rd.*

HOLLOWAY ROAD. (**N.**)
EAST SIDE.

2 Hanington Charles & Joseph (Highbury nursery)
4 White & Coleman, saddlers
6 Roper Henry, bootmaker
8 Shephard James, sign writer
10 Beeston Joseph Robert, plumber
12 McNaughton Miss Emma, dressma
14 Edwards William, beer retailer
16 Bridges William, livery stables
18 Wright Robert, farrier
20 Gorwill William, tinman
22 Davies William, bootmaker
26 Pashley Mrs. Emma, strw. bon. ma
28 Preston Mrs. Sarah, dairy
30 Evans, Jones & Co. undertakers
32 Mason Wm. earthenware dealer

74 Elliott Mrs. Margaret, furniture dealer
Young Alfred, fishmonger
76 Thompson Edwin, herbalist
78 Waller John, chandler's shop
80 Humphreys John, leather seller
82 Dyke Robert, undertaker
88 Webber George, beer retailer
90 Deacon James, pewterer
94 Dyke John & Co. carpenters
98 Barnes James, corn dealer
100 *Lord Nelson*, Robert Virgo
. *here are Aston buildings ..*
104 Rees Edward, rag merchant
106 Seal Thomas, bricklayer
108 Sutton Charles Thos. optician
110 Holley Benjamin, greengrocer
112 Grinsted Henry, butcher
114 Carson David, bootmaker
116 Campling James, dyer
118 Weeks Thos. portmanteau ma
120 Taylor George, confectioner
122 Blowright Thos. furniture delr
124 Baxter Charles, hairdresser
126 Fendick John Brasnett, oilman
128 Nash George, marine store dealer
130 Dixon Charles, ironmonger
132 Swann Samuel, baker
. *here are Highbury hill park & Benwell road.....*
138A, Norton Chas. Douglas, bootma
140 Lawrence John, cooper
142 Messenger George, coffee rooms
144 Fordyce Edw. glass shade wareho
146 & 148 Wootton John George, coach builder
150 Clark George, linendraper
152 Clarke James Arthur, hatter
154 Hayman Wm. Hen. linendraper
156 Edwards David, butcher
158 Hunnings Edward, plumber
160 Trotman John, jun. rustic workr
Working Men's Club & Institute
162 Griffin Samuel, bedstead manfr
164 Shaw Hen. paper hanging warho
166 Davison Edward, chemist
Hollaway Baths, Hy. Harris, prop
172 Bell Stephen, brewery
174 James John, bootmaker
Tilley William Smith, grocer
176 Good William, tobacconist
178 Chegwidden William, draper
180 Walter John, greengrocer
182 Laburnum Walter, beer retailer
184 Thomas Richard, toy dealer
188 *Pied Bull*, Andrew B. Penny (exors. of)
190 Gibbons William, grocer
Ashton John, coffee rooms
192 Palmer John Stephen, oilman
198 Pearce Edwin, auctioneer
200 Usher Mrs. Lucy, bootmaker
202 Close Brothers, grocers
204 Webb & Co. cheesemongers
206 Edwards Joseph, butcher
208 Fricker & Horsford, grocers
210 Almond George, greengrocer
214 *Coach & Horses*, Fred. Doughty
216 I'Anson Robert, fruiterer
218 Evans Charles, linendraper
.... *here is Slaney place ....*
Rose John Henry, wheelwright (Slaney place)
220 Kemp Henry Robert, chemist
.. *here is Pleasant passage ..*
222 Butcher Frederick, glass dealer
224 Shepherd William, butcher
226 Rumble Richd. trimming seller
228 Ody Richard, carpenter
Ayres Misses Blanche & Jessie tobacconists
230 Evans Samuel Daniel, grocer
232 Lovering George Firks, baker
234 Horsey Charles James, butcher
.... *here is Hornsey road ...*
236 Coley Chas. Wm. pawnbroker
238 *Bedford Arms*, Robt. McDiarmid
240 Smith Robt. Davies, bookseller

73. From the Directory of 1871, showing changes in naming and numbering.

in the outer parts of London, or those formerly in the adjoining counties such as Essex or Surrey, should consult Kelly's *Home Counties Directories* (from 1845) and the *London Suburban Directory* (1860–1934). The first edition of the suburban directory reached as far afield as Southall, Romford, Crayford and Malden. Useful maps illustrating the coverage of the London and Suburban directories have been published by P. J. Atkins in *The Directories of London, 1677–1977* (1990). From 1934 the suburban lists were absorbed into an integrated County of London directory.

It may also be worthwhile consulting local directories, which are often more detailed than the London-wide ones. Examples include: *Lucas's Paddington Directory*, and *Ward's Commercial and General Croydon Directory*. Ask at the local borough history library about their collection. In addition, Kelly's entered the market in the mid-1880s with their own local directories (also known as 'buff books').

By working backwards, it is possible to discover an approximate date of construction for houses and streets from their first appearance in street directories. This information can then be checked or refined by using other, more accurate sources, such as contemporary ratebooks or local authority records and maps. For an example, take a typical suburban south London street: Clairview Road is a row of 28 (originally 36) Edwardian-style, two-storey semi-detached houses overlooking part of Tooting Bec Common (Nos 23–30 have been replaced by a block of post-war houses). The street appears on the 1916, 25in Ordnance Survey, but not on the edition of 1894–6, where the site is occupied by four large detached houses and grounds. The *London Suburban Directory* for 1912 shows 31 of the houses numbered and occupied. In 1910, 27 are listed, in 1909 only 17, without numbers, but each with its own evocative house-name, such as 'Hawthorndene', 'Elmscroft' and 'Lawnswood'. The 1908 entry of 11 houses is the earliest, suggesting an approximate construction date of *c.*1907–*c.*1909 for the street. A dig around in the local history library confirms this, as the drainage applications for the street are dated 1908, and provide the builder's name (Messrs

Crunden & Co.). There is also some interesting background information: one of the large houses which used to occupy the site was once home to the potter Henry Doulton, who did much to prevent the enclosure of the common in the 1860s; he sold the house to Charles Derry of Derry & Toms department store.[2]

Although the information listed in Kelly's directories must be treated with some care, it is unlikely that errors would have been published year after year. Kelly paid Post Office letter carriers to submit extracts from the directory to residents for checking, before the next year's issue was published. This was usually carried out at the end of June, with the page-proofs checked on the streets in September and October, and any corrections made before publication in December to meet the Christmas demand. Therefore, as a rough rule, the data they contain applies to the year before publication, i.e. the occupant of a property listed in a directory published in 1924 was probably there during the latter part of 1923. If a building disappears from the directories for a number of years it is probably empty, or could possibly be being rebuilt.

Court Directories. For the upper strata of London society specialist 'Court' directories evolved, listing fellow members of the élite (and sometimes the not-so-élite), intended as a guide for those moving to the capital for the social season. Their contents were entirely confined to private residents. The two best-known were *Boyle's New Fashionable Court and Country Guide and Town Visiting Directory*, published twice annually from 1792 until 1925; and the *Royal Blue Book*, produced between 1822 and 1939. Kelly's *London Directory* also included a court section. *Boyle's* carried the usual alphabetical list of residents, but also had a second list arranged by street-name, making it an early form of specialized street directory. The *Royal Blue Books* were, for a time, even more imaginative in layout: until 1894 parts of the street directory were arranged topographically on the page, as if seen from the air, presumably to make individual houses easier to find for the casual visitor *(ill. 74)*.

Directories such as these, listing only the

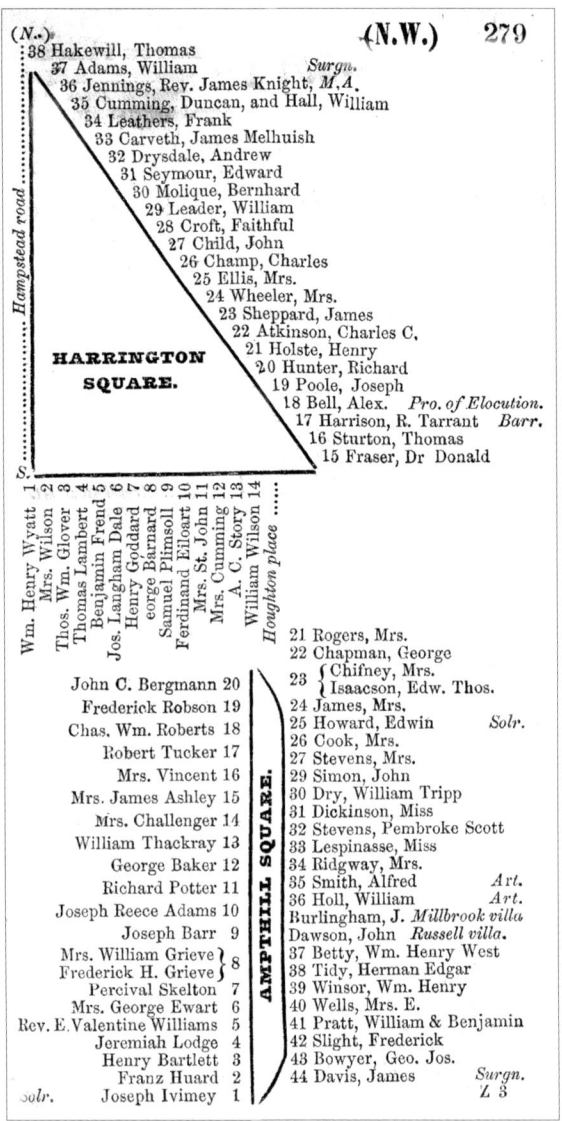

74. *Typical page from a Blue Book of 1861, showing Harrington and Ampthill Squares.*

fashionable and wealthy, and the predominantly West End streets in which they lived, can be used to follow the growth and movement of polite society and the subtly changing boundaries of its playgrounds. And they can also be used in conjunction with biographical works like *Men and Women of Our Time, Kelly's Upper Ten Thousand, The Complete Peerage* and *Who Was Who* to create a more rounded picture of the type of upper-class society particular to each district.

Other specialist directories. It is possible that the occupants of the house under study may have been involved in trade or business in the London area; in which case, if you have a name, it might be worthwhile briefly looking at the commercial and trades sections of the directories, or at specialist trades and commercial directories. These contain alphabetical lists of all types of businesses. Most useful are classified trades directories, divided into separate sections for each trade. Special directories are also available for certain professions such as doctors, lawyers and clergymen (e.g. *Crockfords*).

Census returns

The first census of the English population was taken in 1801 at a time of national emergency, with the country at war, food in short supply, and no real certainty as to the total population. They have been conducted ever since at regular ten-yearly intervals, with the exception of 1941.

Data from the first four censuses of 1801–31 were published in a series of 'abstracts', but these give only summaries of parish-wide statistics, of population and the numbers of inhabited and uninhabited houses, and so are of little use to those seeking information on individual properties. After 1811 the abstracts also list the number of new houses under construction in each area, and the number of families living there, and so can be used to study fluctuations in building activity and population on a local basis. However, in addition to these published sources, parish returns for the pre-1841 censuses survive in some local history libraries and archives. These contain information about identifiable households – such as the name of the head of the household, and the number of people living in each property – which grows with each decade. Some of these records have been indexed by local family history enthusiasts.

Pre-1841 censuses were administered at a local level by the poor-law system and the

75. Census returns: entry for Henry Dove in Highbury Crescent, in 1891 census (see next page).

church. Census-taking in its modern form evolved out of the reform movement of the 1830s, and in 1841 became the responsibility of the recently-created General Register Office. From that year the census forms (or schedules) were left at each house by the enumerators, to be completed by the residents and collected on the morning after census night (usually in March or April to avoid the large movement of population in the summer months). The information in the completed forms was then copied by the enumerators into their books, differentiating between each household. It is these returns which are the major source used by family and local historians.

The 1841 census returns are the first to give the name and sex of each occupant of every property on census night, as well as some indication of their age, vocation and place of birth. All ages above 15 were rounded down to the nearest five (eg 25, 30, 35), and birth-places simplified (whether born in the county of residence or not, or whether Scots, Irish or foreign). Unfortunately there is no clear division of properties in multi-occupancy, as the head of each household is not specified; nor are the relationships within families noted. Thus the 1841 census returns represent a transitional phase between the earlier statistical censuses and the more detailed enumerations of 1851 and after.

From 1851 each individual had to state his or her relationship to the head of the household, marital condition, full age, employment and parish and county of birth (if known). Uninhabited houses and those under construction were also noted. As with other sources of the period, street-names and house-numbers may have changed in the intervening period (see page 66). Households are differentiated by oblique or horizontal lines, and the 1891 census also records the number of rooms in each house.

Carefully interpreted, the returns can offer a surprising wealth of information about the occupants of a Victorian house. The number of people living there, their mode of employment and the presence of resident domestic servants can all be used to piece together the social structure and status of a particular household or street. As an example, take

Highbury Crescent, an elegant sweep of large, semi-detached Italianate villas close to Highbury & Islington Railway Station. The earliest returns for the street date from 1851, giving us a rough construction date, of between 1841 and 1851. (They were in fact developed between *c.*1845 and *c.*1850 by James Goodbody and James Wagstaff, with Wagstaff probably acting also as architect.)[3]

By the time of the census enumeration of spring 1851 all the houses were in occupation, and had already become popular with wealthy merchants, manufacturers and brokers, including two of foreign extraction. At No. 6 resided Raphael Nunes Carvalho, a 41-year-old Jamaican-born West India Merchant, with his wife, Rachel, four children, brother and three servants. Some sense of the family's mobility is given by the fact that the eldest child (Louisa Nunes, aged 15) was born in Jamaica; two others (aged 13 and 11) were born in the parish of St Luke's, Middlesex; and the youngest (Isaac, aged 5) in Lewisham. Their most senior house-servant (Sarah, aged 43) seems to have been brought with them from Jamaica. In 1851 all the households in Highbury Crescent had at least one servant; most had two, three or four — usually, young, single and female, and often hailing from the provinces.[4]

Although the names had changed by 1891, the social class was still much the same: for example John Henry Whadcoat, a 39-year-old Worcestershire man, director of Whadcoat Brothers & Company, bankers, living at No. 18. He and his wife (Mary Jane, 45, from Devon) had seven children with them on the night of the census, aged between 2 and 18, and three resident servants. The youngest son (Horace, aged 2) was born in Islington, but the youngest daughter (Olive, aged 5) was born in Enfield, perhaps indicating how recently the family had moved to the area. Also resident in the Crescent at this time, at No. 22, was the prominent local building contractor Henry Dove, of Dove Brothers, then aged 50 *(ill. 75)*.[5]

In contrast, in 1891 the recently-built terrace houses of the so-called 'Roman' estate, to the east, were filling up with families of a different class. The census returns for Baalbec, Calabria, Gallia and Liberia Roads list schoolteachers, grocer's assistants, clerks, printers, dressmakers and shop assistants among the heads of households. These streets were solidly middle and lower-middle class, but certainly not poor: few houses were in multiple occupancy, employment was high, and some families, such as that of Frederick A. Goodworth, a 29-year-old shipowners' clerk, at No. 23 Liberia Road, could afford a live-in domestic servant (13-year old Lilly Ellis, from East Kennett in Wiltshire).[6]

Information such as the above can also point the way to other sources, such as birth certificates and parish registers. The date of a couple's marriage can be guessed from the age of their eldest child. Employment details for a street or district may indicate the dominant local businesses and industries, and can be followed up by consulting contemporary trades directories.

One of the major difficulties associated with census returns is the problem of ascertaining property boundaries, particularly in the poorer back alleys, courts and rookeries of Victorian London, where buildings were commonly subdivided and rooms partitioned. And the information given is not always reliable: many people at the time were illiterate, or were not aware of their exact date or place of birth. Remember that the census is basically a 'snapshot' of life on one night in a ten-year period, and may not always be a typical or true picture of life in every house and street.

For those who wish to trace an individual or family, and their movements, there are several name indexes to the census returns. The Mormon Church has published a national index to the 1881 census on microfilm, which is available at the Family Records Centre. Other indexes range from simple card indexes and typescript lists to books published by local family history societies: ask at the London Metropolitan Archives or your local history library for any that cover your area.

Census returns are subject to the Official Secrets Act. They are closed to public access for 100 years (on the grounds that the personal information they contain was given in confidence) and the enumerators' books for 1901 are the latest that can be consulted. The 1911 returns should be made available in January 2012.

Electoral registers and poll books

Electoral registers (also known as voters' lists) provide practically the only reliable source of information on the occupancy of houses in recent years. The registers are usually arranged by polling district or ward, and within these alphabetically by street-name, cataloguing every member of each household registered to vote.

The first registers were produced in 1832, after the Reform Act, and some London boroughs, for example Westminster, have registers for the 19th century and early years of the 20th century. These early registers were not always simply a list of names: before 1918 (when all men over 21 were given the right to vote) they stated each person's address and details of their qualification to vote, usually the ownership of a freehold property. Unlike their modern equivalents, the early registers are arranged by parish, with the names of electors listed alphabetically; street order was adopted in 1918. Bear in mind that most women were excluded until the introduction of universal suffrage in 1928, and foreign nationals, who are excluded from British elections, are not recorded. And for some districts it can be difficult, in the early part of the 20th century, to distinguish between members of a household and their resident domestic staff.

From 1696 published **poll books** listing the names of voters in Parliamentary elections, indicating how they cast their votes, are available for much of the Greater London area. The lists were drawn up by returning officers to guard against vote-rigging and deception, and some original manuscripts survive. However, their publication was an entirely private enterprise, undertaken by local printers for profit. The practice ceased in 1872 with the introduction of the secret ballot.

Such lists are by their nature restricted to the more 'substantial' members of society who held the right to vote. Owning freehold property was a common prerequisite.[7]

As the printers themselves decided what information to include, the format and scope varies from book to book. Many are confined simply to registering the votes, and give little else other than an alphabetical list of voters' names. Most however, also give addresses, if sometimes only the parish of residence. The *London Poll Book 1768* is an alphabetical list of names and addresses, but prefixed by the City

Bowyer	Viner William, *Frederick-street*
Bricklayer	Voss Nicholas, *Drury-lane*
Clothworkers	Vincent Francis, *Threadneedle-street*
	Vincent George, *Pater-noster-row*
Coachworkers	Vardon Shadrach, *Holborn*
	Virgo John, *Little Queen-street*
Currier	Varley John, *Redcross-street*

livery company to which each voter belonged.

Some, such as the *London Pollbook 1784*, are classified by occupation, others by area. Occasionally, speeches made by the candidates before the election are included. A few books give additional information such as the address and nature of the freehold property which entitled each man to vote. Below is an extract from Mile End Old and New Town district in the *Middlesex Pollbook 1802*.

Lists like these are clearly of use to local historians and genealogists; for certain areas poll books can run to thousands of names. At a basic level it is possible to identify the homes of certain families, but for those interested in social and political history they have much to offer – insights into local trade and industry, the geographical distribution of voters, and differing voting patterns in different localities. In general such lists are best used in combination with other sources.

For example, by studying the poll books for the Middlesex Elections of 1768–9 in conjunction with Land Tax Assessments and ratebooks, the historian George Rudé was able to show that by that date more voters lived in the urban part of the county, in and around London, than elsewhere. Rudé's analysis demonstrated that John Wilkes's dramatic victory was dependent upon the support of 'middling' tradesmen and small businessmen in this urban sector, particularly in the East End of London, which overcame the natural hostility towards Wilkes from the landowning and professional classes.[8]

Freeholder's Name	Where Freeholder lives	Where Freehold is situate	Nature of Freehold	Occupier's Name
Shakespear, Francis	Lower Thames Street	Mile end Old town	land & house	Mr. Bibbie
Sheridan, James	High Street	Mile end	messuage	Terence Colgrove
Sims, William jun.	Sun Tavern fields	Rose lane, Ratcliff	house	John Marley
Thiswall, Thomas	Mile end Old town	Mile end Old town	house	Churchwarden
Tilley, Richard	Brick lane, Spitalfields	Mile end Old town	house & garden	Carter

NOTES AND REFERENCES

1. *Pigot's Alphabetical Directory*, 1827: *Robson's London Directory*, 1833: *Post Office London Directory*, 1835. For a study of this community see David R.Green, 'Little Italy in Victorian London', in *Camden History Review*, vol. 15, 1988, pp. 2–6.

2. Wandsworth Local History Service, Drainage Applications nos SW1/13, 57, 75.

3. Department of the Environment, list description. Wagstaff and his family were living at No. 1 in the crescent, then known as 'Highbury Lodge', in 1851.

4. 1851 Census, HO107/1501, ff. 514–21

5. 1891 Census, RG12/177, ff. 4–6.

6. 1891 Census, RG12/177, ff. 122–136.

7. For those interested in the laws and regulations governing eligibility to vote in Parliamentary elections, a useful summary is given in: Jeremy Gibson and Colin Rogers, *Poll Books c1696–1872: A Directory to Holdings in Great Britain* (Federation of Family History Societies), 2nd edn, 1990, pp. 5–6.

8. G. Rudé, 'The Middlesex Electors of 1768–1769', in *English Historical Review*, vol. LXXV, no. CCXCVII, Oct 1960, pp. 601–17.

FURTHER READING

P. J. Atkins, *The Directories of London, 1677–1977* (Mansell), 1990

P. J. Atkins, 'The Compilation and Reliability of London Directories', in *London Journal*, vol. 14, No. 1, 1989, pp. 17–28

M. Beresford, 'The Unprinted Census Returns of 1841, 1851, 1861 for England and Wales', in *Amateur Historian*, vol. 5, no. 8, Summer 1963, pp. 260–9

John Cannon, 'Poll books', in *History*, vol. XLVII, no. 160, pp. 166–9

P. J. Cornfield, with Serena Kelly, '"Giving directions to the town": the early town directories', in *Urban History Yearbook*, 1984, pp. 22–35

Jeremy Gibson and Colin Rogers, *Electoral Registers since 1832: and Burgess Rolls* (Federation of Family History Societies), 2nd edn, 1990

Jeremy Gibson and Colin Rogers, *Poll Books c1696–1872: A Directory to Holdings in Great Britain* (Federation of Family History Societies), 2nd edn, 1990

C. W. F. Goss, *The London Directories, 1677–1855* (Denis Archer), 1932

Guildhall Library, *Introduction to London directories filmed by Guildhall Library, 1677–1889*

L. C. Hector, 'The Census Returns of 1841 and 1851', in *Amateur Historian*, vol. 1, no. 6, June–July 1953, pp. 174–7

Edward Higgs, *A Clearer Sense of the Census* (HMSO), 1996 edn

Susan Lumas, *Making Use of the Census* (PRO Readers' Guide), 1993

Jane E. Norton, *Guide to the National and Provincial Directories of England and Wales, excluding London, published before 1856* (Royal Historical Society), 1950 (2nd edn, 1984)

G. Rudé, 'The Middlesex Electors of 1768–1769', in *English Historical Review*, vol. LXXV, no. CCXCVII, Oct 1960, pp. 601–17

Gareth Shaw and Alison Tipper, *British Directories: A Bibliography and Guide to Directories published in England and Wales (1850–1950) and Scotland (1773–1950)* (Leicester University Press), 1989 (2nd edn, 1997)

J. M. Sims, *A Catalogue of Directories and Poll Books in the possession of the Society of Genealogists* (Society of Genealogists), 1964

J. M. Sims (ed.), *Handlist of British Parliamentary Poll Books* (University of Leicester History Department), 1984

J. R. Vincent, *Pollbooks: How Victorians Voted* (Cambridge), 1967

CHAPTER SEVEN

Fire Insurance Records

As with so many improvements relating to London's buildings, the growth and development of the fire insurance business was a response to the terrible destruction wrought by the Great Fire of 1666. Between the 1680s and the 1720s numerous private insurance companies were established (such as the Hand-in-Hand, the Sun, the Phoenix, and the Westminster Fire Office), each offering property owners and occupiers some security from loss through short-term, renewable policies. Initially, their business was restricted principally to the London area, although most – like the Phoenix and the Sun – later expanded into the regions.

Each company maintained its own fire brigade (ill. 76). Policy holders displayed special metal badges (called fire marks) on their insured properties, to indicate to the firemen the buildings for which they were responsible. Each mark was stamped with the policy number (ill. 77). The marks were often decorative, and many of the companies used distinctive symbols (indeed the Phoenix, the Sun and the Hand-in-Hand all became so-called from the design of their fire marks). Although some fire marks can still be seen in situ in London's streets, most have been removed from houses and are now more frequently encountered in private collections or museums.

The insurance offices retained responsibility for fire-fighting in London until the establishment of the Metropolitan Fire Brigade in 1865. Since then most of them have been either wound up or subsumed by larger insurance companies: for example, the Hand-in-Hand was acquired by the Commercial Union Group in 1905.

Fire insurance policy registers

The major source for house historians among fire insurance records is the individual policies. Some can be found with private papers or solicitors' records, or attached to deeds; but by far the best method is to search through the many volumes of policy registers for three of the leading London companies, held by the Guildhall Library.[1] Although these vary from office to office, the information given usually includes: the policy number; the date of the policy; the name, address and occupation of the policy holder (often a lessee or mortgagee, rather than the freeholder) and of any tenants, if applicable; the location and type of building, including a brief description of materials; the value at which the property was insured and the premium; and the date of renewal. Sometimes additional information is given: the Sun registers mention any fire hazards, list the names and occupations of any other people living in the house, and sometimes identify neighbours and their businesses, as potential hazards.

For new policies, the date of registration can be an indication of the date of construction, as insurance was commonly effected as soon as a house was completed, and was frequently a prerequisite for the issuing of a building lease. The first policy holders may indeed be the first lessees (and therefore the builders), and a different name on the renewal may be that of the person to whom the builder assigned his lease, and possibly the first occupant of the house. As policies were usually for a fixed term, it should (in theory) be relatively easy to find the entry for the renewed policy, and note any changes in ownership or occupation, or alterations to the building.

76. *Depiction of firemen of the Sun Fire Office.*

The policies of the Hand-in-Hand Company are the most informative of the three main collections. As well as the data mentioned above, the basic dimensions of the buildings are usually noted in the left-hand margin. For newly erected houses, when street names or numbers were not in common usage, the locational information given is often invaluable in identifying particular houses, as in 'third house from the corner', or, 'adjoining Mr White to the east and Mr Green to west'. Illustration 78 shows a typical late-eighteenth-century example, for a house in Crooms Hill, Greenwich.

A short row of modest houses, Nos 47–57 (odd) Mount Pleasant, near Mount Pleasant Sorting Office, is the only range of buildings to survive from the 18th-century development of the Baynes-Warner (later Jervoise) estate in Clerkenwell, on fields to the west of present-day Farringdon Road. All six houses were insured with the Hand-in-Hand in the summer

77. *A typical Sun Insurance firemark.*

119

of 1720, for about £150–£200 each. The policy holders for Nos 47, 51, 55 and 57 were three of the builders who helped develop the estate: William Newman, joiner, Thomas Scott, mason, and Thomas Dorrington, bricklayer (after whom the street was originally named). The registers inform us that the houses were small and squarish (16–18ft by 28ft), and built of brick. In 1721 Dorrington renewed the policies for his two houses (Nos 55 and 57, identifiable from the descriptions in the registers), but by 1728 the policy holder was Hannah Mayo. Scott's house (No. 51) was later insured by John Sly; other sources inform us that Sly, of Woodford in Essex, had advanced money on mortgage to other builders on the estate.[2] Newman's lease of No. 47 was assigned by him in October 1720 to Robert Pottinger, a sawyer, perhaps as payment in kind for work done on the estate. Pottinger renewed the policy in 1727.[3] (See also Case History One, page 165.)

An example from the Sun Fire Office registers, from 1824, notes the insuring of a row of nine new houses in Mount Square, near Mount Street in Bethnal Green. All were of brick and 'private', except for No. 1 (in the tenure of a carpenter); No. 2 had 'shops communicating'. They were insured for a total of £600 by Thomas Elsom, a local Kingsland Road timber merchant.[4]

As well as confirming the size, method of construction and value of individual buildings, information from fire insurance policies such as these can be used in conjunction with ratebooks and deeds to create a detailed picture of the development process in 18th- and 19th-century London. However, it should be remembered that such records cannot provide an entirely representative record of London's houses, as not all property owners could afford to insure their premises.

Unfortunately, finding policies relating to the building or street under study, should they exist, is not easy. The sheer bulk of the records – the Sun alone issued some 700,000 policies between 1720 and 1799 – makes research difficult, but this is further complicated by the lack of any useful indexes. Only the volumes of the Hand-in-Hand office contain indexes, by policy holder. Often the only successful technique is to browse through the volumes for the years in and around the date of construction of the house, if known, looking out for particular personal or street names. Some Sun and Royal Exchange policies have been indexed for certain periods (1714–31 and 1775–87); these indexes are available at the Guildhall Library. Recently the London Archive Users' Forum's 'A Place in the Sun' project has created a new online index to the Sun's London registers

78. *A typical entry in the Hand-in-Hand Company's policy registers from 1782, recording the valuation of parts of a house on Crooms Hill, Greenwich, with the names of its owner and the occupier of neighbouring property.*

beginning with the years 1816–33, fully searchable on the Access to Archives (A2A) website.

Other insurance records

Only one policy book of the Westminster Fire office survives – volume 'A', for the period September 1717 to September 1721 (policies 1–3021) – now in the care of the Royal and Sun Alliance Insurance Group. Other records of the Westminster Fire Office are at the City of Westminster Archives Centre. No policy registers of the Phoenix are known to exist, but their administrative records are held at Cambridge University Library.

Fire insurance administrative records include such things as board and committee minutes, endorsement books, claims books, accounts and correspondence. For details of such records see H. A. L. Cockerell and E. Green, *The British Insurance Business* (2nd edn, 1994), or consult the Guildhall Library's London subject catalogue (L64.9). Although primarily of interest to those researching the history of fire insurance, these records can be of use to the house historian. For example, minute books of the London Assurance Corporation record that the five houses at Nos 12–20 (even) Rutland Gate, in Knightsbridge, begun c.1838, were financed by the builder John Tombs through loans from the company; by July 1840 Tombs had finished four of the houses, of which two had been let.[5]

Notebooks belonging to fire office surveyors can also be found among the Guildhall's collection.[6] These consist of plans and notes on building materials, decorative features and room uses; but they are limited to only a few years and buildings, and are concerned more with industrial than domestic property. The best-known of the insurance surveyors was the firm of Charles E. Goad & Company, whose large-scale fire insurance plans are now a major source for London building history (see pages 50–52).

NOTES AND REFERENCES

1. These are the policy registers for the Hand-in-Hand (1701–1865, MSS 8674–84), the Sun (1710–1863, MSS 11936–7) and the Royal Exchange (1753–9 & 1773–1883, MSS 7252–3), which can be consulted in the Guildhall Library's Manuscripts Department. The Guildhall also has a few registers for the London Assurance Corporation.
2. LMA, MDR 1726/3/394.
3. Policy numbers 41412–14 in Guildhall Library, MSS 8674/22, pp. 90–1; 8674/24, p. 39; 8674/35, p. 86; 8674/37, p. 273; 8674/51, p. 3; 8674/60, p. 263.
4. Guildhall Library, MSS 11936/494/1006603.
5. Guildhall Library MSS 8733/9, p. 159; 8733/10, pp. 13, 23–4, 43, 68, 71, 102–3; 8733/11, pp. 8, 89, 153–4, 158.
6. Guildhall Library, MSS 11936D, 14316.

FURTHER READING

M. W. Beresford, 'Building History from Fire Insurance Records', in *Urban History Yearbook 1976*, 1976 (Leicester University Press), pp. 7–14

H. A. L. Cockerell and Edwin Green, *The British Insurance Business* (2nd edn, Sheffield Academic Press), 1994

P. G. M. Dickson, *The Sun Insurance Office: 1710–1960* (OUP), 1960

David T. Hawkings, *Fire insurance records for family and local historians, 1696 to 1920* (Francis Boutle), 2003

T. V. Jackson, 'The Sun Fire Office and the local historian', in *Local Historian*, vol. 17, no. 3, Aug 1986, pp. 141–9

Barry Supple, *The Royal Exchange Assurance*, 1970

J. H. Thomas, 'Fire Insurance Policy Registers', in *History*, vol. LIII, no. 179, pp. 381–4

Isobel Watson, 'A kaleidoscope of early 19th-century London', in *Family History Monthly*, July 2004, p. 25

Brian Wright, 'The Fire Mark: a part of London History', in *London Archaeologist*, Winter 1978, vol. 3, no. 9, pp. 243–5

L. M. Wulcko, 'Fire Insurance Policies as a Source of Local History', in *Local Historian*, vol. 9, no. 1, Feb 1970, pp. 3–8

CHAPTER EIGHT

Probate Records and Death Duty Registers

Various documentary records relating to death are used by genealogists to identify familial connections. Those known collectively as probate records – wills, inventories and letters of administration – are also invaluable to the house historian. Wills and administrations can be used to trace the descent of property from one individual to another. Probate inventories, which list the possessions of a deceased person, are somewhat rarer (very rare after *c*.1800), but are worth looking for, as few documents provide as detailed a description of rooms and their contents. These records of probate are supplemented in the period 1796–1903 by records of death duties – the taxes paid to the Inland Revenue on a deceased person's estate.

Wills and administrations

Wills. Today everyone is familiar with the concept of leaving a will to specify how one's property should be distributed after death. Originally two documents were required: a will, covering real estate (or 'realty'), i.e. land and buildings; and a testament, dealing with personal property (or 'personalty'), such as livestock, furniture, plate or money. The two have long been combined in a single document, but their separate histories are still remembered in the will's traditional opening phrase: 'This is the last will and testament'.

It is important to remember when looking for wills prior to the 20th century that their existence was rare outside the world of the upper-class male. Most people had little to leave, or little inclination to make provision in writing, and statistics suggest that only 6–8% of those who died in England and Wales in the

19th century were subject to a grant of probate or administration.[1]

Wills were normally written on paper or parchment but, unless you are lucky enough to come across an original will among personal papers, it is likely that you will see a copy entered in a will register book.

Until Victorian times, it was common for the opening sentences of a will to be of a religious nature, committing the deceased's soul to God, followed by any particular burial arrangements. Robert Dormer, one of His Majesty's Justices of the Court of Common Pleas at Westminster, who died in 1726, requested that his body be 'decently interred without pomp...amongst my Ancestors in the Chancell of the parish Church at Quainton in the Count of Bucks'.[2] After these opening remarks come the name(s) of the executor or executors to act on the deceased's behalf, and lists of any bequests to family and friends, or servants, and sometimes a gift to the poor of the parish. Such information offers an insight into the deceased person's personality, and his or her family relationships, wealth, status, and business associates. For example, Robert Dormer's widow, Mary Dormer, left their family home at Quainton and all the goods in it to her two daughters, provided they resided there for three or four months of each year ('to preserve the memory of my said late dear husband and son and to keep the house Garden and plantations from running to ruine'), otherwise the house was to be sold and the money given to the poor of the parish and the 'poor Debtors in Aylesbury Gaol'.[3] This will includes a detailed list of bequests, mostly of furniture kept at the house, and the family's collection of portraits

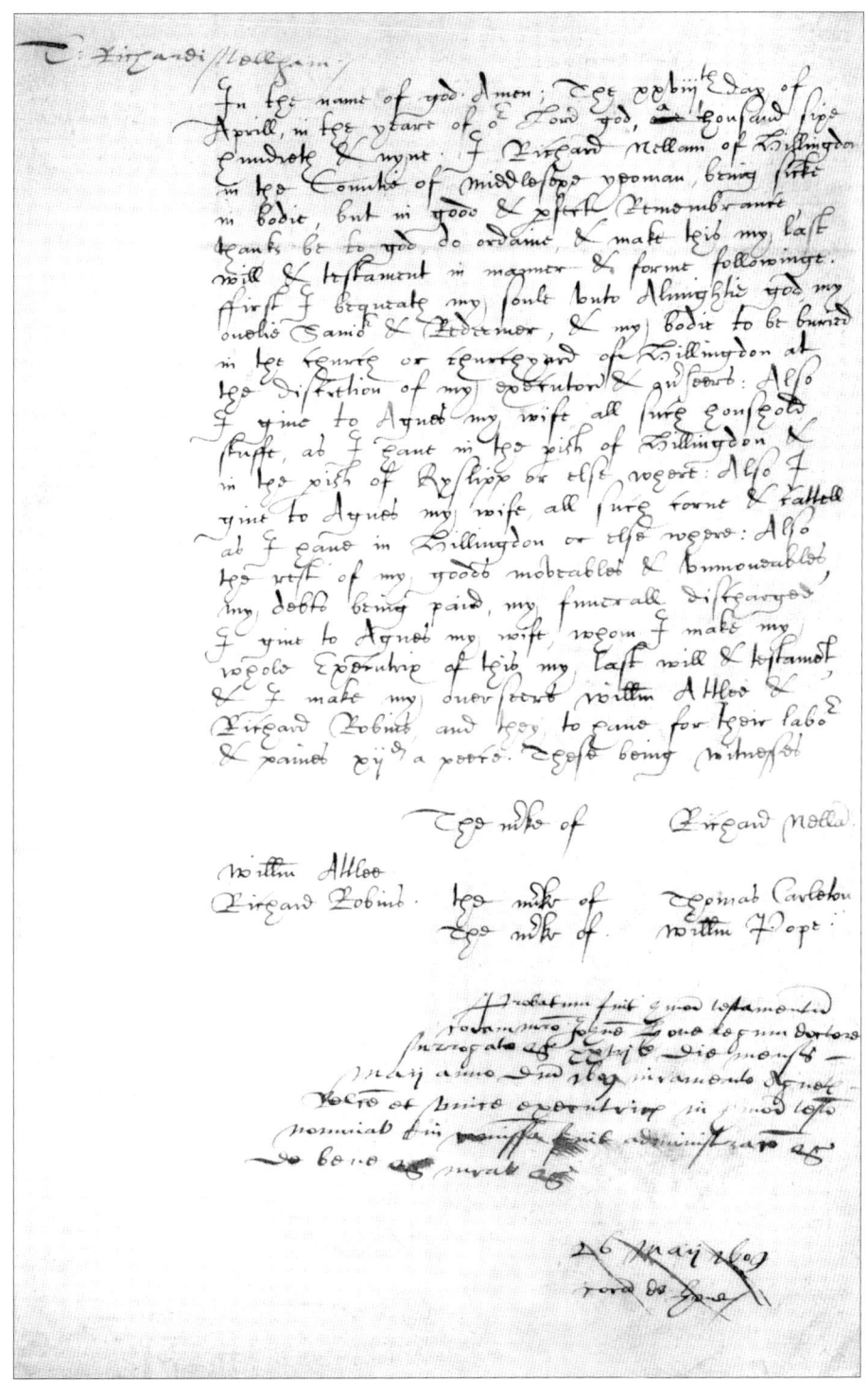

79. *The will of Richard Nellam, yeoman, of Hillingdon, 1609.*

and paintings (including 'a Lady Dormer by Vandyke'). Although principally relating to estates outside the capital, her will does provide a brief glimpse of the nature of their former London house: among the goods passed on to her daughters were 'a walnut Tree Table which stood in the Great Parlour at London', and 'a blew Camblet window Curtaine which hung in the Gallery and Dressing Room in the house at London'.

Remember that a will may not mention all of a deceased person's children: some money, property or goods may have been passed on before the will was drawn up, and a daughter may have married and been given a settlement at that time. An eldest son may have taken over the family business, and, as this would be regarded as his inheritance, would need no bequest in his father's will. In the will of Gabriel Gregory, a south London builder, who died in 1788, this sort of thing is very clearly spelled out. He declares his intention to 'equalize' all his children respecting their bequests, leaving his daughter Mary only £200, as she had already received £300 on her marriage. Gregory had given his eldest son William over £200 'upon and after his going into Business at Sundry times', and had covered £300 of his debt, and says he will leave him nothing else, as he 'hath by his Imprudent Conduct given me great Reason to believe that a further legacy may not be providently managed'.[4]

Although wills rarely describe domestic property in detail, they do often deal with the transfer of real estate. Robert Dormer's will records that he held various houses in London, 'situate in Catherine Street Exeter Street and the Strand', on lease from the Earl of Exeter. These he bequeathed to his wife for the residue of the leases. Excluded from the bequest was 'The Capitall Messuage in the Strand...late in the possession of Samuell Watkinson' and another property in 'Blakes' Court', already devised to Mary by her late father, Sir Richard Blake. The will also lists Dormer's other real estate – houses in Buckinghamshire, Northamptonshire and his own 'Mannor of Ripple' in Worcestershire.

To be valid, a will had to be signed in the presence of witnesses; these are often friends, associates or servants of the testator, but could not include beneficiaries. Occasionally a codicil is added after the main body of text, changing one or more of the bequests or instructions. At the end is a paragraph (before 1733 in Latin), which is the probate, stating when and by whom the will was affirmed.

Administrations. A person dying without leaving a will was said to be 'intestate'. In cases of intestacy, the court would grant next-of-kin or creditors letters of administration, enabling them to administer the estate. Grants of administration occur less frequently than wills, and the information they contain is less detailed, often confined merely to the date and names and addresses of the parties concerned. In some instances a will was made but was invalid (for various reasons, for example because it did not name an executor, or because the executor named had since died or was was unable or unwilling to act), in which case a will should accompany the record of the administration (letters of administration 'with will annexed').

FINDING THE RECORDS: BEFORE 1858 – ECCLESIASTICAL AND OTHER COURTS
From at least the 13th century until 1858 jurisdiction in the cases of wills, testaments and letters of administration was predominantly the responsibility of the Church. Probate – the official approval of a will or administration, enabling the deceased person's property to be released – was usually granted by one of a variety of ecclesiastical courts.

Some 300 ecclesiastical probate courts covered England and Wales. Each diocese had its own bishop's (or consistory) court, and, at a lower level, a number of archdeacon's (or archdeaconry) courts. In addition, there were courts of the bishop's deputy (or commissary) which met on occasions when the archdeacon's court was suspended. The location and type of court where a will or administration was proved depended on the deceased's wealth and the location of his property. Theoretically, small estates were generally dealt with in the local archdeaconry or commissary courts; grants of probate for wealthier people, with *bona notabilia*, i.e. goods worth more than £5

(£10 in the City of London) in more than one archdeaconry in the same diocese, came from the consistory court. If the deceased had *bona notabilia* in more than one diocese, then the will or administration was proved in the highest provincial or prerogative court; in the south this was the Prerogative Court of Canterbury (PCC).

In practice, the system was not always strictly applied. Finding the right court can take some time; and if you do not find a will or administration among the records of the most obvious court, it is advisable to check the other ecclesiastical courts with authority in the area where the deceased lived or is known to have held property, and in the PCC. By the early years of the 19th century the system was beginning to break down, and increasingly wills were proved in the more prestigious PCC; its pre-eminence was consolidated when the Bank of England decreed in 1810 that they would release funds only on a PCC grant of probate.[5]

In addition to the ecclesiastical probate courts, there existed a handful of extra-parochial or 'peculiar' courts, such as the Dean & Chapter of Westminster Abbey, which had probate jurisdiction in the cathedral close and in the villages belonging to the abbey. There were also some secular courts, usually manorial, which had the right to prove the wills of people who died on the manor. For lists of the various peculiar and secular courts and their records, refer to *Further Reading* (below) or information sheets at the principal record repositories.

Records of the church courts are now generally held in the relevant County Record Offices, and, as a popular source among genealogists, are usually well indexed. For the London area the most important collections are those in the LMA, the Guildhall, and the National Archives' collection of PCC records at the Family Records Centre.

FINDING THE RECORDS: AFTER 1858 – THE PRINCIPAL PROBATE REGISTRY

In January 1858 the various ecclesiastical and secular probate courts were abolished, and replaced by a new civil court of probate with a centralized system of principal and district registries. The Principal Probate Registry, or PPR (now the Principal Registry of the Family Division), based in London, holds copies of all wills proved and all grants of representation from January 1858 to the present day. A grant of representation is a document issued by the High Court giving executors or administrators the right to deal with a deceased person's estate. If a will was proved this is called a grant of probate; if not, a grant of letters of administration.

To find a will or grant in the PPR it is necessary to consult the large volumes of annual indexes (called 'calendars'). These list the names of the deceased alphabetically, though before 1871 wills and administrations are listed separately. The calendars are often surprisingly informative, particularly for the years before 1892, giving the names, addresses and occupations of the deceased and his or her executors or administrators, and usually an idea of the value of the estate. The following example is an index entry from 1888:

> CRUICKSHANK, Matthew. Personal Estate £6,693 9s. 1d. in the United Kingdom. 29 October. The Will with three Codicils of Matthew Cruickshank formerly of Glasgow in North Britain Merchant but late of Elim Lyndhurst-gardens Hampstead in the County of Middlesex Gentleman who died 7 October 1888 at Lyndhurst-gardens domiciled in England was proved at the Principal Registry by Hugh Kennedy Wood of 21 Belsize-crescent Hampstead Gentleman one of the Executors

Remember, as with all probate records, that the grant may have been made a year or two, or sometimes longer, after the date of death. Remember, too, that in addition to wills, the PPR also holds the relevant grants of probate, which, though brief and functional, occasionally have information not found in the wills or indexes. For letters of administration, only the grants have survived. Unfortunately reading or copying PPR material at the Principal Registry of the Family Division (currently based at First Avenue House) can involve a hefty charge.

Probate inventories

From the time of Henry VIII until 1782 executors and administrators were required, as part of the probate process, to present to the relevant court an itemised list (or inventory) of the deceased's goods and chattels, with a valuation. This helped in administering the distribution of the estate, particularly in cases of intestacy, and was also used to calculate the probate court's fees. They are most commonly found for the 16th and 17th centuries, and are rare after 1750, unless specifically requested by an interested party, such as a creditor.

Probate inventories were generally confined to personal property – goods moveable and immoveable – such as furniture, merchandise, crops, livestock, loose money, or debts owed. The law treated 'immoveable' property, such as household fixtures, as part of the land, which might not be the testator's to dispose of; it has been suggested that this might explain why William Shakespeare left his wife only his second-best bed.

Although not intended to record real estate owned by the deceased, they are often very informative about domestic property. It was customary to list the goods as they were inspected, room by room, and the names, number and order of the rooms can give an indication of the size, status and layout of the deceased's house. The amount of furniture, and its character and value, may also give some idea of the size or use of a room, and of the wealth of the occupants. Do remember, though, that only the rooms used by the deceased will be listed, and the house may have been in multi-occupation. Other useful data are often featured in inventories – such as the testator's address and profession – which may have been absent from the will. The following is a typical example of a late-17th-century inventory, that of the goods and chattels of Thomas Wellfare of Kensington, prepared by Thomas Peacocke and John Ilford, and dated 1681:[6]

IN THE FIRST CHAMBER One featherbed, one bedstead with a coverlid & blankets & old curtaines, valenes thereto belonging valued at £1.5s.; six paire of sheetes with some old table linnen, £2.; three old chests, one old truncke, one box, 10s.

80. The probate inventory for Nicholas List's house in Whitechapel, 1687.

126

IN THE MIDDLE CHAMBER One featherbed & bedstead with ye furniture thereto belonging, valued at £1.

IN THE HALL One table, five old cupboards, six old chaires, two joynt stooles valued at 13s.4d.; one paire of fireirons, one paire of andirons at 4s.

IN THE MILKEHOUSE Three drinke vessells, six earthen pans with other lumber at 12s.

IN THE KITCHEN The brasse and pewter & iron pots at £1.5s.; one settle with old lumber at 6s.8d.

IN THE STABLE Two geldings, three mares & theire harnesse with other utensills thereto belonging at £18.

IN THE YARD Two carts, one plow, two harrowes at £7.; six cowes at £17.10s. one sow, three piggs, £1.10s.; twenty loade of dung at £2.

Total £53.16s.0d.

Note that both 'chambers' contain beds, and that there are quite a number of 'old' items of furniture. The overwhelmingly rural character of Kensington at the time is evident from the livestock and agricultural tools.

Although descriptions of real estate were not officially required in inventories, any leases or mortgages held by the deceased were often referred to and occasionally transcribed in detail. Reference was also sometimes made to freehold property where it was relevant to the settling of the deceased's debts. As an example, take the estate of Robert Brabourne, gentleman, of the Inner Temple, who died in 1701. In addition to the usual items – money in hand, linen, and personal belongings such as his silver watch and tortoiseshell tobacco box – the inventory includes a detailed list of property held by him, including a brewhouse with rooms over, 'the deceased's dwelling house in Charterhouse Yard with the garden, back buildings, coach-houses, stables, yard and premises', and seven other houses near by. Precise details are given of all leases, rents and mortgages, with the names of landlords and mortgagors, and a valuation of all the buildings.[7]

Probate inventories were either filed away with wills and administrations at the time of the grant of probate, or were kept separately. Most large collections, such as those at the LMA or Guildhall, are well indexed. The collection of PCC inventories at the National Archives are in classes PROB2–5 and PROB31–32.

Many probate inventories relating to specific areas, and indexes to them, have been published, such as F. W. Steer's *Farm and Cottage Inventories of Mid-Essex* (1950), and J. Holman and M. Herridge, *Index of Surrey probate inventories 16–19th centuries* (1986); see J. S. W. Gibson's *Probate Jurisdictions: Where to Look for Wills* for a full list. Lists, indexes and other finding aids are available for all the main London diocesan probate collections, in the Guildhall Library, LMA and Family Records Centre.

Death duty registers 1796–1903

For the period after 1796, records of death duties provide further information about a deceased person's estate and their beneficiaries, and can give a more precise indication of personal wealth at death than probate records.[8] They also serve as a useful index to wills and administrations before the introduction of the Principal Probate Registry in 1858.

Death duties were the taxes paid to the Inland Revenue on a deceased person's estate by their beneficiaries. The first such duty, legacy duty, introduced in 1796, was restricted to legacies and personal estate, and initially was charged only to remoter relatives or 'strangers in blood'. After 1805 its scope was extended to closer family members. Other death duties – succession duty (covering property), and probate duty – were introduced subsequently. The various duties were replaced in 1894 by estate duty, a single tax on all property passed on at death. As with wills, you are more likely to find useful records for those leaving substantial estates; and the later records are often more rewarding than the earlier.

The calculations and payments were recorded in volumes of registers. As with wills, an approximate date of death is needed to find a particular entry. Death duty registers can be difficult to interpret, and the job is made easier if you have already seen the relevant will. The registers record the name and address of the deceased (which is not always given in the will); the date of the will (if there is one) and the court where it was proved or the administration was granted; the name, occupation and rank of each executor or administrator; an approximate overall value for the estate; specific details of individual legacies and beneficiaries, sometimes with expansive accompanying notes; and finally the amount of duty and the date when it was paid. Generally, the wealthier the person the more complicated the entry. The record was often updated in subsequent years, with information such as the marriages and deaths of benefactors, which can help trace the descent of an estate.

The greatest value of the registers is that they show exactly how an estate was distributed. As this may not have been done as intended by the deceased person or as specified in his or her will, the registers may be the only source which shows the eventual descent of a property. They are of particular use in cases of intestacy.

Death duty registers provide a wealth of detail for family historians, too. Before 1805 immediate family were exempt from duty, and the amount to be paid by beneficiaries was dependent upon the relationship to the deceased. Therefore the registers identify precisely the relationships in a column headed 'Consanguinity': codes or abbreviations are used, e.g. 'Stra ND' (stranger, natural daughter) for an illegitimate child, or 'SM' (sister of a mother) for aunt. A list of these is given on information sheets available at the Family Records Centre and the National Archives.

Indexes to death duty records before 1858 state the ecclesiastical court in which a will was proved or letters of administration were granted, and are commonly used by researchers looking for early 19th-century wills. The name of the court is usually in the form of an abbreviation; keys to these abbreviations can be found in the National Archives' handlists and in Jeremy Gibson's *Probate Jurisdictions: Where to Look for Wills*. But remember, in the early period death duties were limited, and the registers will not contain *every* grant of probate and administration after 1796.

Indexes to death duty registers (IR27) and the registers for 1796–1857 (IR26) can be consulted on microfilm at the Family Records Centre and the National Archives; original registers for 1858–1903 (IR26) are stored at Hayes and must be ordered in advance at the National Archives.

NOTES AND REFERENCES

1. Anthony J. Camp, *Wills and their Whereabouts*, 1974, p. xxxviii.
2. The National Archives (TNA), PROB11/611, sig. 202, f. 131v.
3. TNA, PROB11/635, sig. 6, ff. 42–3.
4. TNA, PROB11/1170, sig. 485, f. 308.
5. Jane Cox, *Affection Defying the Power of Death: Wills, Probate & Death Duty Records* (Federation of Family History Societies), 3rd edn, 1998, p. 19.
6. This inventory is included along with many others in the Kensington and Chelsea area in Brian R. Curle, 'Kensington and Chelsea Probate Inventories 1672–1734' (typescript, 1970), p. 33.
7. TNA, PROB5/4809.
8. This is because, until 1858, real estate was not included in the valuation of a deceased person's estate at probate

FURTHER READING

A. J. Camp, *Wills and their Whereabouts* (Society of Genealogists), 1963 (and later editions)

Jane Cox, *Affection Defying the Power of Death: Wills, Probate & Death Duty Records* (Federation of Family History Societies), 3rd edn, 1998

R. Sharpe France, 'Wills', in *History*, vol. l, no. 168, Feb 1965, pp. 36–9

J. S. W. Gibson, *Wills and Where to Find Them* (British Record Society), 1974

J. S. W. Gibson, *Probate Jurisdictions: Where to Look for Wills* (Federation of Family History Societies), 4th edn, 1994

Eve McLaughlin, *Somerset House wills from 1858* (Federation of Family History Societies), 3rd edn, 1985

Eve MacLaughlin, *Wills before 1858* (Federation of Family History Societies), 2nd edn, 1985

R. R. Sharpe (ed.), *A Calendar of Wills proved and enrolled in the Court of Husting, London, 1258–1688*, 2 vols, 1888–9

F. W. Steer, *Farm and Cottage Inventories of Mid-Essex* (Chelmsford, Essex RO), 1950

F. W. Steer, 'Probate Inventories', in *History*, vol. XLVII, no. 161, Oct 1962, pp. 287–90

Wills in the Public Record Office (Baltimore), 1968

CHAPTER NINE

Illustrations

Written historical documents can tell us a lot about any of London's streets and houses, but for an immediate and clear impression of the character and appearance of a building there is nothing to compare with a good illustration. Old photographs, prints, paintings or drawings offer an invaluable and often unique record of our built heritage.

Apart from a very few prints and book illustrations, the earliest images of London's housing are the mid-16th and mid-17th century 'map-views', such as the 'copper plate' map of *c.*1558 *(ill. 1)*; although unlikely to give a true representation of each and every house, these maps do provide a vivid overall picture of the capital's early-modern character (see also Chapter 1, pages 49–50).

By the 18th century, views of streets and buildings were being engraved for published histories of London, and for periodicals such as the *Gentleman's Magazine*. The rise of antiquarianism encouraged artists to draw and paint buildings and archaeological remains, and to depict them accurately, primarily to record their appearance. Topographical views also became popular as a subject for paintings, prints or book illustrations, reaching their pinnacle with the work of Canaletto, who came to London in the 1740s. And the emergence of architecture as a profession brought with it the growth of architectural draughtsmanship. But in all these cases, it was usually the large public buildings, parks, grand vistas or aristocratic mansions that caught the artist's or architect's eye, rarely the mundane reality of a lower-class residential street. London's topographical artists continued in the tradition of Canaletto well into the 19th century,

their views appearing in published collections such as *Select Views of London and its Environs* (1804), Elmes and Shepherd's *Metropolitan Improvements* (1827), and Thomas Shotter Boys's *Original Views of London* (1842). Subject matter gradually became more diverse – see for instance the published street views of 1838–40 by John Tallis *(ill. 81)*, or the British Library's two volumes of lovely pen and watercolour street-scenes of Deptford, Greenwich and Lewisham of the 1830s and '40s, by various artists, which provide a remarkable record of these south-eastern districts before Victorian house-building took off *(ill. 82)*.[1] But apart from a few exceptions (such as R. B. Schnebbelie or George Scharf), by and large London's artists of the 1830s and '40s rarely responded to the dramatic changes that defined early Victorian life in the capital — the relentless urban expansion, the technological triumphs of new road and rail improvements, the poverty of the burgeoning slums. These subjects began to find expression in illustrations made for the pictorial magazines of the 1840s and later, such as the *Illustrated London News* and the *Builder* (see Chapter 10), but soon this field of 'pictorial reportage' was to become monopolized by photography.

The first **photographs** of London – the daguerreotypes and calotype prints of the 1840s – were generally architectural views of major sites and monuments, such as Westminster Abbey or Trafalgar Square. With the invention of the wet collodion process in the 1850s and further improvements in camera technology, by the 1860s photography had emerged as an important recording medium, and photographers were employed to chart the progress of metropolitan improvements and engineering projects such as

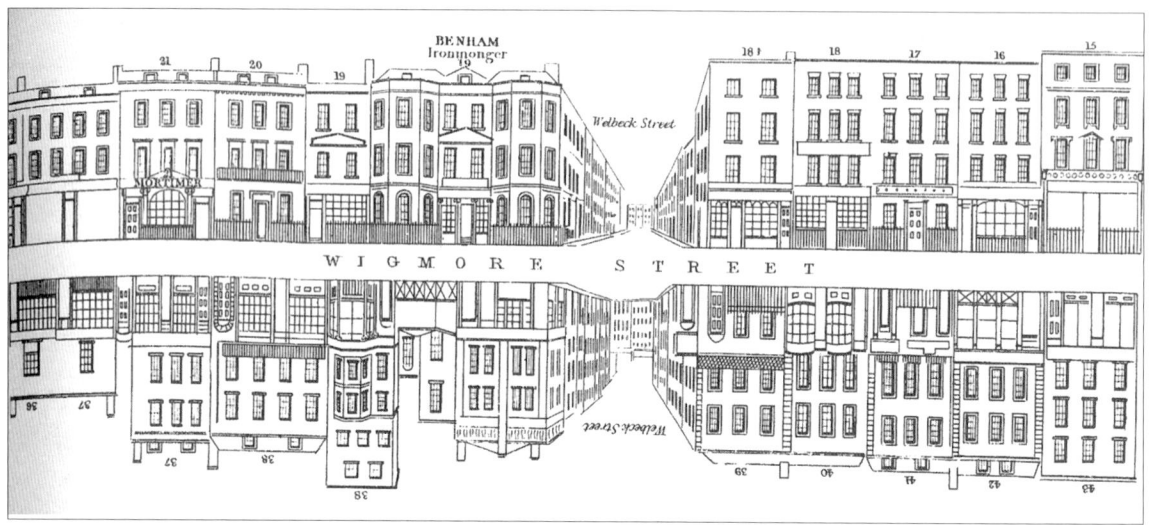

81. *Houses in Wigmore Street, off Cavendish Square, St Marylebone, from Tallis's* London Street Views, *1838–40.*

82. *Topographical view from the British Library's collection: Edward Barnard's house on Deptford Green, c.1840.*

the Holborn Viaduct or Metropolitan Railway (see *ill. 16*). As well as the new road and rail works, photographers of the 1860s and '70s also began to record the old fabric that these improvements were sweeping away. The Society for Photographing Relics of Old London (SPROL) was in the van of an emerging late-19th-century conservation movement, that was to include the Society for the Protection of Ancient Buildings and the Survey of London. During the 1870s and '80s, SPROL used photographers like Henry Dixon and Alfred and John Bool to take views of many of the capital's characteristic but fast-disappearing old buildings.

The Victorian era also witnessed the emergence of photography as social documentation. In the 1870s gelatine dry-plate negatives were introduced, which greatly reduced exposure times, making naturalistic street 'snapshots' a possibility. Pioneered by men such as John Thomson and Paul Martin, street photography played an important role in bringing to light the terrible living conditions suffered by many Londoners, helping to change public perception of the poor and usher in a new era of social welfare *(ill. 83)*.

Photographs gradually acquired greater commercial potential, and as the processes became simpler and cheaper, street views and scenes became increasingly popular with the public. Picture postcards of bustling London street-scenes (known as 'Topographicals') became common from the 1890s, and by the Edwardian era, views of even the most humdrum middle-class streets were being taken by local photographers, and were often hawked for sale from door to door *(ill. 114)*. Such postcards are now collectable, and books of photos and postcards from the late-Victorian and Edwardian era have become a popular form of local history publication in recent years. Also in the 1890s, the introduction of half-tone printing finally enabled photographs to be used cheaply and extensively as illustrations in books and magazines, bringing photography to a wider audience and giving it a new and important role in publishing.

From the 1890s, London's expanding government authorities relied heavily on photography as a means of recording their work, such as

83. *Victorian social photography: an elderly female 'Crawler', slumped on the steps of the St Giles's Workhouse in Short's Gardens, photographed in about 1877 by John Thomson.*

slum clearance, or the provision of new housing or other local improvements *(ill. 84)*. Today these photographs – both those of the London-wide London County Council and of the various local boroughs – are one of the most valuable sources of information on London's changing cityscape. In addition to these 'public authority' photos, some of the big private architectural practices and construction firms, such as Mowlems, commissioned photographers to record their new works, and estate agents, too, used photography widely in advertising; many of these photographs have also made their way into London's archives.

In recent years conservation and 'heritage' organizations, such as the now-defunct Royal Commission on the Historical Monuments of England (RCHME) and English Heritage, took many photographs of buildings, including London houses, which were thought to be of historic or architectural interest.

84. House in Adam Street, Rotherhithe, 1904, demolished for Rotherhithe Tunnel.

The main collections

Most London local archives have their own collections of **photographs**. These, and the principal large London-wide repositories, such as London Metropolitan Archives and the Guildhall Library, are the best place to begin looking for old images of houses, and there are also important national collections with extensive London material, such as the National Monuments Record (NMR), now maintained by English Heritage. These three bodies now provide on-line searching, the Guildhall through its Collage site, the LMA as part of the European Visual Archive Project, and the NMR on English Heritage's Viewfinder web pages. These three bodies are also founder members of *PhotoLondon*, a conglomerate of major holders of London photographs, whose website offers information and links to collections in the capital's libraries, archives and museums. There are also valuable photographic collections at the Museum of London, the V&A

Museum, the Royal Institute of British Architects Library, the British Museum and the National Archives. In addition to the archives, there are a number of well-known commercial photo libraries, for example: the Hulton-Getty Picture Collection, with over 6 million illustrations, including engravings as well as photos; the Mansell Collection (now part of Time & Life Pictures); and Aerofilms.

As well as trawling through archives and collections, it is also worthwhile searching relevant books, journals and newspapers for illustrative material. Books of local history, local newspapers, or specialist periodicals like the *Builder* are a good source of images of houses (see also Chapter 10). Also, if your area has been covered by the major works of London building history, such as the *Buildings of England*, the *Survey of London*, or the *Victoria County History*, they may have included drawings or photographs which would otherwise be hard to find. Westminster City Archives, for example, keeps a useful card index of book photographs and illustrations of buildings in their area.

For **paintings**, **prints** and **drawings**, local archives and the main London repositories mentioned above are still the best starting place; but there are also specialist architectural and topographical collections with important London material, such as the Crace Collection and King's Collection in the British Museum's Department of Prints & Drawings; the Buckler Collection in the British Library's Manuscripts Department; the Sir John Soane Museum; and the Gough Collection of English topography at the Bodleian Library. (Some larger local studies archives, such as that at Westminster, keep a microfilm set of the Crace collection for ease of use.)

Using old photographs, prints and drawings

Old photographs, particularly if of a known date, offer the most direct and authoritative evidence of the form of a building. For example, what did Acris Street in Wandsworth (covered in Case History Two) look like when it was newly built? Luckily we have a picture-postcard view from about 1919 (see *ill. 114*), showing clearly that the buildings themselves have changed little

85. Typical Gustave Doré engraving of London slums from the Pilgrimage: Houndsditch (see next page).

86. *View of old houses in Fore Street, Lambeth, c.1866, by William Strudwick.*

since then, but suggesting also how much more attractive a street of late-Victorian terrace-houses looked in the days before widespread car-ownership. Or what did Thomas Carlyle's house in Cheyne Row, Chelsea, look like when he was living there? Luckily someone photographed the man himself standing proudly outside, and there is even a photo of him working in the sound-proofed attic study he designed for himself, to keep the noise from the street at bay.[2]

Old photographs have an immediacy and truthfulness that is often harder to find in contemporary paintings, prints or drawings. Compare, for instance, the photos of working-class or slum houses and occupants in this book with engravings by Gustave Doré *(ills 18, 19, 85)*: Doré's work is loaded with atmosphere and pathos, and is rightly highly regarded for its visceral exposure of the horrors of Victorian street life. But to achieve this he often exaggerated the height of buildings, the narrow-

87. *Old houses in Fore Street, c. 1830. Lithograph by Giles Firman Phillips.*

photographs taken by William Strudwick, in conveying the tumbledown, shabby nature of these slum houses, of a type once common along the Thames foreshore *(ills 86, 87).*

To appreciate the value of using illustrations to understand changes to streets of houses over time, let us look at a short row of houses formerly known as Cobham Row, in Clerkenwell, now part of the south side of Rosebery Avenue, on the corner with Farringdon Road *(ills 88–91).* Today about two-thirds of this frontage is taken up by the bulk of Clerkenwell Fire Station, the rest by what look like two old houses, one faced in dark brick, the other in light, each with a two-bay wide frontage. On the west (right-hand) corner is a curved, modern cement-fronted building, adjoining another old house around the corner. A second look shows that the two 'old' houses either side of the corner block have no doors; all are in fact part of the same new development, the brick-fronted houses designed in facsimile to match the only genuinely pre-1900 structure, the house next to the Fire Station (now No. 40 Rosebery Avenue). There are two very fine watercolours of the same stretch of frontage of 1852 and 1887, by two of London's foremost topographical artists of the period, Thomas Hosmer Shepherd and J. P. Emslie respectively *(ills 89, 90).* Shepherd's closer view concentrates on an impressive double-fronted house on the corner site; both images show our 'genuine' house next door, still with its two-bay wide frontage, deep window reveals and semi-circular overdoor light, in style and scale looking very much like a typical house of the 1810s or 1820s. Emslie's view shows the first, much smaller fire station building on the east (left-hand) corner; but what is especially interesting is the row of four houses between this and our house at No. 40. Each is three 'bays' wide, has distinctly smaller proportions, and what look like windows with flush-fronted frames – a sure sign that this fabric is early Georgian. Later photographs show how the fire station expanded over the site of some of the houses: by 1910 only our No. 40 and the houses either side were left *(ill. 91).* From what we can see of the impressive corner house, it has changed little; but the

ness of the streets, and the overcrowding of the people and traffic (relying heavily on what he claimed was a photographic memory), as can be seen by comparing his well-known view of Ludgate Hill with Victorian photographs. If you have doubts about the veracity of an artist's image, it is always worth checking what you see against the large-scale Ordnance Survey maps of the period.

However, if we accept a little artistic licence, prints and drawings, like photographs, also offer a clear and immediate picture of the character of a street or area. For example, take Fore Street, in Lambeth, a street of old riverside houses demolished in the 1860s for the construction of the Albert Embankment. There is information about the houses among the records of the Metropolitan Board of Works, which carried out the improvement, and we can get an idea of the class of occupant and their density from the censuses of 1851 and 1861; but no written material matches the early-19th-century prints of the street, or the later

88.   Modern Rosebery Avenue, showing the fire station with No. 40 adjoining.

89. Houses at the corner of Cobham Row and Cold Bath Square in 1852, by T. H. Shepherd: the present No. 40 Rosebery Avenue (with dormer window) is to the left of the corner house.

90. The same corner in 1887, by J. P. Emslie, showing the original fire station building and old houses adjoining (later demolished for its extension).

91. Nos. 40 (right) and 42 Rosebery Avenue in 1910.

house on the other side (No. 42), so obviously early Georgian in Emslie's view, has been given new, larger windows, a new doorcase and an attic storey with dormer windows, making it look much more like our house in style and age; if it were not for the Emslie view, it would be very difficult to guess the true age of this now demolished house from photographs. Later photos show the fire station expanded to its full extent, and the corner site cleared, awaiting redevelopment.

Comparing illustrations of different dates in this way, where they are available, is one of the best ways of charting basic changes to a structure. Take, as another example, one of London's best-known monuments, the row of late-16th-century houses in High Holborn, part of the buildings of Staple Inn. Their black-and-white half-timbered exterior conforms to most people's idea of what a true 16th-century London building should look like. But is it genuine? Compare the 20th-century images of Staple Inn in Illustrations 4 and 92 with earlier images in Illustrations 93 and 94. These latter views clearly show a plainer, plastered façade, without the rows of jutting bay or oriel windows with leaded lights. Is the present facing therefore a 20th-century Liberty's-style sham?

92. *Staple Inn, Holborn, 1920s etching by Hampton.*

The truth, as always, is more complicated than that. It seems that Staple Inn's original timber frontage was given a protective layer of plaster after the Great Fire, and its projecting bay windows (which constituted a fire hazard) were taken down and stored in the cellar of the Great Hall. When the buildings were acquired at auction by the Prudential in the 1880s, their architect, Alfred Waterhouse, advised removing the plaster and re-instating the bay windows, which remarkably were still intact after over 200 years in the Hall cellar. Interestingly, this 'restoration' was at the time opposed by the Society for the Protection of Ancient Buildings, which objected to the destruction of the 17th-century plaster facing. By the mid-1930s the timbers were all fractured, rotten or infested, and had to be replaced, so what we see today is basically a 1930s facsimile of an 1880s restoration of a Tudor frontage.[3]

Aerial photographs, or photos taken from high buildings near by, are rarer and therefore harder to find, but where they exist these can show houses in their context in a way that would be impossible for the photographer at ground level *(ills 17, 20, 29, 95)*. Some idea of planning, street layout, back gardens and other factors become immediately apparent. Also of interest to the house historian are any old interior photographs or paintings, which can show fixtures and fittings, give clues as to a house's layout and décor, and therefore the socio-economic status of the inhabitants. Interior views of poor houses are rare (see *ill. 18*); most of those that do survive tend to be of wealthier households, often filled with Victorian bric-à-brac and clutter, as only the middle- or upper-middle classes and above could af-

93. *Staple Inn in 1883, by Philip Norman.*

94. *Staple Inn c.1800.*

ford to hire a photographer to record their home and belongings.

One final piece of advice when studying old photographs and prints: look, look and look again, as the more you look, the more you will see. Some details are apparent immediately, but others take time to emerge. And don't be too quick to judge. For instance, take the view of Moss Alley, in Bermondsey (now demolished), taken in May 1912 *(ill. 96)*. At first sight this looks like yet another photo of a late-Victorian or Edwardian London slum court and its occupants. The tall buildings and narrow alley certainly make it a forbidding place. But look again at the house on the right-hand side. Its window and door surrounds look freshly painted, the shutters are neat, and the paving is relatively free of rubbish; in fact everything looks well maintained. The people,

95. High level view of houses inTabard Street, Southwark, June 1916, showing back yards etc.

too, are clean and well turned-out, and all of the older children are wearing shoes. This is a poor street, certainly, but there are none of the barefoot, dirty children in rags, or any other suggestions of the grinding poverty seen in photos of the East End, St Giles's or other London slums *(e.g.ills 19, 83)*. This impression is borne out to an extent by the 1901 census returns, which show most of the street's householders to have been employed in local industries.

NOTES AND REFERENCES

1. British Library, Add. MSS 16,945–6.
2. The photograph of Carlyle's attic study is reproduced in John Richardson, *The Chelsea Book, past and present* (Historical Publications Ltd), 2003, p. 20.
3. For a recent account of the history of Staple Inn, see Arthur Tait, *The Story of Staple Inn on Holborn Hill* (Institute of Actuaries), 2001

FURTHER READING

Bernard Adams, *London Illustrated 1604–1851* (Library Association), 1983

M. W. Barley, *A Guide to British Topographical Collections* (Council for British Archaeology), 1974

John Betjeman, *Victorian and Edwardian London from old photographs* (Portman Books), 2nd edn, 1987

Anthony Byatt, *Picture Postcards and their Publishers* (Golden Age Postcard Books), 1978

A. W. Coysh, *The Dictionary of Picture Postcards in Britain 1894–1939* (Antique Collectors' Club), 1984

Rosemary Eakins, *Picture Sources UK* (Macdonald), 1985

Robert Elwall, *Photography Takes Command: The Camera and British Architecture 1890–1939* (RIBA Heinz Gallery exhibition catalogue), 1994

Hilary Evans, *The art of picture research*, 2nd edn (David & Charles), 1979

Hilary and Mary Evans, *Picture Researcher's Handbook*, 4th edn (Van Nostrand Reinhold International), 1989

Mireille Galinou and John Hayes, *London in Paint. Oil Paintings in the Collection of the Museum of London* (Museum of London), 1996

A. Griffiths and R. Williams, *The Department of Print and Drawings – User's Guide* (British Museum Press), 1987

96. *Moss Alley, Bankside, in 1912.*

Jason Hawkes, *Over London: A Century of Change* (HarperCollins), 2000

Peter Jackson, *George Scharf's London* (John Murray), 1987

Peter Jackson, 'London Illustrations in the *Gentleman's Magazine*, 1746–1863', in *London Topographical Record*, vol. XXVI, 1990, pp. 177–213

Peter Marcan, *Artists and the East End* (Peter Marcan Publications), 1986

S. T. Miller, 'The value of photographs as historical evidence', in *Local Historian*, vol. 15, no. 8, Nov 1984, pp. 468–73

Ira Bruce Nadel and F. S. Schwarzbach, *Victorian Artists and the City* (Pergamon Press), 1980

Lynda Nead, *Victorian Babylon: People, Streets and Images in Nineteenth-Century London* (Yale University Press), 2000

George Oliver, *Photographs and Local History* (Batsford), 1989

J. F. C. Phillips, *Shepherd's London* (Cassell), 1976

David Piper, *Artists' London* (Weidenfeld & Nicholson), 1982

Michael Pritchard, *A Directory of London Photographers 1841–1908* (PhotoResearch), revised edn, 1994

Royal Institute of British Architects, Drawings Collection, *Catalogue of the Drawings Collection of the RIBA*

Mike Seaborne, *Photographer's London 1839–1994* (Museum of London), 1995

Gavin Stamp, *The Changing Metropolis: Early Photographs of London 1839–1889* (Viking), 1984

Don Steel and Lawrence Taylor (eds), *Family History in Focus* (Lutterworth Press), 1984

John Thomson, *Victorian London Street Life in Historic Photographs* (Dover Publications), 1994 (a reprint of *Street Life in London*, 1877)

Victoria and Albert Museum, *Topographical index to measured drawings*

John Wall, *Directory of British Photographic Collections* (Heinemann), 1977

Macolm Warner et al, *The Image of London: Views by Travellers and Emigrés 1550–1920* (Trefoil Publications/ Barbican Art Gallery exhibition catalogue), 1987

Roger Whitehouse, *A London album: early photographs recording the history of the city and its people from 1840 to 1915* (Secker & Warburg), 1980

Gordon Winter, *Past Positive: London's Social History recorded in Photographs* (Chatto & Windus), 1971

C. E. Wright, 'Topographical Drawings in the Department of Manuscripts, British Museum', in *Archives*, vol. III, no. 18, 1957, pp. 78–87

CHAPTER TEN

Other Types of Record

This final chapter brings together a group of unrelated sources, both published and documentary, none of which would have fitted very comfortably in the preceding chapters, viz. newspapers and periodicals, legal records, bomb-damage records, and business records. None of these can be regarded as the average house historian's first port of call, and most are difficult and sometimes unrewarding to use. Yet each is a valuable source of a particular type of information on London and its buildings that would be very difficult, if not impossible, to find elsewhere, and so their existence and potential usefulness should always be borne in mind.

Newspapers and periodicals

The information given in old newspapers, magazines and periodicals can often add flesh to the barer bones provided by other historical sources. The biggest obstacle to their use, however, is the dearth of useable, detailed indexes. Even if you have a rough date for a particular story, making your way page by page through several weeks' or even months' runs of a local paper is a time-consuming and frustrating process. Some local studies libraries have compiled place-name indexes, but these are few and far between, and usually rather limited.

The most effective way to access historic newspaper material is to look at collections of **newspaper cuttings**. Most local history archives keep a collection of cuttings on all sorts of topics, including houses and local buildings, from all types of newspapers and magazines, both local and national. These are usually arranged alphabetically by street-name, by subject, and/or by building type.

Early newspapers. The first English-language weekly newspapers and 'newsbooks' appeared in the early 17th century. The trade grew during the political strife and regulatory freedom of the 1640s, but was curtailed by the re-introduction of stricter press controls at the Restoration. In 1665 the *Oxford Gazette* was published as an official state-run newspaper for the Court, in exile from the plague in Oxford. Renamed the *London Gazette* in 1666 (following the Court's return to the capital), this was the only regularly-produced newspaper of the late 17th century. Still running today, it is the world's oldest surviving periodical. Its official nature was evident in its contents, dominated by Court and foreign news, and lists of appointments. The *Gazette* also listed bankruptcies (one of its greatest uses). But the lack of domestic news in the *Gazette* left a gap in the market, and by the early 18th century a considerable number of news-sheets and papers were being published in London, catering for both a metropolitan and provincial readership. These included the *Post Boy*, *Daily Courant*, *Daily Journal*, *Daily Post*, *Public Advertiser*, and the *Daily Advertiser*. These early newspapers concentrated on politics, domestic and foreign, relying heavily on other papers for their copy, and reserving a considerable amount of column-space for advertising, which brought in valuable revenue. It is the classified adverts, particularly those for auction sales or new leases, which provide the greatest amount of detail on London houses, but with no indexes finding a relevant entry is a matter of luck or intuition. Here are a few typical examples:

'*To be Lett at* Twickenham, A New-built Brick House, four Rooms on a Floor, with Offices adjoying, and a handsome Garden, late in the Possession of Mr. James Cole deceased. Enquire at the House' (*Post Boy*, 16–18 Aug 1722)

'A Parcel of Land to be Lett to Build on, near Mariner-Square. Enquire at the Cocoa-Tree Chocolate-House in Pall-Mall' (*Daily Courant*, 14 Jan 1725)

'*To be Sold by Auction, by* JOHN YOUNG, Tomorrow, the 17th instant, at the White-Hart Tavern in Holborn, to begin at Four in the Afternoon, THE Lease of a Brick Dwelling-House, four Stories high, three Rooms on a Floor, lately fitted up after a genteel Manner, situated in Chancery-lane, fronting Lincolns-Inn Gardens, in the Occupation of Mr. Loaftis, at 45*l*. per Annum, to come of the Lease 21 Years at Michaelmas last (*The Gazetteer and London Daily Advertiser*, 16 Dec 1762)

Local newspapers. The earliest local papers confined their content to news of domestic or world affairs, usually taken verbatim from the main London press, and it was not until Victorian times that they became more comprehensive in their coverage of local events. Also, the number of titles increased greatly following the repeal of stamp duty in 1855, and in London grew further with suburban expansion. For the social or local historian their content is invaluable: accounts of the opening of new railways and buildings, charitable work, sporting events, announcements, obituaries, and many other aspects of economic and cultural life.

For information on houses, as with the early London press, the classified advertisements are often the best source, especially if you are interested in house prices, rents or the type of accommodation available in a particular area at a particular time. Sometimes 'feature articles' appear on local sanitary problems, slum clearance or new housing provision, but hopefully most of these will have found their way into the cuttings files. Some London papers had a wider coverage than just their local area:

97. Typical auction advertisement from the Hampstead and Highgate Express, December 1890.

the *City Press*, for instance, despite its name, covered stories in areas beyond the City's limits, including Holborn, Islington and the East End. It is also a good source for information on demolitions and new developments in the City from the 1860s onwards, with regular reports on 'City Improvements'. In March 1860, Mr Raiby was given as the builder of two new first-class houses, Nos 93 and 94 Cannon Street; and on the same day it was reported that several houses were being pulled down in Sparrow Corner, Minories, to allow for the enlargement of the Victoria Dock Company and Great Northern Railway Company's goods' station.[1] Also good for regular London-wide stories (and more classified ads) is the *Standard* (from 1827, now the *Evening Standard*) and its principal competitor, the *Evening News* (from 1881).

Most local history libraries or archives should have a collection of old newspapers for their area, either in original form or, more frequently these days, on microfilm. Alternatively the British Library Newspaper Library collection includes most of the UK's local and provincial newspapers; its catalogue is now searchable online.

For a list of London local newspapers, see J. S. W. Gibson *et al*, *Local Newspapers 1750–1920, England and Wales, Channel Islands, Isle of Man* (1987; 2nd edn 2002). Also the NEWSPLAN 2000 project, which aims to preserve and make available old local papers, has a website catalogue of titles in London and the south-east with details of where they can be seen *(see www.newsplan.co.uk)*.

Later national newspapers and magazines. Britain's cultural and social transformation during the industrial and economic revolutions of the late 18th and early 19th centuries is reflected in the growing number of newspapers: about 10 titles were being published in London in the 1760s, but the figure had risen to 52 by 1811.[2] Of the national titles that emerged during this and later periods, many are still with us today. *The Times* (produced since 1785) for a long time dominated the market, though it was later challenged, initially by the *Daily Telegraph* (from 1855) and the *Manchester Guardian* (from 1821), and later by the cheaper, popular press, such as the *Daily Mail* (from 1896) and *Daily Express* (from 1900).

Only *The Times* has a detailed index, available both in published form and on CD-ROM in major reference libraries like the Guildhall Library and British Library. Being a national paper, the focus of its articles on housing tends to the general rather than the specific, on subjects such as the increase of house-building in nineteenth-century London, suburban expansion, or slum dwellings. But particular streets or areas do get coverage from time to time, such as Hampstead Garden Suburb, which featured regularly in articles and correspondence in the early 1900s, during its planning and early development.[3] Accounts of individual properties are rarer, but when found, can often be informative. For instance, in September 1880 *The Times* reported on a court case regarding an infringement of local bye-laws in Upper Tottenham, on the Stoneley South estate, where a Rotherhithe builder, Louis Etheridge, had been putting up houses with 'improper' foundations.[4] But the most frequent references to London domestic properties are the regular reports of house fires or other disasters. At the end of November 1837 two houses on Commercial Road, Nos 6 and 7 'London terrace', fell with a loud crash, alarming 'the whole of the inhabitants of that numerously populated neighbourhood'. Foundations had been 'giving way' in the terrace for some time beforehand, on account of a nearby common sewer. One family was at dinner on the first floor of No. 7 at the time of the accident, but managed to scramble to safety before the house literally 'tumbled to pieces'.[5] In recent years *The Times* has developed an on-line digital archive, which allows full text searching of all articles from 1785 to 1985, greatly widening the paper's potential as a historical source; subscription is costly, but increasingly the facility is becoming available in good reference libraries.

Improvements in printing technology in the early- to mid-19th century made possible new types of lavishly-illustrated publications. These 'illustrated newspapers' – more like modern magazines, which they prefigured, than daily papers – were immediately popular with a public eager for images of recent events. The *Illustrated London News*, launched in 1842, claimed to be the world's first illustrated newspaper, and was certainly the best-known and widest-read of the British versions. Its range was broad: news of the progress of British troops abroad was a constant, as were natural and man-made disasters, and royal stories. In terms of architecture and building development, most news items related to the provision of new churches, schools, hospitals, or other public edifices. Accounts of houses tend to be of the mansions of the wealthy, but there are sometimes reports on new estate developments, or fires and other damage to houses, usually under a heading such as 'Metropolitan News', or 'Accidents'. In June 1844 the paper reported that the 'usually quiet' neighbourhood of Notting Dale, Bayswater, had been thrown into 'consternation' by the destruction by fire of a new row of eight dwelling-houses, recently erected immediately behind Norland Crescent, and two adjoining carpenters' workshops, which had held all the workmens' tools.[6]

Other titles similar to the *Illustrated London News* include the *Illustrated Times*, *The Graphic*, and *The Sphere*.

The architectural press. The technical improvements that introduced the illustrated newspapers also brought a new breed of architectural magazines in the 1840s, well-illustrated and cheap to buy, reflecting the growing status of the architectural and building professions.

The Builder was the first, longest-running and most influential of the weekly architectural journals, with regular, detailed articles on all sorts of building work. It has appeared every week since February 1843 (following a 'one-off' first issue in December 1842), and continues to appear today as *Building* (its name since 1966). The wide range of subjects covered included not just new building projects, but archaeological discoveries, ancient monuments, and professional issues, as well as lists of tenders and many well-illustrated adverts. Naturally the bigger public buildings get more coverage, but accounts of ordinary house-building occur from time to time. For instance, in November 1882 the paper reported on the development of the Dulwich College estate (or 'Old Manor House estate') at West Dulwich, where about 180 'suburban villas' were being erected between Knights Hill and Gypsy Hill, at rentals from £60 to £120 per annum, all under the superintendence of the estate's architect, Charles Barry.[7]

There is a good index to each *Builder* volume, which includes a separate index of the buildings illustrated, both by building type or name and by architects' name. Again, London housing is occasionally featured. On 5 February 1881, illustrated plans and elevations were reproduced of typical two-storey houses then being erected on the Crownfield Road estate, between Stratford and Leyton *(ill. 98)*. These were 'cottage-flats' or 'maisonettes', each house being intended for two families, with fitted kitchens and wash-houses on both floors; they were designed by William Crisp, ARIBA, for the Rural Property Investment Association Ltd.[8]

However, the richest seam of everyday information about house construction and development in London comes in the weekly lists of building contractors' tenders, which are not indexed. The data are basic, but precise, for example: in July 1878, for the erection of seven houses in Maygrove Road, Kilburn, designed

98. The Crownfield Road estate, between Stratford and Leyton, as illustrated in The Builder, *1881.*

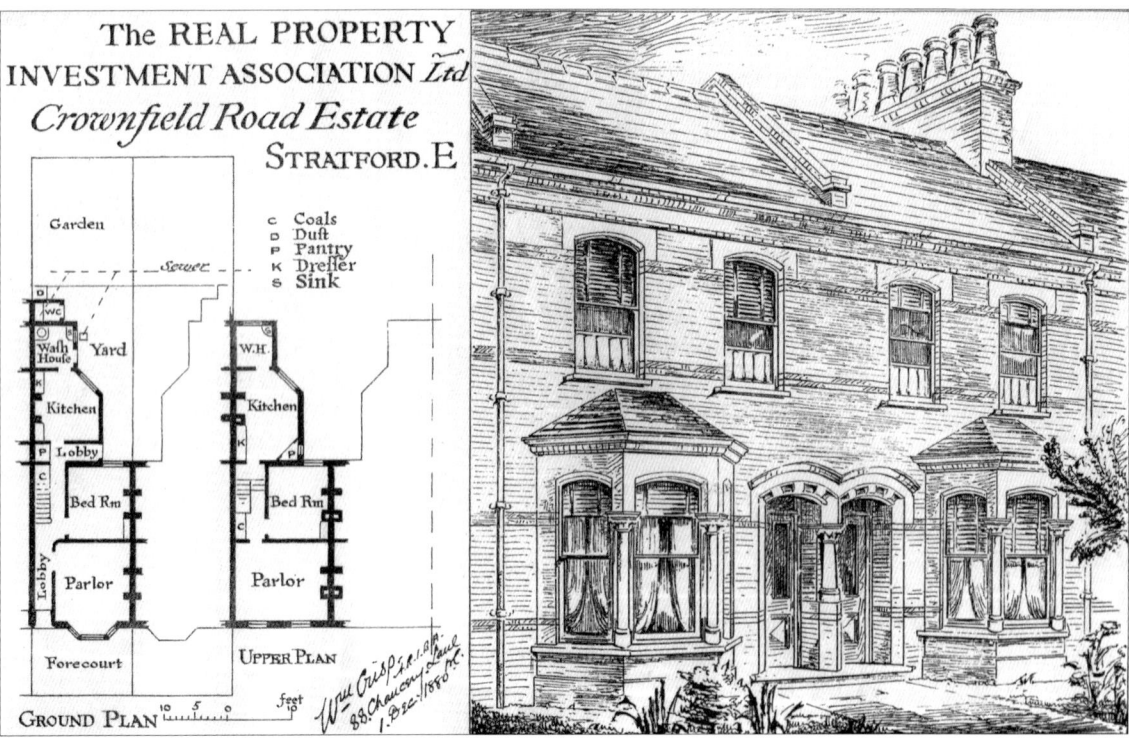

by Mr W. Smith, architect (lowest tenderer Taylor); in February 1891, for a pair of new semi-detached houses in Hardy Road, on the Westcombe Park estate, Blackheath, designed by Mr A. Broad of Croydon, architect (lowest tenderer Soper, accepted); or from August 1868, for 'finishing' Nos 2–5 on the Kidbrooke Park Estate, Blackheath, designed by J. Whichcord, architect (lowest tenderer Easman & Cockerell).[9]

The *Survey of London* has compiled an index of inner London entries in the *Builder* for the years 1842 to 1892, arranged by old LCC metropolitan borough, which includes tenders and shorter news items not generally found in the magazine's own indexes. This is available for consultation on microfiche at the London Metropolitan Archives. Also, a very useful index has been published to all the illustrations featured in the *Builder* for the years 1843 to 1883 (see *Further Reading*, below, under Ruth Richardson and Robert Thorne).

Later rivals to the *Builder* are also well worth consulting, if you think the property you are interested in may have been covered in the architectural press but does not appear in the *Builder*. See, for example, *Building News* (from 1855), the *Architect* (from 1869), the *British Architect* (from 1874), the *Builders'* (later *Architects'*) *Journal* (from 1895), and the *Architectural Review* (from 1896). The best place to consult architectural periodicals is the British Architectural Library, at the Royal Institute of British Architects, where many are easily accessible on open shelves, but the library now charges a fee for annual membership (daily tickets are also available). Alternatively, good runs of the principal titles (e.g. the *Builder, Building News, Architect & Building News* and *Architects' Journal*) can be found at the London Metropolitan Archives.

Other specialist periodicals and magazines. Many other serial publications are of use to local and house historians. For instance, the *London Journal* regularly publishes work on all aspects of London history, including suburban housing, such as Tanis Hinchliffe's essay on Highbury Park, Bernard Nurse's study of the development of the Dulwich College estate, or Miles Horsey's article on 'Between-the-Wars' speculative housebuilding.[10] The *London Topographical Record* is another good source, the 1995 edition, for example, containing studies of early-Victorian suburban development, of pre-1830s St John's Wood, and of the pre-1820 development of Mile End Old Town (by Sir John Summerson, Malcolm Brown and Isobel Watson, respectively).[11] The *Transactions of the London & Middlesex Archaeological Society*, too, though principally concerned with recent archaeological discoveries, also publishes more general articles on London building development and local history; see for example Carol Bentley's study of poor working-class housing in Bethnal Green in the early 1900s.[12] Other useful specialist periodicals include the *Georgian Group Journal*, *Architectural History* (the journal of the Society of Architectural Historians of Great Britain), as well as a host of local history society publications. Ask at your local history archive what kind of journals or newsletters have been published by the local history society for your area.

Legal records
Before the rationalization of the civil legal system in 1875 under the Supreme Court of Judicature, there were many civil courts that dealt with property disputes. These can be divided into two different but complementary groups: the *common law courts*, such as the King's Bench and the Court of Common Pleas, where litigants could seek compensation, but could not have their rights restored or broken contracts enforced; and the *equity courts*, such as Chancery and the Exchequer, which, although they could not award damages, could administer justice and take remedial action through the 'equity of reason'. Cases regarding inheritance and the restoration of property to its rightful owner, or relating to the non-payment of rent, mortgage defaulting, or broken leases or contracts, were generally heard in the equity courts. All the same it was not uncommon for action to be taken in both types of court simultaneously, or for cases to move between one and the other, adding to the complications in using legal records.

Legal records are voluminous and difficult

to use, and are not recommended to the beginner. It is unlikely that you will find information about an individual house or property unless you know that it was the subject of a dispute that ended up in court. Even then, you will need to have a good idea of the date of the case and the name of the plaintiff, as nearly all legal records relating to a civil case are filed annually by the plaintiff's surname.

This guide focuses on the principal legal source for London historians, the proceedings of the Lord Chancellor's Court of Chancery. Other equity courts, such as the Court of Exchequer and Court of Requests, followed the same or similar procedures, but their records are harder to use.

Chancery proceedings. The first stage in a Chancery suit was for the plaintiff (or *complainant*) to set out his grievances in a *bill of complaint* for the court; this was usually drawn up by a lawyer. In response to the charges in the bill, the defendant was required to provide a written *answer*, in which he might make countercharges against the complainant. Sometimes the complainant replied to the answer with a *replication*, and the defendant could respond again with a *rejoinder*. This process — known as 'pleading' — continued until the issues in dispute in the case had been agreed by both sides.

Once the pleadings were over, the business of gathering further evidence began. Both sides drew up lists of questions (called *interrogatories*), which were put to approved witnesses with some knowledge of the dispute (known as *deponents*), whose written answers (or *depositions*) were the principal form of evidence after the pleadings. The court also kept *affidavits*, which were voluntary statements of further evidence made under oath during the case. Sometimes the judge would ask a court official (or *Chancery Master*) to investigate matters further, by gathering more documentary evidence (called *exhibits*) and reporting back. Finally, the court made its judgement, in the form of a *decree*.

Not all the documents in any one case were filed together by the Chancery officials, but were put into separate series depending on

their nature or type, usually relating to the different stages in the progress of the case. It is the *pleadings*, which defined the exact nature of a dispute, that give the most detailed information about individual properties and their owners. Finding the pleadings for a particular case is not easy: there is no comprehensive index, and the papers were filed in a complicated system, usually by the surname of one of the plaintiffs. Few of the indexes indicate the location of the property in dispute, but London and Middlesex parish names are given for cases heard between 1649 and 1714.

In her book *The birth of modern London*, Elizabeth McKellar used Chancery pleadings from this period as her principal source of information on the London building world of the later 17th and early 18th centuries.[13] These provided her with detailed data on all aspects of the speculative building process, enabling her to shed fresh light on the methods and activities of Nicholas Barbon and other developers. Chancery cases supplied her with a valuable insight into (among other things) the form of building agreements, the pattern of double employment among the building craftsmen (many of them holding more than one job), rates of payment, the cost of bricks, and the types of wood used in house construction.

Few other classes of document provide this level of detail. To take an individual example, in 1694 Robert Dormer of Lincoln's Inn, who owned a 'large new built and well finished' brick house in St John's Court, Clerkenwell, agreed to let it to Edward Woodward. The following year Dormer entered a complaint in Chancery, saying that, despite their agreement, Woodward had taken up residence without signing a lease or paying any rent.[14] In his support, Dormer listed the repairs agreed to be done by him for Woodward, including: 'making good' the wainscotting in the Dining Room, Passage and Chamber; repairing the weatherboarding, rails and banisters 'on the top of the house'; putting a new outer gate in the courtyard; and erecting 'A New house of Office in the Garden'. Dormer added that these improvements had cost him over £100, employing 'divers able and sufficient Artists' to do the work. Woodward's reply included the information that he believed the house to have been built 'about 1674'. He complained that Dormer had not carried out all the repairs as agreed, pointing out that he himself had fixed the drain between his house and that of Lord Lisle, a neighbour, which had been flooding the buttery, wash-house and basement vaults with water, 'being a very great annoyance'. Woodward also supplied a complete inventory for the court, listing all the rooms in the house and their fittings. Thus we have a very good impression of the size and status of the house, its building materials and even its layout, as well as a date of construction.

A further example of the illuminating nature of Chancery pleadings is given in Case History One (see page 166).

As for the other classes of Chancery records, which record the remaining stages in a suit, these are unlikely to provide more information about property than the pleadings. However, for those who would like to know more about a Chancery case, or follow its progress from stage to stage, excellent information leaflets on Chancery and other legal records are available at the National Archives, and guides to the subject are listed in *Further reading* (below).

Bomb damage records

During the Second World War, London's civic authorities kept detailed records of the destruction caused by enemy bombing, and these are invaluable to anyone researching the history of a street or area that they think may have been hit during an air-raid.

The best place to begin is with the series of bomb-damage maps commissioned by the London County Council's Valuer's Department, principally as an aid to post-war redevelopment planning. These are coloured versions of the 1:25,000 scale OS maps of London, the seven colours coded to signify the extent of the damage to each property, ranging from yellow for 'minor' blast damage at one end of the scale, to black at the other for 'total destruction'. A glance at any of the sheets covering the East End shows with frightful clarity the extent of the devastation suffered there. In addition to the colour-coding, large and small circles on the maps plot the impact points of V1 and V2

missiles respectively. Laminated reference copies of these maps are now available on open access at London Metropolitan Archives.

For those who wish to go further, there are London-wide daily reports of incidents logged by the fire brigade, and a series of similar 'daily situation reports' by the various local ARP or Civil Defence units. These usually give the addresses of properties affected, names of owners or residents, describe the types of bombs or missiles and the extent of the damage, and list the number of people killed and injured. For example, for the night of 19–20 March 1941 – one of the worst nights of the Blitz, when there was a massive assault on the Docks – the daily returns of fire reports run to nearly 50 closely-typed A3 pages. The streets of east London were badly hit, there being numerous incidents in Poplar, Stepney, Bow, and also in Lewisham, Blackheath, Greenwich and Eltham, though most of these were from incendiary bombs, and the damage relatively concentrated. However, in May Day Gardens, Blackheath, high-explosive bombs demolished 37 houses (Nos 34–64 and 45–83), and badly damaged 104 others; 9 people were killed and 21 others injured.[15] These daily reports are arranged in chronological order, so you need to have a good idea of the date the incident occurred. Some local archives also have collections of the local ARP or Civil Defence units' incident records: Hackney Archives, for example, has an extremely informative series of local Civil Defence 'diaries' for part of the borough, with reports and photographs.

The National Archives also has summaries of daily incidents, arranged region by region, compiled for the Ministry of Home Security (ref HO/203). This department also created numerous bomb-damage survey plans and papers between 1940 and 1945 (ref HO/198). However, these 'bomb census' maps and papers, compiled to help assess the pattern and intensity of bombing across the country, are not so easy to use or as useful for individual property enquiries as the LCC maps at London Metropolitan Archives.

Many photographs were taken of bomb-damaged areas, not only by the services, the LCC and the metropolitan boroughs, but also

99. *American officers being shown the destruction caused by a flying bomb at the Ben Jonson School, Stepney, 27 July 1944; damaged and demolished houses in Monsey Street, behind.*

by interested residents *(ills 99, 100)*. These and a wealth of other supplementary wartime material, such as diaries, letters or personal papers, can be found in national and local collections. Heather Creaton's *Sources for the History of London 1939–45* is the definitive guide to the subject (see *Further reading*).

Less well-known are the German airship and bomber raids of World War One, during which over 1,000 British civilians were killed and some 3,000 injured. In London, 29 attacks took place between May 1915 and May 1918, and similar sets of air-raid reports and fire calls survive for these as for World War Two.[16] Fire-call returns for the night of 23–24 September 1916 chart the progress of a Zeppelin airship, weaving a path of destruction through south London. After dropping a bomb on No. 30 Ellison Road, Streatham, it caused considerable damage to rolling stock and vehicles at Streatham Common Railway Station, before inflicting further damage and death in Estreham Road, Greyhound Lane, Gleneagle Road and others, following the main road (now the A23) to Brixton and Kennington. No. 19 Baytree Road, Brixton, the 7-room home of the Lorimer family, was hit and entirely demolished *(ill. 101)*. The records give the bald facts: Alexander, aged 10, and Maxwell, aged 2, were injured and taken to hospital; their brother Bunty, aged 5, and a female, 'name and age unknown', were killed.[17] Maxwell — who became the comedian Max Wall — briefly recalled the traumatic event in his memoirs. His father Jack Lorimer, a Scottish music-hall artiste known as the 'Hieland Laddie', was at the time on tour in South Africa with his wife. The unfortunate 'unknown' female was Betty Hobbs, a friend of the family who regularly looked after the boys during their parents' frequent absences. Alec and Max survived because the large iron bedstead they were sleeping on turned over, protecting them from the falling rubble.[18]

100. Bomb damage caused by a V1 rocket on Lewisham Hill, June 1944.

101. Bomb damage to houses in Baytree Road, Lambeth, caused by a Zeppelin airship raid in the 1st World War.

Business records

At first glance, business records may not seem to offer much to anyone researching the history of a house or street. But you may wish to learn more about the builders or craftsmen involved, about the landlord or the developer, or about the architect who provided the design. Alternatively, your research may have uncovered one or more businessmen among former residents, about whom you would like to learn more.

Company archives. If the firm or company still exists, it is worth writing to the secretary to ask if any old records have survived, and if they can be made available to the public. In addition to the records required by law (such as lists of directors and share-holders), some companies may retain old minute books, letter-books, deeds and other material that could be of interest. The Business Archives Council (BAC) has published directories of member companies who maintain an archive; the most recent edition is the *Directory of corporate archives*, edited by Lesley Richmond and Alison Turton (4th edn, 1996).

For defunct companies, records exist at both national and local levels, and the best places to start are at your local archive, at London Metropolitan Archives, the National Archives, or by checking the whereabouts of company material via the National Register of Archives (now part of the National Archives). The Business Archives Council also regularly publishes lists of business records deposited in record offices.

Of particular interest to house historians are records of firms of **builders** and **contractors**. Where these survive, they can be extremely informative, often including account books, letter-books, or even ledgers listing all the projects undertaken by the firm. A list of building contracts worth over £500 for the period 1901–70 survives at the London Metropolitan Archives for the south London builders Holliday & Greenwood Ltd (later part of Higgs & Hill Ltd). This gives dates and addresses of houses built or altered by the firm, and names of clients and architects. For instance, most of the housing and flats erected in the early and mid-1960s in and around Fairfax Road and Marston Close in South Hampstead were the firm's handiwork. The records reveal that these works were carried out for a number of different developers (Cyril Leonard & Co; Studland Properties; and Ferrymead Properties Ltd), give the value of each contract (for example over £22,000 for 2 houses at Nos 9 and 11 Fairfax Road), and name the architect (R. Jelinck-Karl).[19] The records also include photographs and scrapbooks. Many other big London building firms have left behind good records, such as Trollope & Colls Ltd, John Mowlem & Company, Higgs & Hill Ltd, Reader Brothers and Dove Brothers.[20] And many local archives also have records of local builders and craftsmen: for instance, Hackney Archives has the records of the Hackney builders H. Bartlett; and Waltham Forest Archives & Local Studies Library holds the memoirs of the local 18th-century carpenter and builder Joel Johnson.

Some **architects** and **architectural practices** have left behind similar records of their work. The principal collection of architects' papers is at the Royal Institute of British Architects' (RIBA) British Architectural Library; the two standard biographical dictionaries of architects (by Howard Colvin and the RIBA, see *Further reading*, below) usually refer to any surviving documentation. The RIBA's British Architectural Library also maintains biographical files of architects, which usually contain lists of their works, obituaries, and any applications for membership to the institution.

Also worth considering are records of **estate agents** (see page 94) and **solicitors** that have been deposited in local and main archives, as where these survive they often include deeds, accounts and correspondence relating to housing. The records of Messrs May, May & Merrimans, solicitors, now held at London Metropolitan Archives, include leases, abstracts of title, wills and other documents (dating from 1796 to 1927) pertaining to Nos 11–14 Bruce Grove, in Tottenham.[21]

City of London Livery Companies. For older properties, particularly those built in the 18th century, if you have the name of one or more of the building tradesmen or craftsmen involved in its construction from title deeds or insurance records, it is worth consulting the archives of the City of London Livery Companies, kept at the Guildhall Library Manuscripts Department. Medieval in origin, these 'companies' were associations of individuals, bound together by sets of rules which regulated and monopolized their particular profession. They dominated trade in and around the City until the 19th century, by which time their power had declined, and today they act mostly as fund managers and property owners.

Their records are principally those of administration and membership. Court minutes record decisions about policy and general practice, and also the admission of new members. Of most interest are the records and lists of apprentices and members (or 'freemen'), which provide much useful biographical and social information. For instance, John Warden, a Holborn carpenter, one of a family of building craftsmen active in the area in the early 18th century, was made a freeman of the Carpenters' Company in October 1720, having served seven years apprenticeship to his father, also John, a Clerkenwell carpenter. Warden later 'translated' to the Plumbers' Company, in 1738.[22]

Official records: company registration and regulation. After the records of the companies themselves, the best sources of information on business history are the post-1844 records required by legislation for the registration of public and private joint-stock companies. These documents were kept in files by the Registrar of Companies, each company having its own identifying registration number. Files of returns for companies that are still active (or 'live') are today held at Companies House, where they are available for public consultation, though this usually involves a fee. Files for dissolved (or 'dead') joint-stock companies are held at the National Archives, in classes BT31 and BT41. In both cases the papers held are similar, usually including some of the following: the company's name and registered address; lists of directors and shareholders; articles of association; details about share capital; a prospectus; and (for dissolved com-

panies) details of their winding-up and dissolution. Most of the files for private companies dissolved after 1907 have been destroyed, but minimal details for these can still be found in the 'class sheets' in BT95.

A company's official registration number is essential in tracking down these records. There are finding aids at the National Archives and at Companies House, and at the Guildhall Library. Registered company details were published in *Joint Stock Returns* (for 1856 to 1900) and *Investors' Guardian* (for 1901 to 1962).

For companies not covered by the post-1844 joint-stock legislation, such as chartered companies, there are regulatory papers and correspondence among the records of the Board of Trade at the National Archives (class BT). Other 'official' sources held there include details of bankruptcies among the records of the Court of Bankruptcy (class B1) and Commissioners of Bankruptcy (B3).

Records of the London Stock Exchange. Public companies who wished to have their shares traded on the London Stock Exchange had to apply for authority to deal, and those wishing to have their share price quoted had to apply for listing. Records of both types of application survive for 1850–1954 among the collections of Guildhall Library Manuscripts Department, giving the company's objectives, capital history, voting rights, borrowing procedures and other details. Guildhall Library also holds annual reports for public companies quoted on the Stock Exchange after 1880 and before 1965; these usually include directors' reports, balance sheets, letters, and details of share prices. The reports are bound together by category, as in the *Stock Exchange Yearbook* (e.g. all property companies were filed together, as were all railway companies).

In addition, Guildhall Library has prospectuses for public companies quoted on the Stock Exchange from 1824; these were intended to advertise the company and encourage investment. For instance, a prospectus from the 1880s for the City of London House-Owners' Corporation, Limited, states the capital (£250,000 in £5 shares), lists the names of the company's directors, bankers, architect & surveyor (Mr

William Wimble of 9 Queen Victoria Street), valuers & agents, auditors, solicitors and secretary (Lieut-Col. F. Lean), and states its main objective: 'not any novel or speculative enterprise offering fabulous gain or ... heavy loss', but simply to offer its shareholders a 'remunerative as well as steady and perfectly safe medium of investment for large or small sums' by purchasing and managing a selection of 'well-situated' business premises in the City of London.

Yearbooks, Directories, and other records. For businesses and companies there is a host of specialist yearbooks and directories, both old and new.

The *Stock Exchange Yearbook* (held from 1875 onwards at the Guildhall Library) was intended as a 'reliable and inexpensive digest of information' relating to public security and joint-stock companies. It lists the names of public companies quoted on the stock exchange, divided into sections by their type, under headings such as 'Government Stock', 'Railways', 'Banks', 'Gas and Water', etc; there is also an alphabetical index by company name. The lists provide useful if basic information: names of directors, dates of formation, the function or aims of the company, its capital history, etc.

Forerunners or alternatives to the *Stock Exchange Yearbook* include the *Railway Intelligence* (for railway companies), and *Burdett's Official Intelligence*. Other useful publications include the *Banking Almanac*, and the *Red Book of Commerce*. Individual prominent businessmen can be traced through **trade directories** and other directories such as *Who's Who*, *Who Was Who*, the *Directory of Directors*, and *Notable Londoners*. Notices of bankruptcy were published in the *London Gazette*, and liquidated companies were listed in *Perry's Gazette* and *Stubbs Gazette*. Most of the above titles are available at the Guildhall Library.

Specialist newspapers survive for most trades and industries, for example the *Railway Times*, *The Engineer*, or the *Hotel Keeper*, and this **trade press** is a valuable source for business history. As for more general newspapers, *The Times* is the best, because of its wide coverage and user-friendly indexes (see above), and *The Economist* has also been indexed for the whole of the 20th century.

Finally, **trade catalogues** – illustrated catalogues of goods produced – are a good source for the types of fittings, furnishings and household appliances that were common in the home in the 19th and early 20th centuries, but their survival is patchy. They often include an engraving of the firm's office or works, and other useful information.

NOTES AND REFERENCES

1. *City Press*, 3 March 1860, p. 6.
2. Jeremy Black, *The English Press 1621–1861*, 2001, p. 74.
3. e.g. *The Times*, 27 Dec 1904, p. 5c; 28 Dec 1904, p. 5c; 29 Dec 1904, p. 9a; 30 Dec 1904, p. 10e; 20 June 1905, p. 7c; 6 May 1907, p. 4b; 3 Oct 1907, p. 6b; 22 July 1908, p. 19d; 15 Aug 1908, p. 11c.
4. *The Times*, 24 Sept 1880, p. 4b.
5. *The Times*, 1 Dec 1837, p. 7b.
6. *Illustrated London News*, 15 June 1844, p. 383.
7. *The Builder*, 18 Nov 1882, p. 649.
8. *The Builder*, 5 Feb 1881, pp. 161, 165.
9. *The Builder*, 20 July 1878, p. 764; 7 Feb 1891, p. 117; 8 Aug 1868, p. 596.
10. Tanis Hinchcliffe, 'Highbury New Park. A Nineteenth-Century Middle-Class Suburb', in *London Journal*, vol. 7, no. 1, 1981, pp. 29–44; Bernard Nurse, 'Planning a London Suburban Estate: Dulwich 1882–1920', in *London Journal*, vol. 19, no. 1, 1994, pp. 54–70; Miles Horsey, 'London Speculative Housebuilding of the 1930s: Official Control and Popular Taste', in *London Journal*, vol. 11, no. 2, 1985, pp. 147–59.
11. Sir John Summerson, 'The Beginnings of an Early Victorian Suburb', in *London Topographical Record*, vol. XXVII, 1995, pp. 1–48; Malcolm Brown, 'St John's Wood: The Eyre Estate Before 1830', *Ibid.*, pp. 49–68; Isobel Watson, 'From West Heath to Stepney Green: Building Development in Mile End Old Town, 1660–1820', *Ibid.*, pp. 231–56.
12. Carol Bentley, 'The Brady Street Scheme: Homes for the poorest Londoners in the early 20th century', in *LAMAS Transactions*, vol. 51, 2000, pp. 189–207.
13. Elizabeth McKellar, *The birth of modern London. The development and design of the city 1660–1720*, 1999, *passim*.
14. The National Archives, C10/243/20.
15. LMA, LCC/FB/WAR/3/7.
16. LMA, LCC/FB/WAR/2/66; LCC/FB/WAR/3/1–2.
17. LMA, LCC/FB/WAR/3/1.
18. Max Wall (with Peter Ford), *The Fool on the Hill*, 1975, pp. 43–6.
19. LMA, B/HOL/1.
20. LMA, B/TRL (for Trollope & Colls); LMA, Acc/2809 (Mowlems); LMA, B/HIG (Higgs & Hill); LMA/4430

(Reader Brothers); Islington Local History Centre (Dove Brothers).

21. e.g., LMA, B/MMN/11/69–75, 76–113, 149–93.

22. Guildhall Library MSS Department, MS 21,742/2.

FURTHER READING

Newspapers and Periodicals

Jeremy Black, *The English Press 1621–1861* (Sutton), 2001

Lucy Brown, *Victorian News and Newspapers* (Clarendon Press), 1985

George Boyce, James Curran and Pauline Wingate (eds), *Newspaper history from the seventeenth century to the present day* (Sage / Constable), 1978

Colin R. Chapman, *An Introduction to Using Newspapers and Periodicals* (Federation of Family History Societies), 1993

Jeremy Gibson, Brett Langston and Brenda W. Smith, *Local Newspapers 1750–1920, England and Wales, Channel Islands, Isle of Man. A Select Location List* (Federation of Family History Societies), 2nd edn, 2002

Dennis Griffiths (ed.), *The Encyclopedia of the British Press 1422–1992* (Macmillan), 1992

Frank Jenkins, 'Nineteenth-Century Architectural Periodicals', in John Summerson (ed.), *Concerning Architecture* (Allen Lane / Penguin), 1968, pp. 153–60

Eve McLaughlin, *Family History from Newspapers* (Federation of Family History Societies), 1987

K. A. MacMahon, 'Local History and the Newspaper: An Experiment in Group Study', in *Amateur Historian*, vol. 5, no. 7, Spring 1963, pp. 212–17

George R. Mellor, 'History from Newspapers', in *Amateur Historian*, vol. 2, no. 4, Feb–March 1955, pp. 97–101

Michael Murphy, *Newspapers and Local History* (British Association for Local History, The Local Historian at Work no. 5, Phillimore), 1991

Ruth Richardson and Robert Thorne, *The Builder Illustrations Index, 1843–1883* (Builder Group and Hutton & Rostron) 1994

Lucy Maynard Salmon, *The Newspaper And The Historian* (Oxford University Press), 1923

Legal Records

R. E. F. Garrett, *Chancery and other Legal Proceedings* (Pinhorns), 1968

Dorian Gerhold, *Courts of Equity. A Guide to Chancery and other Legal Records* (Pinhorns), 1994

Henry Horowitz, *Chancery Equity Records and Proceedings, 1600–1800: A Guide to Documents in the Public Record Office* (HMSO), 1995

Henry Horowitz, *Samples of Chancery Pleadings and Suits: 1627, 1685, 1735 and 1785* (List & Index Society), 1995

Mark M. Hughes, 'Notes on some Finding Aids to Chancery Proceedings in the Library of the Society of Genealogists', in *Genealogists' Magazine*, vol. 18, No. 3, Sept 1975, pp. 129–31

Elizabeth McKellar, *The birth of modern London. The development and design of the city 1660–1720* (Manchester University Press), 1999

Bomb Damage

James Bishop, *The Illustrated London News Social History of the First World War* (Angus & Robertson), 1982

Heather Creaton, *Sources for the History of London 1939–45. A Guide and Bibliography* (British Records Association, Archives and the User No. 9), 1998

John D. Cantwell, *The Second World War: A Guide to Documents in the Public Record Office* (HMSO, PRO Handbook 15), 1998 edn

Clive Hardy and Nigel Arthur, *London at War* (Quoin Publishing Ltd in association with Hulton-Deutsch Ltd Collection), 1989

John Hook, 'They Come! They Come! The Air Raids on London during the 1914–1918 War', typescripts of 1990, 1991 (in London Metropolitan Archives)

John Hook, 'Air Raids on London during the Great War', 3 vols, typescript, 1990 (in London Metropolitan Archives)

David Johnson, *The London Blitz* (Scarborough House), 1990

Joanna Mack and Steve Humphries, *London at War. The Making of Modern London, 1939–1945* (Sidgwick & Jackson), 1985

Joseph Morris, *The German Air Raids on Great Britain, 1914–1918* (Sampson, Low & Co), 1925

Winston Ramsey (ed.), *The Blitz Then and Now* (Battle of Britain Printing International Ltd), 3 vols, 1987–1990

C. M. White, *The Gotha Summer. The German daytime air raids on England, May to August 1917* (Robert Hale), 1986

Philip Ziegler, *London at War 1939–45* (Sinclair-Stevenson), 1995

Business Records

John Armstrong, 'An Introduction to Archival Research in Business History', in *Business History*, vol. 33, no. 1, Jan 1991, pp. 7–34

John Armstrong and Stephanie Jones, *Business Documents. Their origins, sources and use in historical research* (Mansell), 1987

Howard Colvin, *A Biographical Dictionary of British Architects 1600–1840* (Yale University Press), 3rd edn, 1995

C. R. H. Cooper, 'The Archives of the City of London Livery Companies and Related Organisations', in *Archives*, vol. XVI, no. 72, Oct 1984, pp. 323–53

Ian Anders Gadd and Patrick Wallis (eds), *Guilds, Society & Economy in London 1450–1800* (Centre for Metropolitan History / Institute of Historical Research / Guildhall Library), 2002

Francis Goodall, *A Bibliography of British Business Histories* (Gower), 1987

Guildhall Library MSS Section, *A handlist of Business Archives at Guildhall Library*, 2nd edn, 1991

Charles Harvey, 'Business Records at the Public Record Office' in *Business Archives*, no. 52, Nov 1986 (N. S. vol. 5, no. 3), pp. 1–18

John Orbell, *A Guide to Tracing the History of a Business* (Gower), 1987

T. Rath, 'Business Records at the Public Record Office in the Age of the Industrial Revolution', in *Business History*, vol. XVII, no. 2, 1975, pp. 189–200

Lesley Richmond and Bridget Stockford, *Company Archives: The Survey of the Records of 1000 of the First Registered Companies in England and Wales* (Gower), 1986

Lesley Richmond and Alison Turton, *Directory of Corporate Archives* (Business Archives Council), 4th edn, 1996

RIBA, *Directory of British Architects 1834–1914* (Continuum), revised edn, 2 vols, 2001

Stephanie Zarach (ed.), *British Business History: A Bibliography* (Macmillan), 2nd edn, 1994

CASE HISTORY ONE

The small Georgian terrace-house: Nos 55 and 57 Mount Pleasant, Camden

Nos 55 and 57 Mount Pleasant are the end pair of a short terrace of six modest Georgian houses (Nos 47–57, odd) close to Mount Pleasant Sorting Office, on the Camden–Islington border *(ills 102, 103)*. Although the neighbouring houses have been converted to commercial use, this pair appears to be occupied still as family residences, and have had modern apartments added recently at the rear, on their back gardens. The size and proportions of the six houses, and surviving elements of original fabric – flush-fronted sash windows with segmental heads, rubbed red-brick window dressings at Nos 47 and 49, and

102. Nos 51–57 Mount Pleasant.

103. *Nos 47–57 Mount Pleasant.*

104. *The Dorrington Street name plate in Mount Pleasant.*

the double pitch roof at Nos 55 and 57 – suggest an early-18th-century date; perhaps they are a survival of London's early-Georgian middle-class suburbia. We have one apparently invaluable guide to their age: on the front of Nos 55 and 57 is a stone street-name tablet, incised with the inscription 'DORRINGTON STREET 1720' *(ill. 104)*. But the *Buildings of England* volume for the area states that, though this seems 'appropriate' (i.e. in terms of its date), it is not *in situ*, having been moved from another street in Holborn some way to the south, near Leather Lane.[1] So when exactly and by whom were these houses built? And what is the story of the name tablet?

Phase 1: Basic London-wide and local sources for the period – maps, directories, ratebooks and photographs

As the houses are clearly Georgian, there seems little point in examining Ordnance Survey maps for clues to their origins, but the earlier editions of the five-foot-scale OS, of the 1870s and 1890s, do provide some useful if puzzling information *(ill. 105)*. Firstly, the maps show the houses in surroundings very different from today's post-war topography: to the east and south are streets and squares of similar-sized houses, suggesting that our pair was once part of an almost solidly residential area, perhaps an estate development. Secondly, both editions clearly show seven houses here, west of the Apple Tree public house, not the present six. What happened to the seventh house, which would have abutted on the end of our pair?

105. The Mount Pleasant area in the 1870s. From the first edition of the five-foot-scale OS.

Also, according to the earlier map, this eastern stretch of Mount Pleasant was not so-called in the 1870s: the three rows of houses here were then known by the names Cobham Row, Baynes' Row and, for our terrace, Dorrington Street – the same as on the name tablet. The maps also make it clear that the houses, though now in Holborn, in the London Borough of Camden, were formerly within the parish of St James, Clerkenwell, which is now part of the London Borough of Islington. The administrative boundary was moved east of the houses before the 1890s survey, probably as part of the reorganization of London's local government in 1889–90. This information is very important for planning documentary research. It is likely that sources will be divided between two locations: early parish material (such as ratebooks) and early deeds should be in the local history library for Islington; information on the house's later history may be in the Camden library; general sources, such as photographs, illustrations, local directories, etc, may well be found in both.

Widely-available earlier maps of London that cover this area – e.g. by Richard Horwood (1799–1819), John Rocque (1747), and Ogilby

& Morgan (1676) – simply confirm our suspicion that the houses were built in the early 18th century. They appear, along with the surrounding estate, on Rocque's and Horwood's maps (*ill. 106*) but not on Ogilby & Morgan's, where the site is shown as fields. However, it is always worth looking at as many old maps as possible, particularly any local ones. One of these, of the parish of St James Clerkenwell, drawn up around 1720 for Strype's edition of John Stow's *Survey of London,* still shows fields of pasture on the site of our houses. Though this map is based largely on an earlier one ('Taken from ye last Survey'), it is reliable, having been brought up-to-date, showing many improvements known to have been made in the area in the early 18th century – so our houses must have been built between c.1720 and 1747.

So how best to narrow down our construction date further? At this early stage, the best way to establish a rough chronology of development is to work backwards through the *Post Office Directories* and ratebooks.[2] Although this may sound laborious, there are few more accessible or reliable basic sources, and the work will also provide an invaluable body of information – on dates, names and changes of oc-

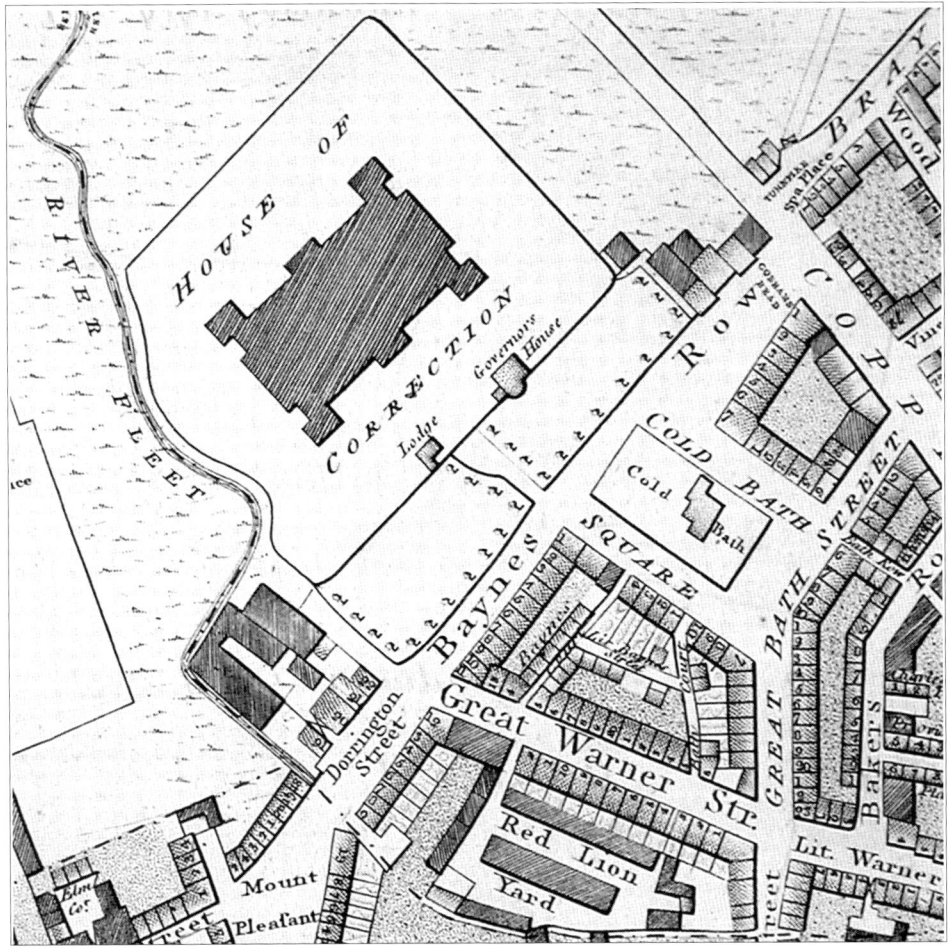

106. *The Mount Pleasant area from Horwood's map, 1813 edition.*

cupants, the renumbering of houses and re-naming of streets, etc – which we can refer to later on. We should also see some indication of the disappearance of our mysterious seventh house.

Since the 1960s, the *POD*s always list Laystall Court (the block of flats now standing to the west of Nos 55 and 57) immediately after the houses. However, working backwards, we find a No. 59 Mount Pleasant (our seventh house) listed in 1953 and before, and other houses (Nos 61–75) are also listed up until 1944. So it appears that our mystery house was demolished in the 1950s for the construction of the flats.

In the post-war *Directories*, the whole row of houses was occupied by small businesses. In the 1940s and '50s, No. 55 was shared by two: a builders (Crisp, Fowler & Co), and a hairdresser (Francesco Pisani); in 1955, No. 57 was occupied by a masseur (Percy Mansi). So the two houses were not always solely in residential use. Note also the Italian-sounding surnames, for in Mount Pleasant we are on the northern fringe of the part of Holborn and Clerkenwell once known as 'Little Italy', the principal colony of Italian immigrants in London in the 19th and early 20th centuries.

Working back further, we find a bootmakers (William Glanvill & Son) at No. 57 from *c*.1870 until 1894, and a succession of small businesses – a picture-frame maker, a paper-stainer, a tailor, etc – at No. 55. The pre-1875 *Directories* and ratebooks refer to the houses as Dorrington Street – not Mount Pleasant – and list Nos 55 and 57 as 6 and 7 respectively; the seventh house (No. 59) is No. 8 Dorrington Street. There is no ratebook entry for No. 8 before 1796, when Charles Vine is given as its first occupant; so it seems that our 'disappearing' seventh house was not as old as its neighbours, but was added to the end of an existing row in about 1796. Further back is another change of numbering, Nos 2–7 Dorrington Street being known as 13–18 before 1796. The ratebooks show the houses to have been in almost continual occupation from the 1740s to the present day. It is not until we reach the early 1730s and 1720s that things begin to change; three are empty in 1728, including the Apple Tree, the pub on the other corner, which first appears in that year. Only five of our six houses are listed in 1723. There are no surviving ratebooks for Clerkenwell for the period between 1723 and 1696; but, given the gaps in occupation, and what we already know from the maps, it looks likely that our terrace was reasonably

newly built in the early 1720s. Our first five known ratepayers in 1723 (for Nos 47–55) were: John Slaughter (£20), Mr Sly (£20), William Barker (£20), William Banes (£30), and James Palefield (no rateable value). No. 57 is not entered.

One valuable lesson from this first trawl through the most basic documentary sources is the importance of being aware of changes to street-names and house numbers – otherwise it might not be evident that the No. 55 Mount Pleasant of today, the No. 17 Dorrington Street of 1780 and the No. 6 Dorrington Street of 1850 are in fact one and the same house. For the post-1850 period, the London County Council regularly published revised editions of its reference volume of changes to London street-names. The 1901 edition tells us that the names Cobham Row, Baynes' Row and Dorrington Street were abolished on 25 June 1875, when the houses there became a continuation of Mount Pleasant.[3]

There is no shortage of old 20th-century photographs and other, earlier illustrations of houses in the area; but the two which show our row *(ills 107, 108)*, offer no extra clues to the date of construction. However, the more recent

107. Nos. 47–57 Mount Pleasant in 1971.

108. Nos 47–57 Mount Pleasant in 1947.

109. Houses in Baynes' Row, showing street-name tablets.

photo shows Nos 55 and 57 still largely in commercial use in 1971, confirming that to-day's ground-floor arrangement is a recent alteration. And the older photo, of 1947, clearly shows the name tablet; so if it was moved from elsewhere, this was done some time ago. But could it not be genuine? Another old photo-graph, of nearby houses of similar date in Baynes' Row (now demolished), reveals that one of these buildings, too, had tablets placed in the brick facing: an elaborate one, bearing the initials of the builder (John Pankeman), and another, simpler street-name tablet, al-most identical to ours at Nos 55–57 *(ill. 109)*.

Phase 2: Casting the net wider – the Middlesex Deeds Registry and Fire Insurance policies
We now know that our houses were probably built in the early 1720s, and we have the names of some early occupants. But by whom and why were they built? Although we are concen-trating on primary documentary sources, now is a good time to consult any published his-tories of the area, which may provide a clue to landownership and building development hereabouts. There are two for Clerkenwell: one published in 1863–5, written by William Pinks;

and another, of 1828, by Thomas Cromwell. Each provides a short account of our district.[4]

As the OS maps suggested, the houses at Nos 47–57 Mount Pleasant were part of an estate development, known as the Baynes-Warner or Jervoise Estate. The land here, between the Clerkenwell parish's western boundary at the Fleet and Coppice Row (one of the main routes north, on the approximate route of present-day Farringdon Road) had been purchased in 1696 by Walter Baynes, a lawyer, and John Henley, a merchant taylor. At this time the estate comprised fields of pasture (known as Sir John Oldcastle's Field and Gardiner's Field or Farm) and some buildings, one of which was a celebrated wayside inn, the Sir John Oldcastle (thought to contain remains of the manor house of Sir John Oldcastle, Lord Cobham, the medieval catholic martyr). Henley's share in the estate was subsequently acquired by John Warner, a banker and goldsmith (and friend of Baynes), who died in 1721, bequeathing it to his son, Robert. Cromwell describes Baynes, the other owner, as having bought the estate 'with an eye to the building speculations'. In about 1697 Baynes converted an ancient spring on the estate into a cold bath, which he advertised as a curative for many ills and ailments, charging the public for its use. In the 1720s and '30s the southern half of the estate, Sir John Oldcastle's Field, was built over with streets of terrace-houses. In a list of the streets of the estate, Cromwell mentions Dorrington Street, which he says took its name from Thomas Dorrington, a London bricklayer, to whom Baynes and Warner leased the ground for building. After the deaths of Baynes and Warner, the estate came into the ownership of Jervoise Clarke Jervoise (died 1809). It was finally broken up and sold in 1811.

Armed with this information, we can search the National Register of Archives to see if estate records survive. Unfortunately there are no entries for our area under the names Baynes, Warner or Jervoise. However, it is always worth asking local librarians and archivists if they know of any such records. An informal enquiry at London Metropolitan Archives revealed that among their collection of family and estate archives are boxes of uncatalogued deeds re-

lating to the Jervoise estate in Holborn and Clerkenwell, deposited by a firm of solicitors with Bedfordshire Record Office in the 1940s and '50s, and since then transferred to the LMA via the Middlesex Records Office.[5]

Even so, ploughing through 10 or more boxes of uncatalogued estate papers would be a big, time-consuming job, especially if we are interested principally in only two houses. Instead, now we have the names of early ratepayers, estate owners and/or developers, and a rough construction date, it is much better to begin by looking through the Middlesex Deeds Registry (MDR) for building leases. If necessary, we can return to the estate papers later for more background information, or to get a deeper understanding of the chronology and process of estate development.

Looking through the MDR indices under the names Baynes and Warner from c.1720 brings immediate results. This row of houses was the first to be built on the estate, and is easily identifiable from the registers, being next to the parish boundary at the River Fleet (then known locally as Turnmill Brook), a major local landmark. The registry for 1720 records the building leases for two of the houses, the present Nos 51 and 47 (the latter described as 'the fourth house from the brook'), leased to Thomas Scott, a City of London mason, and William Newman, a joiner of St Clement Danes, respectively.[6] Our pair at Nos 55 and 57 appears in the registry for 1721. The houses are described as 'near adjoining' a bridge over the Fleet called the New River Bridge, and as abutting on the parish boundary at Turnmill Brook – and, as Cromwell suggested, were leased by Baynes and Warner to Thomas Dorrington, a City bricklayer. So then, as now, they were the end pair of the terrace, and we now have no reason to doubt the name tablet's authenticity.[7] All the building leases in Dorrington Street were for 61 years, and the dates when they were issued (August 1720 for Nos 51 and 47, March 1721 for Nos 55 and 57) give a reasonably accurate date for their completion.

It was typical of 18th-century estate development for landlords to issue leases of this type, for houses singly or in pairs, to different building tradesmen. Note the variety of trades

– mason, bricklayer, joiner, carpenter. The men would not have built houses individually, as might be inferred from the leases, but would have worked together on the whole row, in return for a financial interest. Most of them assigned their leases to others shortly after the houses were finished, either through sales or mortgages; builders, then as now, were frequently in need of ready cash.[8]

The MDR entries provide other information about the early stages of the Baynes–Warner estate's development. For example, the leases did not include the 'airy' or area in front of the houses, which was to be reserved, for the benefit of future inhabitants of the estate, to lay pipes or conduits draining from other houses (as yet unbuilt) into Turnmill Brook. Another MDR entry for a Baynes–Warner lease mentions a clause requiring the lessee to insure his house with the Hand-in-Hand Insurance Company, and even gives a policy number. It is likely that this requirement was standard, and applied to all builders on the estate; so there is a good chance that the Hand-in-Hand policy registers, which survive for this period, would also record the construction of our pair of houses – which they do. In fact, all six houses were insured with the Hand-in-Hand in the summer of 1720, for around £150–£200 each, confirming the date of completion, and the names of policy-holders (for example Newman, Scott and Dorrington) accord with those of ratepayers and lessees. But what, if any, new information do the insurance policy registers provide? Hand-in-Hand policies were renewable every 7 years, so theoretically it should be possible to work forward through the registers to discover the names of later owners and occupiers. For instance, in July 1721 Dorrington renewed the policies for his two houses, but that August he assigned them to Katherine Gaunt (this was presumably a mortgage). By 1728 the policy-holder was Hannah Mayo, who is listed as a ratepayer at Nos 55 and 57 in the 1730s and '40s; this sort of research could be carried on into the 1860s (when the records cease), if so desired. The Hand-in-Hand registers also give brief descriptions and measurements of buildings, so it should also be possible when working through later years to check for

any alterations or additions to the houses. There are no obvious changes: the most important piece of structural information is that, then as now, the houses had no back extensions (or 'closet wings'), but were simple brick boxes, about 16–18ft by 28ft.[9]

Phase 3: Further research – estate papers, census returns, local government records and other sources

For those who wish to go further with their research, the uncatalogued estate papers will provide a wealth of information about the history of the district – how it was administered, the types of industry carried on there, and (from information about the lessees and residents) an insight into its social character. For example, although predominantly developed with small houses, the estate was not solely residential. There are numerous references to inns and alehouses. Some papers refer to the lease of a site to the parish authorities for a new Clerkenwell Workhouse, built in 1727. Other larger buildings erected on the estate included a distillery (in the 1730s) and a smallpox hospital (in the 1750s). Some papers concern the sale of the largely undeveloped northern half of the estate to the Middlesex justices as the site for a new prison, or 'House of Correction', which from the 1790s until the 1880s stood on the site now occupied by Mount Pleasant Sorting Office.[10] The presence of such buildings – particularly the prison – had an impact on the character of the area, which gradually lost any lingering pretension to gentility. We know from the *Directories* that by the 1840s and '50s many of the houses were being used for some form of trade or light industry. In his *The Great World of London*, of 1856, Henry Mayhew said 'few persons in easy worldly circumstances care to reside in the neighbourhood of a prison', and he described the houses in Mount Pleasant facing the main entrance of the House of Correction as having been 'degraded', and converted to use as old furniture stores, or lodging houses for single men.[11]

Also among the uncatalogued papers are particulars for the auction sale of the estate in 1811. Our pair of houses (then known as 6–7

Dorrington Street) are described as two free-hold 'convenient' dwelling-houses, brick-built, containing two rooms on a floor, with a yard to each house and workshops, at the time leased by the Jervoise estate to one Samuel Agland for a term expiring at Lady Day 1832, at an annual rent of £30.[12] It should be possible to go back to the Middlesex Deeds Registry and discover who bought the houses at the sale, and follow their descent thereafter.

What about our builder, Thomas Dorrington? As he was described as a 'Citizen and Bricklayer', he must have been a member of the City of London's Tylers' & Bricklayers' Company. Records of many of the City guilds and livery companies are kept at Guildhall Library. A list of early-18th-century freemen of the company includes Thomas Dorrington, and from this and other entries it becomes clear that he was one of a family involved in the trade: he was made freeman in 1717 'by pat-rimony', i.e. by having his fees paid by his father, an existing member of the company, also called Thomas. Other Dorringtons listed include Matthew Dorrington, 'bound over' as an apprentice in 1714 to Thomas senior (and after his death to Thomas junior), and made freeman in 1721 having completed his appren-ticeship; and Joseph, 'bound over' to Matthew in 1721 and made freeman in 1728.[13]

There are many other possible avenues of research for those who wish to know more about the area's development, rather than just the age of the two houses. An abstract of title among the estate papers refers to litigation between the two owners, Baynes and Warner, in the form of a Chancery case over a proposed division of the estate into two separate freeholds.[14] Legal records can be difficult to locate and unravel, and are only really worth looking for if you know that a case was heard, and have the names of the people involved and an approximate date; but they can often pro-vide invaluable background information on the history of a property which would be im-possible to find elsewhere. In this instance, the Chancery proceedings confirm Cromwell's view that Baynes was the driving force behind the area's development — he claimed to be the sole 'improver' of the estate, dealing with the

builders himself and overseeing all the legal work. The Chancery papers also provide the name of the man who surveyed the estate and designed the layout of the houses: Richard Grimes, a City carpenter, who, from a study of the estate papers and deeds registry, emerges as one of the estate's principal builders.[15]

The increasing availability and ease of ac-cess to census enumerations will tell us more about the social status of residents from mid-19th century until 1901. In 1851 No. 55 (then known as 6 Dorrington Street) was divided into three separate households (presumably one to each floor), with 7 occupants: Thomas Grimshaw, a 45-year old Clerkenwell-born brazier, and his wife, Sarah; a second Thomas Grimshaw, a retired brazier, born in Lancaster, and his wife Elizabeth; and Mary Poley, an umarried schoolteacher. No. 57 (or 7 Dorrington Street) was unoccupied. In the 1871 returns both houses were sub-divided, each into three households, with a total of 6 families (16 adults and 23 children) in residence. By 1901 26 of the 29 occupants were of Italian origin (compared with only 3 in 1871), reflecting the growth of the Italian community in the area.[16]

For a more detailed account of the houses' recent history – something that is often hard to unearth – the local planning department (Camden) has a publicly accessible statutory register of applications. From these we learn that No. 55 was converted to a betting-office in 1962, and had a new shop-front inserted in 1969 – the one in our 1970s photo (ill. 107). More importantly, the applications for the in-ternal and external alterations to restore the two houses to family dwellings are also there, from 1995-6, so we now know when the ground-floor was rearranged, and the name of the architect of the scheme, which included the new residential 'units' in the rear yards. In the same file are the applications and correspond-ence of 1953–8 relating to the construction of the block of flats at Nos 59–75 Mount Pleasant, to designs by the Holborn Borough Architect, which confirms what we had already concluded from the *Post Office Directories*.[17]

Summary

Most of inner London's 18th-century middle-class suburbs were built up in a similar fashion to the houses and streets of the Mount Pleasant area described above. For anyone researching terrace-house or estate development in this period, the classes of documents used here – old maps, ratebooks, estate papers, fire insurance records, and (for London north of the Thames) the Middlesex Deeds Registry – should prove invaluable, and offer enough basic information to construct a basic outline or chronology of development.

NOTES AND REFERENCES

1. Bridget Cherry and Nikolaus Pevsner (eds), *London 4: North*, 1998, p. 301.

2. The ratebooks for Clerkenwell are at the Islington Local History Centre, Finsbury Library.

3. LCC, *Names of Streets and Places in the Administrative County of London*, 1901 edn, p. 762.

4. For accounts of the estate see Thomas Cromwell, *History and Description of the Parish of Clerkenwell*, 1828, pp. 298–315; and William J. Pinks, *The History of Clerkenwell*, 1880 edn, pp. 124–5.

5. The uncatalogued Jervoise estate papers are at London Metropolitan Archives (LMA), in Acc/137/1–234 and Acc/35/1–46.

6. London Metropolitan Archives, Middlesex Deeds Registry (hereafter MDR) 1720/4/335; 1720/6/268.

7. MDR 1721/6/112–14.

8. MDR 1720/4/334; 1720/5/181; 1721/6/114.

9. Policy numbers 41412–14 in Guildhall Library, MSS 8674/22, pp. 90–1; 8674/24, p. 39; 8674/35, p. 86; 8674/37, p. 273; 8674/51, p. 3; 8674/60, p. 263.

10. LMA, Acc/137/113–117, conveyance of 27 Dec 1736, Baynes to Warner.

11. Henry Mayhew, *The Great World of London*, 1856, p. 278.

12. LMA, Acc/137/212–234, sale particulars, 1811.

13. Guildhall Library, MS 3053/3.

14. Abstract of title in LMA, Acc/137/212–234.

15. PRO, C11/1512/8; C11/1152/8; C11/1624/6.

16. Censuses for 1851, 1871, 1901.

17. London Borough of Camden Planning and Environment Department, Statutory Register Files, under 'Mount Pleasant'.

The Victorian terrace-house: Acris Street, Wandsworth

Acris Street, in Wandsworth, south-west London, is a typical late-Victorian sub-urban street of middle-class terrace-houses. Of red brick, with white- or cream-painted render dressings, the houses have trademark splayed bay windows, attractive tiled entrances, and black-and-white terrazzo paths, and have been well maintained by their 'up-and-coming' owners *(ill. 110)*. But when, exactly, were they built? Are they contemporary with the almost identical houses in the

immediate neighbourhood, in Melody, Trefoil and Cicada Roads? Who built them? And for what sort of people were they intended?

Phase 1: Basic London-wide sources for the period

The 1916 Ordnance Survey (OS) 25in sheet for the area clearly shows all these streets fully developed, in pretty much the same form they take today, so they are certainly not later than

110. Acris Street today.

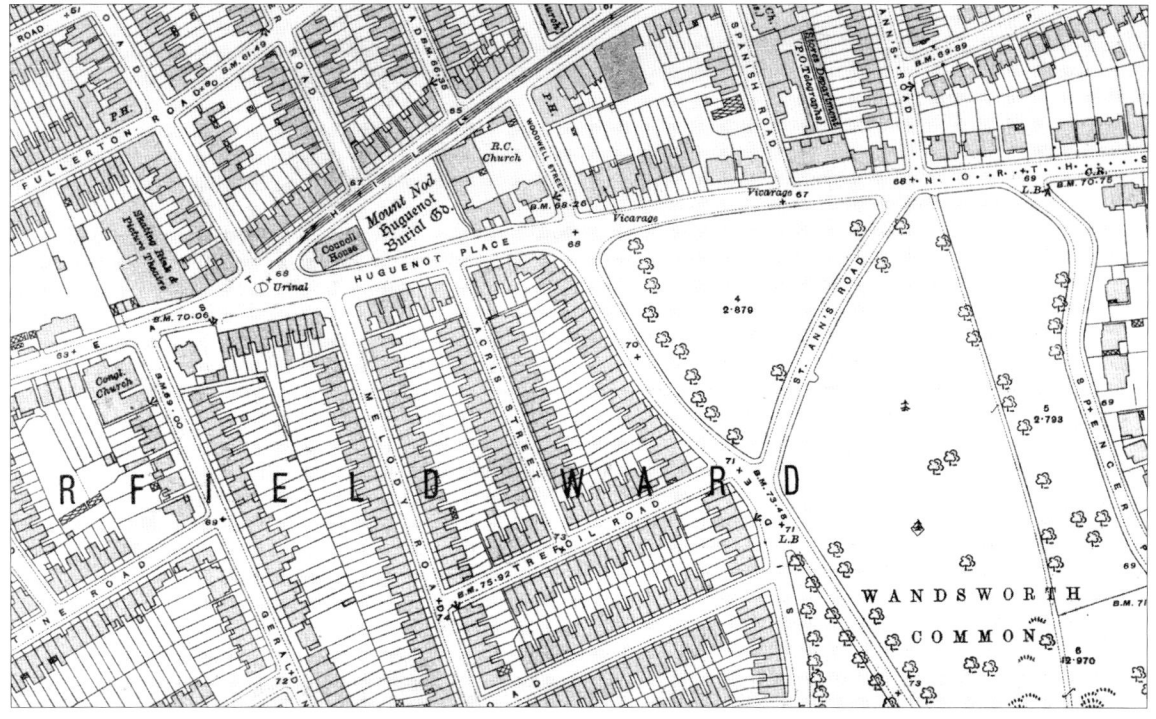

111. The Ordnance Survey of 1916, showing Acris Street in the centre of this excerpt.

112. The Ordnance Survey of 1894. The site of Acris Street is still occupied by the grounds of large houses.

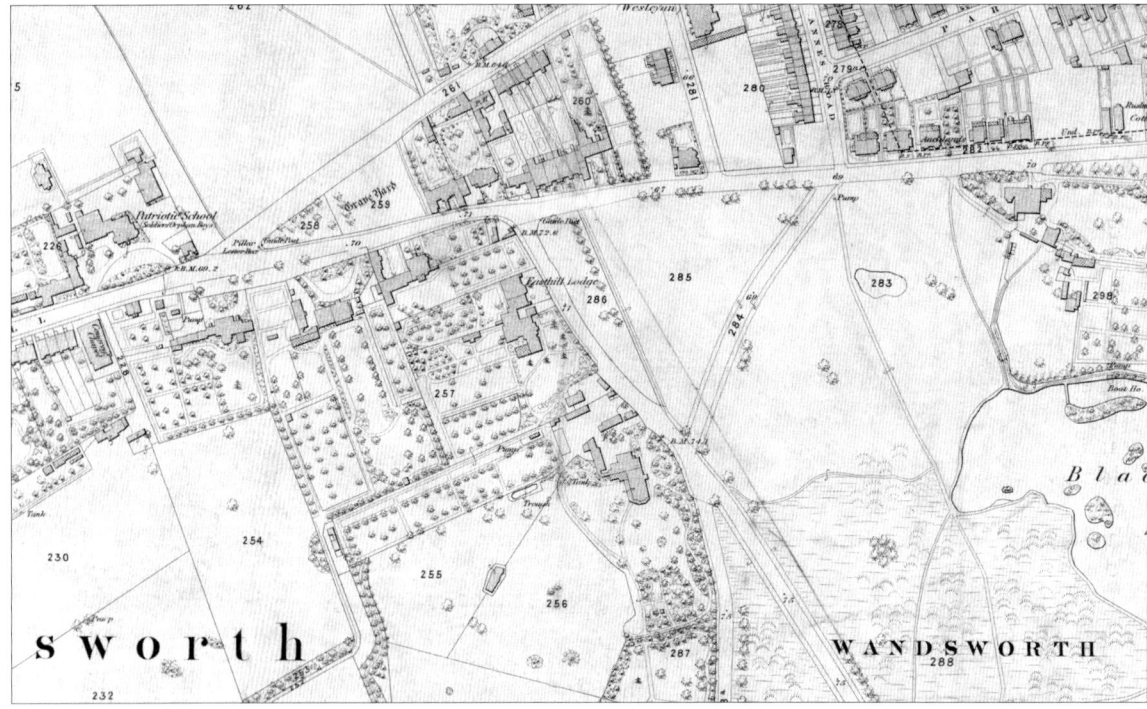

113. *The Ordnance Survey of the 1870s, before Acris and its neighbouring streets were developed.*

Edwardian *(ill. 111)*. The 1894–6 map shows Melody, Trefoil and Cicada Roads built up, but there is no sign of Acris Street: its site is occupied by two large detached buildings, Easthill Lodge and Ivy House *(ill. 112)*. None of the streets appears on the 1867–70 edition of the OS, which shows this area on the west side of Wandsworth Common entirely given over to fields and half-a-dozen-or-so large private residences *(ill. 113)*. So, already, having consulted only one source, we can say with confidence that Acris Street post-dates its immediate neighbours, which had been built by *c.*1894, and seems to have been part of a comprehensive residential development on the west side of the common, south of the main east–west road (East Hill).

A leaf through local *Directories* for the same period confirms the above, and gives a further insight into the chronology of development. All the streets are listed in full in the 1900 *London Suburban Directory*; none appears in the 1890 version. By 1893 (i.e. in the 1894 *Directory*) substantial runs of houses have been let in Cicada Road and Melody Road; only two are listed in Trefoil Road. By 1895 many of the gaps have been filled, and by 1897, of these three streets, only Cicada Road is not complete or fully occupied. The 1900 *Directory* is the first to list Acris Street. These directories also give the occupations of some residents, including two music-teachers in Melody Road, an architect in Cicada Road, and a dressmaker in Acris Street. This sort of information is a valuable guide to the social status of the area (something we shall return to later), especially for the post-1901 period, for which census returns are not yet available. One other point is worthy of note. In some streets, one or two builders appear briefly as residents during these early years: Albert Eaton at No. 56 Melody Road in 1894; George Gay at No. 2 'Holland's Terrace', in the same road, in 1896; and William Henry George at No. 20 Trefoil Road in 1898. It was common practice for a builder to set up headquarters in one of his own new houses (or a pub if one was included in the development) whilst he was completing his street or terrace; this would be sub-let or sold once work had finished. So it is likely that these are some of the men who built our little estate. Names of terraces, often short-lived, can also be a clue, as frequently they were called after the person who built them. We have two in Melody Road – 'Holland's Terrace' and 'Cecil Terrace' – names that had fallen out of use by 1898.

What we need now are more accurate dates for the streets, and some idea of the pattern of landownership in the area at the time, which should help identify the estate developer. For houses of this period in London, perhaps the quickest way to learn more about their constructional history is to consult the IR58 fieldbooks at the National Archives, drawn up around 1911–13. Although you may be lucky in having a local history library with good runs of drainage applications, estate papers, deeds or other records which can provide the same sort of information (and more) for your house, the advantage of the IR58 books is that they recorded *every building* in the country at that time, and give the names of owners, lessees and dates of leases. Although the fieldbooks can vary in quality from district to district, for this area they are particularly instructive.[1]

The fieldbooks reveal that the majority of the houses on Melody and Trefoil Roads were built on land owned by Henry Nicholas Corsellis, of 64 East Hill (a local address); all were held on 99-year leases from December 1891. These would be the original building leases, though most would have been sold on or 'assigned' by this time, and their commencement date probably corresponds to the initial agreement between landowner and builder, rather than the completion of the houses (which would be a year or two later); this compares well with what we have learnt from the OS maps and *Directories*. In Acris Street the story is slightly different: here Captain A. H. N. Corsellis and Mr H. M. Ellis are given as 'head lessees', the freeholders being Magdalen College, Oxford. A note on the back of the first entry helpfully declares 'H.N.Corsellis dec.', so we know that our potential original owner/developer was dead by *c.*1912 and had bequeathed his estate to a son or other relative. All the leases in Acris Street were for 92 years from

March 1894 — only two and a bit years later than the adjoining streets, but late enough to miss the survey for the 1894-6 edition of the OS.

In the IR58 books these houses are described as 'attractive' and 'modern', in 'good condition' and 'well-fitted', some with electric lighting, although this was probably not an original feature, as electric lighting was rare in suburban houses until after the invention of the tungsten-filament bulb in 1907. In all cases the layout, number and type of rooms are given, and can be compared with the present-day arrangement. In Acris Street the houses generally had on the ground floor (from front to back): two 'parlours', a kitchen, scullery, outdoor water-closet and small garden. On the first floor were three bedrooms and another wc; and a fourth bedroom and a bathroom were situated on the floor above. For tax purposes a valuation is given for each house (about £400), and there are also references throughout to previous sales of leases, with prices.

Unusually, the entries for Melody Road give the names of some of the building contractors, and these confirm our suspicion from the *Directories*: Nos 1–51 (odd) were built by Mr Eaton, Nos 69–75 by Mr George ('this end of the road is not so good', say the notes), Nos 80–98 (even) by Mr Driver, and Nos 100–122 by Mr Gay.

So, having consulted only three basic London-wide sources, already it is clear that Acris Street was the last component in a small estate development of the 1890s, undertaken by H. N. Corsellis, using a number of local builders, replacing a group of big detached houses with streets of the latest suburban terraces. We also know something of the pattern and rate of development, the number of builders (there were at least four working in Melody Road), the original layout of the houses, and an idea of the sort of people for whom they were built. For a fuller story, and some background to this little district's history, it is time to look at the holdings of the local history library, and some of the more complex metropolitan sources.

Phase 2: Local archives and further London-wide sources
Old photographs are worth looking for when researching the history of Victorian houses.

114. Acris Street newly built, c. 1919.

The Wandsworth Local History Service has photographs and old postcards of Acris and its neighbouring streets *(ill. 114)*; but although these are evocative, with children in period dress standing or playing in the streets, they are not accurately dateable, nor do they provide any further clues to the exact date of the houses.

The first local government documents to check for houses of this period are the Building Act Case files of the London County and Greater London Councils held at London Metropolitan Archives. These are often a good source of information on the construction of new houses and streets, and subsequent alterations, but there are no index entries for Acris Street, or for any of its neighbours – these must have been among the 60% of files that were destroyed following the abolition of the GLC. If no Building Act Case files survive for your street it is always worth checking the lists of Building Act applications in the published volumes of Minutes of the Metropolitan Board of Works (MBW) and London County Council (LCC). There are numerous applications listed under the name Corsellis for the period *c.*1888

to *c.*1896, for various new streets in Battersea, Clapham and Wandsworth, so obviously the family was heavily involved in building development in this part of south London.[2] And one entry for 1891 provides us with a useful new piece of information: a name for the Corsellis family's little estate. On 29 September that year the LCC approved an amended plan for the building of new streets on the Bramblebury Estate, Wandsworth Common, to be known as Melody, Cicada, Dault, Trefoil, Jessica, Quarry and Geraldine Roads.[3]

Another good source for Victorian housing, held at a local level, is the series of drainage applications submitted to the local authorities by builders, and here we come up trumps. Wandsworth Local History Service has a good collection, the vast number of late-19th-century applications testifying to the rapid pace of development in the area at this time. There are four applications relating to Acris Street, made between 1 October 1895 and 16 June 1896, for a total of 46 houses, all submitted by the builder W. H. George of Trefoil Road.[4] Of these, the 39 houses built in Acris Street itself comprised the earliest application; the seven others were built slightly later in the plots at the northern end, with shops facing the main road (Huguenot Place/East Hill). The plans that accompany these applications are site maps and simple, sketched outlines of houses, showing the approximate layout of the buildings and the positioning of the drains and sewers *(ill. 115)*.

We now have a much more reliable date for the commencement of building works in our street and the name of the builder. Armed with this information, we can make an assault on the enormous series of post-1870s district surveyors' returns at London Metropolitan Archives, to pin down the exact date of house construction. In the part 1 entries for the Wandsworth West District for 1895 are two notifications from W. H. George, dated 7 November 1895, one for building work to commence on 19 houses on the east side of 'Acris Road', one for 20 houses on the other side. All are for dwelling houses, 25ft high, of three storeys. Work would have begun very shortly afterwards, and leafing through the part 2 entries for the succeeding years we find that most of the houses were completed 'in carcase' and the relevant fees paid by George in the early months of 1897, but four of the houses were not finished until March 1898.[5]

Returning to the drainage applications for the other streets, there are six from 1892 relating to Cicada Road, for a total of 51 houses, each from a different local builder (G. Treland, William Hanbury, William Pierce, S. Rashleigh and Arthur Lindfield), and others of 1893-4 involving still more builders (W. E. Ireland, W. H. George and Albert Eaton).[6] In Melody Road the story is similar, with the bulk of the houses being started in 1891 and 1892 (by G. Driver, W. Gay and Albert Eaton), with further applications in 1893 and 1894 (from Eaton, George and Ireland).[7] Trefoil Road was begun in 1893 and 1894, with only two builders working in this much shorter street (Eaton and George).[8] A glance at entries for other streets in the area (e.g. Dault Road, Geraldine Road, Jessica Road and Quarry Road) shows that these, too, date from the same 1892-6 period, and were the work of many of the same builders. Should a researcher wish to embark on a detailed study

of the development of this small patch of Victorian Wandsworth, there is plenty of data here and in the district surveyors' returns that could be used to analyse the scale and speed of development, the number of builders, and so on. However, there is no sign of a builder named Holland or Cecil, so our terrace-names in Melody Road did not, after all, commemorate the house-builders — a salutary lesson in the dangers of assumption.

Returning to the card index, under the estate name, 'Bramblebury', we find another application that we might otherwise have missed, for 38 or 39 houses on the west side of Wandsworth Common, with a good plan, indicating the room divisions, wall thicknesses, and the

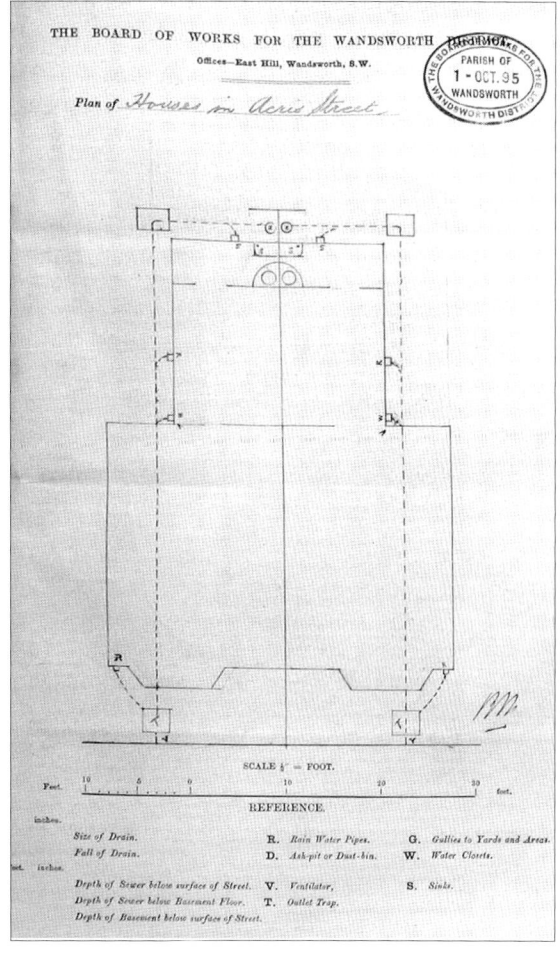

115. From the drainage records for Acris Street, 1895.

positions of the staircases and fireplaces.[9] There are other references to Bramblebury in the local library's collection. One occurs in the transcript of an auction sale of real estate in 1835–6 by Earl Spencer, lord of the Manor of Battersea and Wandsworth. A number of the lots relate to our area, such as three or four small estates on the south side of East Hill and west side of Wandsworth Common. One of these comprised a residence and outbuildings in over an acre of grounds, held on lease by Mrs Lydia Harrison, afterwards known as Bramblebury House. An additional note in pencil states: 'Trefoil Road and Cicada Road were cut through this plot'.[10] There is also a late-Victorian photograph of the house, amid pleasant grounds, and an 1890 reference to a fête for local Liberals and Radicals, held there with the kind permission of Mrs Dickinson (presumably a later owner or resident).[11] Although only one of the many detached houses in the area, Bramblebury House seems to have given its name to the entire development. Some of the other houses were photographed before demolition, including Easthill Lodge and Ivy Lodge, which occupied the site of Acris Street; there are prints in both the local collection and at the LMA *(ill. 116)*.[12]

But what of our family of developers, the Corsellises? Wandsworth Library's card index of personal and place names provides three sources of information. One is a notice from the *Daily Chronicle* of the death in December 1910 of our developer, Henry Nicholas Corsellis, late of Hambledon in Surrey, a solicitor in the firm of Corsellis & Berry. His effects were valued at £190,000. The second source is an obituary, from the *Putney & Wandsworth Boro' News*, of H. N. Corsellis's father, Arthur Alexander Corsellis, who died in 1888. This gives some useful background: A. A. Corsellis, the only surviving son of Lt-Col. Henry Nicholas Corsellis, had also been a solicitor, the senior partner in the Wandsworth firm of Corsellis Son & Mossop, and had served as a County Justice, and as Clerk and Solicitor to the Wandsworth District Board of Works for nearly 30 years. He had retired to Torquay by 1884, to a house named 'Layer Marney', where he died. The third and most interesting piece is in the library's Local En-

quiry file, in reference to a family called Attwood. Most local history libraries keep letters of enquiry, and copies of the staff replies, and these are often a quick route to information that otherwise would be difficult or time-consuming to locate. In this instance we have summaries from the census returns for 1861–81 for the Corsellis family home in Wandsworth, 'Marney Lodge', on East Hill (now No. 85), where A. A. Corsellis lived with his wife and growing family of children, and an average of four female servants. Corsellis's place of birth is listed as the West Indies, though the age of his wife and children suggests that he had come to England by the mid-1850s. Also given is the 1881 census return for Henry Nicholas Corsellis and his family at 2 Crowland Villas, Apsely Road, Wandsworth; this confirms that A. H. N. Corsellis, the leaseholder of Acris Street, was one of his children.[13]

Unfortunately there is no mention of the Corsellises involvement with the Bramblebury Estate. But it is clear from the above that this was a well-to-do family, of some standing in the area, whose successful solicitors' business and links with the local board of works would have enabled them to understand the mechanics of estate development, and would have provided them with the means and contacts to undertake such a speculation.

We now know in considerable detail when and how the street was built, and the names of many of the people involved. But who were the first occupants? For what type of people were the houses intended? Luckily the 1901 census, the first to cover Acris Street, recently became available to the public. An analysis of the 1901 returns for each house in the street shows that the most common types of profession among the early inhabitants were in the rapidly-growing 'white-collar' sector. Fifteen of the 56 heads of household in the street – nearly 27% – were employed as clerks of one sort or another: Civil Service clerks, bank clerks, solicitors' clerks, etc. So this was a middle-class street, certainly. But it was perhaps more mixed and varied socially than the regularity of the bay-windowed house-fronts might have suggested. There was a good number of salesmen and shop assistants, and some representatives

116. Easthill Lodge in 1893, on the site of Acris Street.

from skilled trades such as tailoring and printing. And there were a few specialists – a journalist and author, an art-metal worker and a stained-glass artist. A few residents could be bracketed in the wealthier upper sections of the middle classes: for example Lars Bristol, a 52-year-old Norwegian-born electrical engineer, the head of a large business, the sole occupant of No. 24, if we exclude his live-in servant. Eleven of the 56 households in Acris Street could afford to pay one servant. But only about half of the houses in the street were in single-family occupation; the rest were shared. A typical example of the latter was at No. 16, where a house decorator, his family and two boarders lived with the family of a factory-yard foreman – a total of nine people. In all there were 212 people living as 56 households in the 38 houses of Acris Street. The most crowded house was at No. 26, where a widow and her five daughters shared with a commercial traveller and his extended family, a total of 12 people.[14]

Phase 3: Further research

What type of sources are available to the dedicated researcher, who may wish to delve even deeper into the history of Acris Street and its immediate neighbourhood?

We know from the IR58 fieldbooks that the freehold of Acris Street was owned by Magadalen College, Oxford. Many historic colleges like Magdalen have their own archives, and an investigation of their holdings may shed more light on the street's development. The best place to begin, before writing to the college archivist, would be the volumes of Magadalen College catalogues published by the Historical Manuscripts Commission, and other lists held at the National Register of Archives.

More research could be carried out if desired on the Corsellis family and their involvement in local politics and building development. For example, we know of other streets in Battersea and Wandsworth in which they were involved; their histories could be unravelled using the same methods as above. As for the family itself, a quick search in the National Register of Archives catalogue produced only one entry for Corsellis – on the face of it unpromising – for deeds and estate papers in Essex Record Office of a family of that name of Wivenhoe Hall in Essex, relating to their holdings there.[15] In his will, A. A. Corsellis referred to his house in Torquay by name as Layer Marney, and the solicitors' business in Battersea was part of a building called Marney Lodge; so the family obviously had connections with Essex, and was proud of them. At this stage following a hunch provides an interesting result: a guidebook to Layer Marney Tower, the well-known sixteenth-century tower in Essex, lists four generations of Corsellises as owners and lords of the manor. The Essex Record Office collection also includes a family's pedigree, showing their descent from Zaeger Corsellis of Roussellier, in Flanders, a useful lead should more research be required on the family's background.

Finally, what of the more recent history of the street and its residents? What changes have taken place? Information about subsequent occupants may be difficult to trace: post-1901 census returns are not yet publicly available, but lists of later occupants can be found in local *Directories*, in electoral registers, and in collections of local deeds and leases. Some of the street's Victorian houses (Nos 19–33) have been demolished and replaced by more recent housing. This isolated example of redevelopment could well be as a result of World War Two bomb-damage (the houses adjoining at the rear on the west side of the Common have also been rebuilt); a look at War Damage maps and records would confirm this. For more recent alterations to the fabric, applications held by the local planning department should be publicly accessible and should record any major changes.

Summary

This research has shown Acris Street to be a fairly typical example of a late-19th-century suburban street. Similar terraces are to be found all over the capital, in a variety of sizes and styles: in east London, in Hackney, Walthamstow, Ilford; in north London, in Harringey, Muswell Hill, Finsbury Park, Islington; but south-west London is particularly rich in them – Fulham, Battersea, Wandsworth, Tooting, Streatham, all are lined with row after row of Victorian terraces. It is likely that the story of Acris Street's development is also fairly typical. By using the classes of records listed above, it should be possible to unearth the history of many of London's Victorian streets and terrace-houses.

NOTES AND REFERENCES

1. The fieldbooks for these streets are at TNA, IR58/ 88651, 88656, 88679, 88680, 88686.

2. For example, London County Council (LCC) *Minutes*, 20 July 1888, p. 176, para 94 ; 3 August 1888, p. 295, para 96; 29 September 1891, p. 917, para 54; 1 August 1893, p. 862, para 10; 21 January 1896, p. 36, para 6.

3. LCC *Minutes*, 29 September 1891, p. 913, para 12.

4. Wandsworth Local History Service, Drainage Applications nos W12/2019, 2031; W13/2110; W14/2244.

5. LMA, LCC/AR/BA/04/062/066; LCC/AR/BA/ 04/079/062; LCC/AR/BA/04/088/062.

6. Wandsworth Local History Service, Drainage Applications nos W9/1428, 1446, 1465, 1505, 1509; W10/ 1585, 1596, 1613, 1671.

7. As above, nos W9/1415, 1476, 1480, 1482, 1512; W10/1613, 1636, 1665; W12/2011.

8. As above, nos W10/1570–1, 1708, 1769.

9. As above, nos W9/1467, 1507.

10. *Wandsworth Notes & Queries*, pt VI, 1899, p. 107.

11. Wandsworth Local History Service, photo 2188; cuttings 728.3BRA.

12. As above, photos 17, 21: also LMA photo 62/703 (95.0WAN).

13. Wandsworth Local History Service, Local Enquiry File, under Attwood, Llewellyn; *Putney & Wandsworth Boro' News*, 5 May 1888, p. 5.

14. TNA, RG13/484, pp. 182–6.

15. NRA 7417 Elwes; Essex RO refs D/DEt/ M24; D/DEt/T22; D/DEt/F2; D/DEt/F33.

CASE HISTORY THREE

Between-the-Wars Suburbia:
Nos 137–147 Cornwall Road, Ruislip Manor, Hillingdon

Live in Ruislip where the air's like wine,
It's less than half an hour on the Piccadilly Line[1]

Cornwall Road is a wide, curving, tree-lined road in the largely residential area known as Ruislip Manor, between Ruislip and Eastcote, in the London Borough of Hillingdon, on Greater London's north-western limits. The rather uniform houses here seem to belong to the lower, 'functional' end of the capital's inter-war suburban sprawl: most are grouped together in fours in short 'terraces' – as is the case with Nos 137–143 – interspersed with a few pairs of semidetached houses, such as Nos 145–147 *(ill. 117)*.

Like many of London's outer suburbs, Ruislip was until about 100 years ago almost entirely free of concentrated building development. For centuries it was a village centre surrounded by fields and farmland. The watershed was the coming of the railways in the early 20th century, opening up the area initially to daytrippers, then to developers and commuters. Ruislip underground station opened on the Uxbridge branch of the Metropolitan Line in 1904, and main-line services were introduced from Paddington and Marylebone to Ruislip and South Ruislip (originally Northolt Junction) stations in 1906 and 1908. Extra Metropolitan Line passenger halts opened at Eastcote (1906) and Ruislip Manor (1912), and by 1933 the Piccadilly Line was also running its trains along the tracks between Rayners Lane and Uxbridge. Ruislip was one of many north-western suburbs which sprang up alongside these and other new routes – known collectively as 'Metro-land' – making

117. Cornwall Road, with Nos 145–147 at the far right.

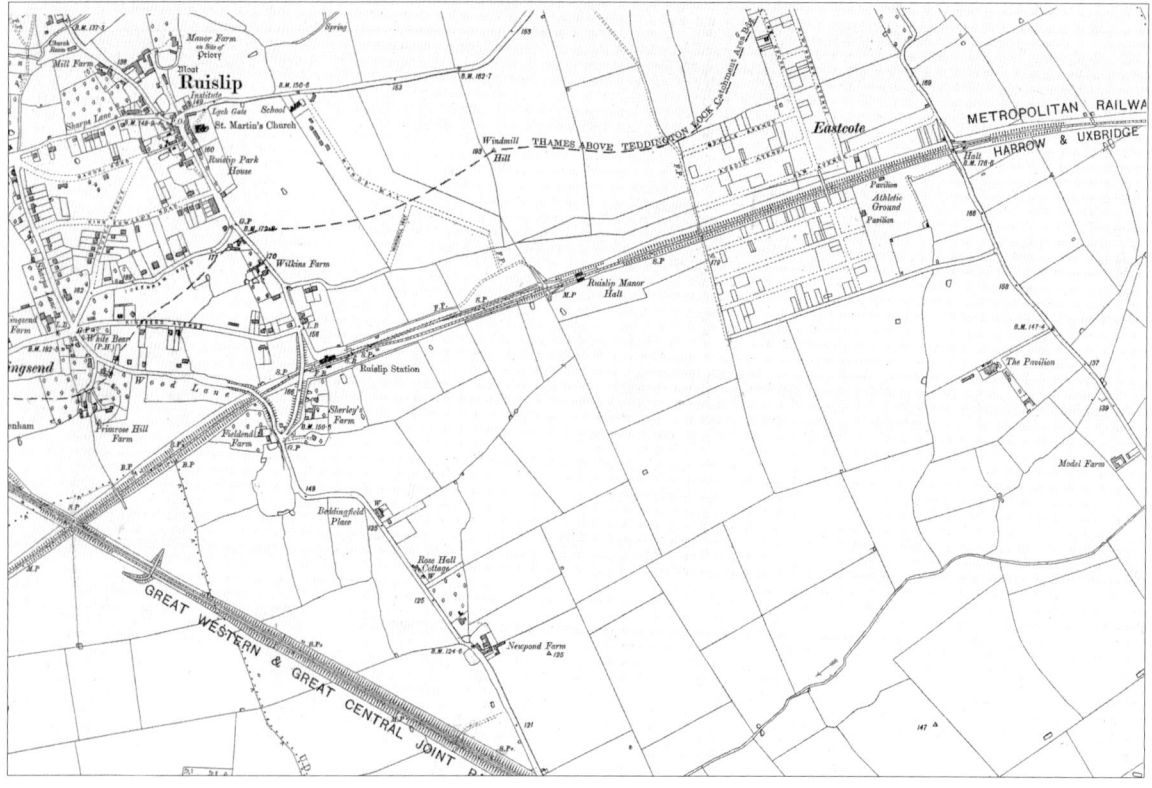

118. *Ordnance Survey map of the Ruislip Manor area in 1916.*

the area one of the fastest-growing parts of the country at the time.

So when were our houses in Cornwall Road built? Who were they built by, and for what kind of resident were they intended? How do they relate to contemporary developments in other parts of Ruislip, and are they typical of suburban development outside London in the early- and mid-20th century, or are they in any way special or unusual?

Phase 1: Basic sources – Ordnance Survey maps, directories, ratebooks and electoral registers
Ordnance Survey maps of the 1890s clearly show the rural character of this area between the villages of Eastcote and Ruislip. By 1916 the two railway lines have been driven through and now we see the first tentative fingers of suburban development to the west of Ruislip, between the station and Kingsend, in Kingsend Avenue, King Edward's Road and Manor Road, for example; and east of the village, on the

north side of the underground line, in Manor Way and Windmill Way *(ill. 118)*. A new grid of streets can also be seen in genesis at Eastcote. But our area, to the south of Ruislip Manor Halt (now Ruislip Manor Station) is still farmland. By the next edition, of 1935, the area has changed completely. North of the Metropolitan Line, Ruislip and Eastcote villages have been engulfed by an almost solid mass of suburban housing. To its south, the area now known as Ruislip Manor has been laid out and many of the streets, including Cornwall Road, lined with houses. However, the impression is one of an estate still under construction, with large gaps to the south and west, towards the Yeading Brook. Cornwall Road itself is unfinished at its north-eastern end, where it meets Victoria Road. It is not until the next edition, of 1946, that we see the estate north of the brook completed, much as it is today *(ill. 119)*.

So Cornwall Road seems to have been almost finished by 1935, as one of the first streets

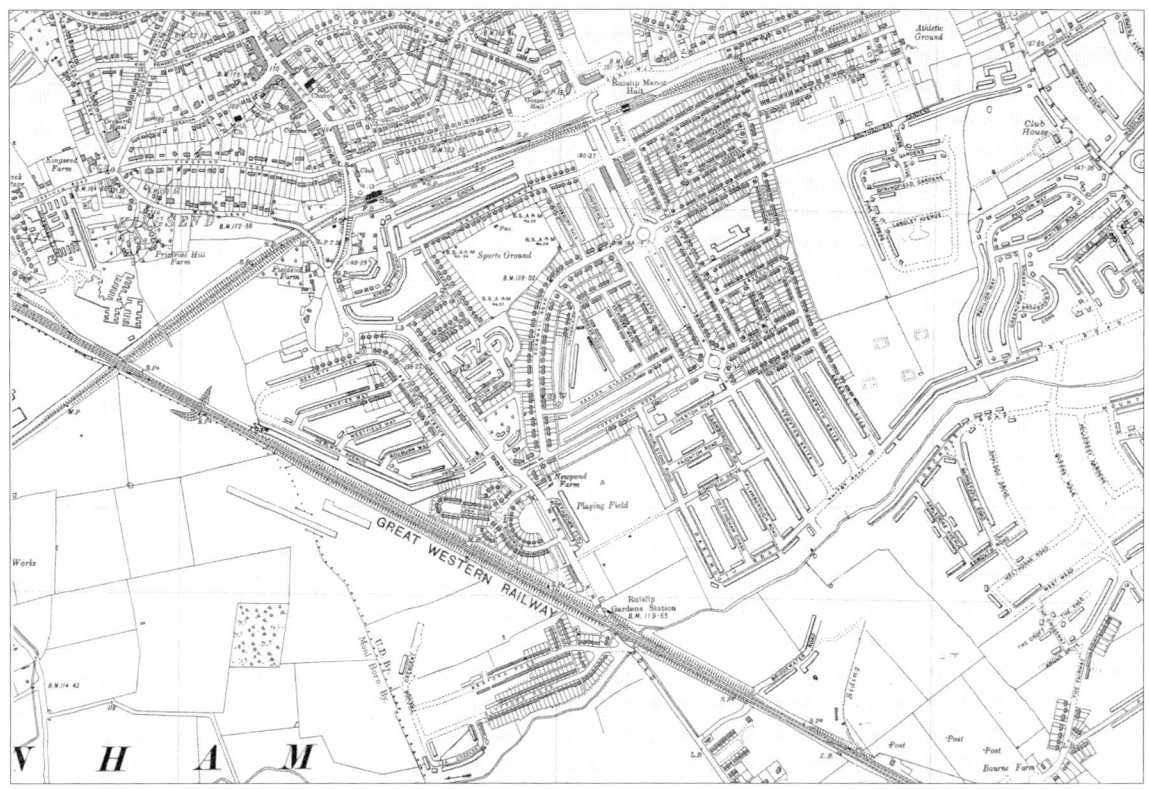

119. Ordnance Survey map of the Ruislip Manor area in 1946. Cornwall Road is the long curving road in the centre, south of the sports ground.

of a large estate development. But when exactly were the houses built? Ruislip is in the former county of Middlesex, outside the pre-1965 administrative county of London, and not all of the sources used in the two previous case studies in more central areas will be applicable or available here. But nearly every district should have local street directories, electoral registers and possibly ratebooks, and for Ruislip Manor these are the easiest and quickest way to pinpoint the street's construction date.

Kelly's *Directory of Pinner*, which covers Ruislip, has no mention of Cornwall Road in its 1933 or 1934 editions. Quite a few houses are listed in Linden Avenue, and a handful of others in Chudleigh Way and Dulverton Road, on the eastern part of the estate, which seems to have been built up first. Unfortunately the 1935 edition was not available, but by 1936 Nos 1–163 are listed on the north side of Cornwall Road, with only a few gaps (presumably some houses were not yet occupied), and Nos 2–138

on the south side; this corresponds with what is shown on the 1935 OS map. By 1937 most of the gaps have been filled, and the house-numbering sequence has extended to Nos 167 on the north side, and 142 on the south; by 1939 we have reached Nos 169 and 144. A glance at the names of other streets on this part of the estate reveals a similar story, with Torrington Road, Salcombe Way, Seaton Gardens, chunks of Victoria Road and others being developed in 1935–7. The intensity of house-construction in the area during the 1930s is evident simply from the number of pages Ruislip occupies in the street directory, leaping from 23 pages in 1931 to almost a hundred by 1939.

Electoral registers (also known as voters' lists) for the same period confirm the information from the directories, and make up for the missing 1935 volume, revealing that the majority of the houses at Nos 1–161 and 2–138 had filled up in time for their occupants to make the 1935 register, with most of the unoccupied

179

houses being taken the following year. But it is the ratebooks that provide the clearest picture of our street's chronology. The first entry for Cornwall Road dates from April 1934, for a house and garden at No. 138, on the north side. Eight more (Nos 122–136) had been rated and occupied by the end of May 1934, some with typically evocative suburban names such as 'Southwold' or 'Beecholm'. At this early stage of the development there was still some confusion among the rate-collectors as to the exact location of certain houses: a group of four was originally given plot numbers in Cornwall Road, but this was later changed to West End Road. By the end of June 1934 our houses at Nos 137–147 had been taken, along with Nos 121–135 and 106–120. A pattern emerges, of the builders beginning at the northern end of Cornwall Road, on the south side at the junction with Ashburton Road, on the north side at Rosebury Vale, and gradually working their way southwards. Nos 78–104 and 109–119 were finished next, then Nos 62–76 and 65–107, in June and July 1934, with the remainder (Nos 2–60 and 1–63), and some new houses beyond Rosebury Vale (Nos 149–163) being finished by March 1935. Some of these later houses, though listed, had not yet been occupied by March 1935, and in some of these cases the rates were being paid by George Ball Ltd — presumably our builder.[2]

Phase 2: Local archive collections – photos, deeds and ephemera, and local government sources
Now we need some background to flesh out the story of Cornwall Road's development. Hillingdon Local Studies and Archives Service, at Uxbridge, has a box of papers relating to the Ruislip Manor estate for the period 1930 to 1939, including conveyances, agreements and estate plans.[3] From these we learn that the estate was owned by King's College, Cambridge, which in 1930 agreed to sell its freehold title to a development company, Southern Park Estates Ltd of Baker Street, London, for £32,000. However, the sale seems not to have gone through, as by 1933 George Ball (Ruislip) Ltd had contracted with King's to buy the land, and had received approval from Ruislip-

Northwood Urban District Council to develop the northern part of the estate (about 186 acres on the north side of the Yeading Brook, as far south as Torrington Road and Filey Waye), with 2,322 houses, at a density of no more than 14 houses to the acre. The accompanying plans show Cornwall Road to have been the first road lined with houses on the west side of Victoria Road (the estate's main north–south axis and shopping street). Later agreements show that by July 1934 Ball's company had agreed to reduce the number of houses to 2,238 to allow room for a school (provided by Middlesex County Council), a church, a public house and several open spaces. By 1938 Ball had begun to lay out more streets and houses on the southern part of the estate on the north side of the brook, either side of Victoria Road (some of these are indicated on the 1935 OS map), and by 1939 was planning another grid of streets south of the brook, towards South Ruislip (this part of the estate was not finished until after the war). Most of the maps and plans are signed by William F. Hobbs of Harrow, Architect & Surveyor, whom the company probably employed to design the estate's street layout and housing, subject to the approval of the council's surveyor. Also, most of the agreements refer to a Town Planning Scheme of 1914, which had to be amended to allow Ball's development to take place.

But the most valuable source in the box at Hillingdon is a mid-1930s 'Manor Homes' sales brochure, produced by George Ball (Ruislip) Ltd to attract prospective residents to the new suburb. It has various photographs of roads being laid and houses under construction, and even one of a spectacular fireworks display on the estate, in September 1933 (we shall return to this later). Best of all are photographs and plans of the different types of housing built by Ball in the first phase of development in Ruislip Manor, from two-bedroom terrace-houses at £450 freehold, to four-bed houses with a garage, at £745 *(ills 120, 121)*. These are particularly valuable, as there are no drainage plans in the local archives collection to give an idea of the houses' original layout, and there are few photographs of the area, other than one terrific early shot near to the

120 and 121. Photos of typical Manor Homes houses from the George Ball brochure, retouched to suggest an idyllic landscape setting: a row of £745 houses (above) and a pair of £665 houses.

122. Photo of 1933, taken from the railway station, during the early days of the Manor Homes estate, showing the estate office, saloon cars ferrying customers, and a signwriter at work on a hoarding.

station, with no buildings save George Ball's estate office, an advertising hoarding to catch the eye of tube travellers, and saloon cars ferrying buyers along a bare concrete road (Victoria Road) to view the house plots *(ill. 122)*.

Returning to the brochure, despite the standardization in design, and the similarities in style across the different types, our Cornwall Road houses are easily recognizable. Nos 137–143 have end houses of the most expensive four-bedroom type, with two of the first-floor bedrooms extending over a brick-built garage; the inner houses (Nos 139, 141) would have been of the £595 three-bedroom type. Our semi-detached pair at Nos 145–147 would have had the same accommodation as Nos 139 and 141 – a hall, two reception rooms and kitchen on the ground floor, with the bedrooms, a bathroom and separate w.c. above – but were priced higher at £665 for their greater privacy and bigger gardens *(ill. 123)*. Walking the streets, and looking again at the estate and OS Maps, it becomes apparent that Cornwall Road was one of the better roads (if not the best) on this first part of Ball's development. Its generous size, at 60 feet wide, marks it out: only Victoria Road is as big, the other streets all measuring 40 feet in width. It is also one of the few streets to have been planted with trees, and furthermore has none of the longer, cheaper 'terraces' of six houses found commonly in other streets; most of its houses are of the £595 type and above.

The brochure's accompanying blurb proclaims that the Manor Homes houses ('palaces in miniature') were intended for those who spent their days in the 'big city', enabling them to return 'in the quiet dusk of the evenings, to Nature's stronghold outside the town'. These inexpensive houses were specially aimed at 'the man of moderate means', who need no longer be confined to 'less attractive' locations, the cheapest £450 houses being offered on hire-purchase for repayments of just 11s 3d per week. All the houses were fitted with electric lighting, and interior decoration was carried out to the 'purchaser's own choice'. Ball seems to have had a particular market in mind, building cheap houses mostly in little terraces, rather than the more expensive semi-detached form found in other suburbs, to appeal to the better-off working-class population trapped in poorer districts of the capital. But our case study houses were not the cheapest on the estate, and were perhaps aimed more at lower-middle-class 'white-collar' workers than those on the other streets. Without access to census returns for the period, or first-hand local knowledge, it is difficult to discover exactly where the early residents of Cornwall Road came from. However, it is likely that the majority of people who chose to leave London for a suburban house with a garden would have been young married couples, in their twenties or early thirties, with a young family, and so it is possible that some of them may appear on the 1901 census as small children. This is not a very reliable method, but searching for the most unusual half-dozen or so male names from the electoral registers and ratebooks does bring up three infants of the right name in Walthamstow and Poplar – exactly the sort of north London working-class areas Ball would have been aiming at – and two south of the river in Camberwell and Peckham.

Hillingdon Local Studies Library also has in its collection the minutes of the Ruislip–Northwood Urban District Council, which should give a further insight into the area's inter-war development. Those for 1932 to 1935 and November 1937 to April 1938 are indexed, which makes finding information about George Ball and the Manor Homes estate relatively easy; those for the intervening period are not. Early entries show the council worrying about the density of Ball's original plans. Density per acre had been prescribed by the 1914 Town Planning Scheme already referred to, and the council asked Ball to build at no more than 70 houses per 5-acre unit.

There were also concerns about the appearance of the houses. In June 1933, before development had gone very far, the Ruislip Association asked for assurance that Ball's houses would be 'of a type and character suitable to the District'. The council promised to watch the development closely, and the following May, at a meeting with representatives of Ball's company, asked for more variation in the elevational treatment of the houses, 'to avoid monotonous repetition'. The developers promised to 'bear this in mind', but pointed out that they had already provided eleven different types of elevation.[4]

In terms of Cornwall Road itself, the minutes have some snippets of information. The name, suggested by George Ball Ltd, was approved by the council in March 1934, and street-lamps were being erected there the following May. Cornwall and Victoria were the only roads of the estate considered fit by the council for tree-planting (which the council was willing to carry out if the developers or occupants provided the trees), as the narrower roads had service pipes running directly under the footpaths. As a result the council asked Ball to modify the intended layout of the houses to the south of Yeading Brook so as to allow trees and shrubs to be planted in 'islands' and at road junctions.[5]

Phase 3: Going further? Other types of record, and secondary sources

Do we want more background? Was this development a purely independent speculation by Ball? How does it relate to the development of the rest of the Ruislip–Northwood area, also carried out in the 20th century? Departing momentarily from our trawl of primary sources, there are numerous published works of local history which can fill in much of the background to Ball's house-building activities of the 1930s, and explain the 1914 Town Planning Scheme, to which it is connected (see *Further Reading*, below).

From these we learn that most of the land in Ruislip was owned by King's College, Cambridge, who had been Lords of the Manor since 1451. Concerned at the character of suburban development near by in the early 1900s, in 1909 the College entered into an agreement with Garden Estates Ltd, a development firm connected with the pioneering and successful Hampstead Garden Suburb scheme, to develop the College's entire estate - some 1,300 acres - on 'Garden City' principles. Their interest was transferred in 1910 to a new development company, Ruislip Manor Limited, and a town-planning competition held, which attracted considerable interest. From the 62 entries received, that of A. & J. Soutar of Wandsworth was selected by the eminent judges, Sir Aston Webb and Raymond Unwin. The area covered by the plan was over four miles long, extending from Northolt Junction in the south to Copse Wood, near Northwood station, in the north. The Soutars' plan was enlightened, with separate 'zones' for houses, shops, and leisure activities, and featured a gradation of house-densities for different social groups, starting in the north with large houses (at three to the acre) near Park Wood for wealthier residents, and gradually changing in character towards the south, with the smallest houses (at ten to the acre) south of the Metropolitan Line. Although laudable for the low density of its housing, and other amenities, the Soutars' plan

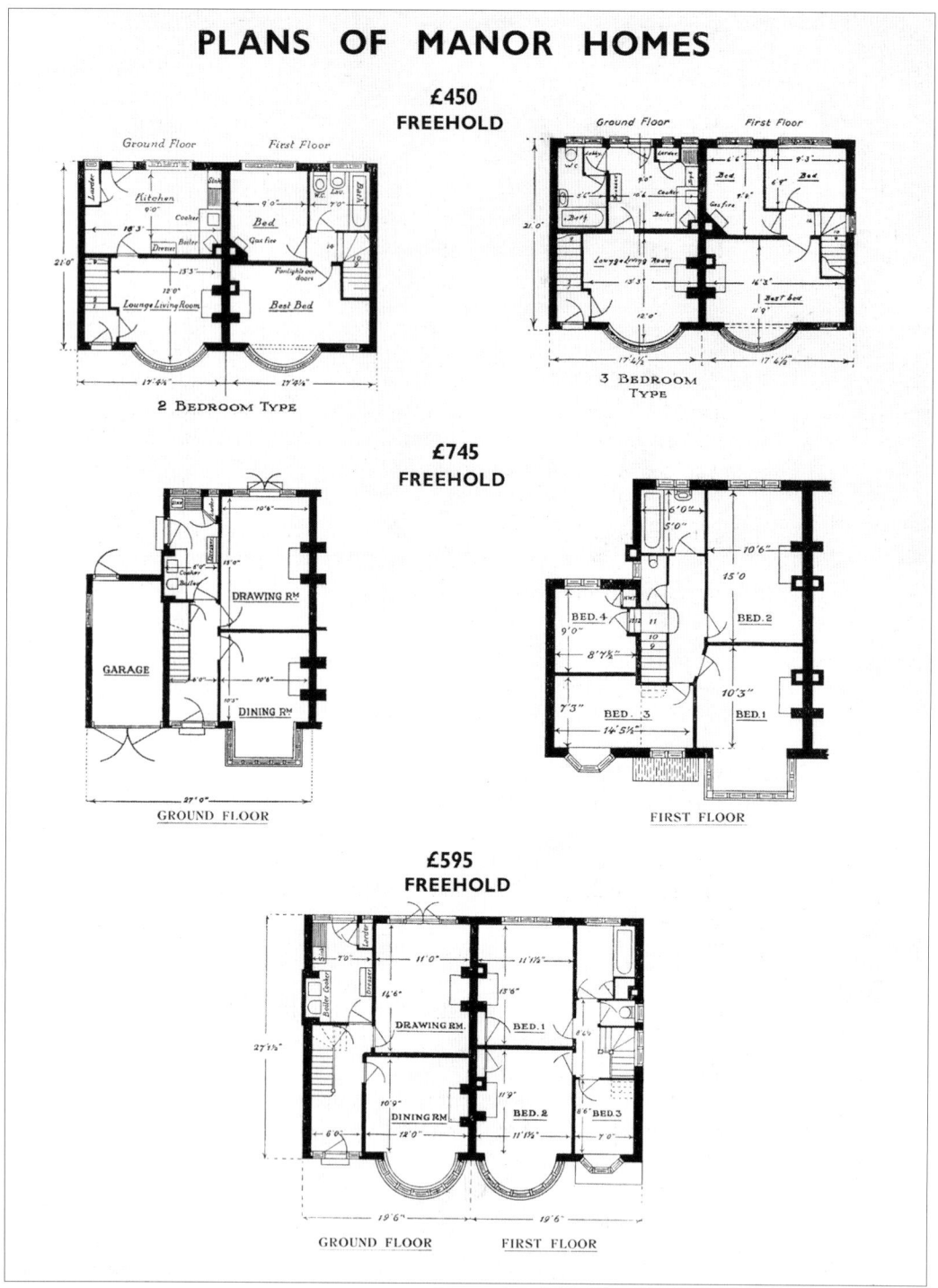

123. *Plans of Manor Homes houses, from the same George Ball brochure.*

124. Fireworks display on the theme of 'The Defence of London', at the launch of Ruislip Manor.

was rigorously geometric, with little feel for the local topography, centred on a new main north–south road from which diagonal streets fanned out to the further reaches of the estate. And they showed little regard for the area's historic fabric, such as Manor Farm and some sixteenth-century timber-framed buildings on the High Street, which were to be swept away.[6]

Fearing that such an enlightened plan might be undermined by 'objectionable developments' on adjoining land, the district council exercised its powers under the recent Housing and Town Planning Act (1909), and promoted an extended joint scheme for the 6,000 acres surrounding and including the Ruislip Manor estate, and Soutars' plan was adapted to suit. It was this dual municipal and private plan that was given Local Government Board approval in 1914.[7] Under the new scheme some working-class cottages were built between 1911 and 1914 by the Ruislip Manor Cottage Society, a specially formed subsidiary, in Manor Way, Manor Close and Windmill Way; these were

intended to house workers for the wealthier residents in the north of the suburb. But the outbreak of war in 1914 brought work to a halt, and the plan was never fully implemented. The large houses planned by the Soutars in and around Park Wood were never built. After 1918 development in the area was slow to restart, but by the mid-1930s it seems that the remaining parts of the district covered by the 1914 plan had been sold to private developers and builders, who thereafter developed their own estates, to an amended version of the plan, with the council's approval. Of these George Ball's Manor Homes estate was undoubtedly the largest. Although the big, speculatively built estates in and around Ruislip are somewhat limited in architectural terms, they seem to have benefited from their connection with the 1914 scheme in terms of their planning and housing densities, which are better than in some other inter-war Middlesex suburbs.

One last point, from Eileen Bowlt's account of the area, requires us to reassess slightly the social background of the estate's residents; they were not drawn solely from London's working-class areas. She relates that 'a substantial number' of the houses in Ruislip Manor were taken by men from Tyneside and the north, who had come south looking for work in the London area during the industrial slump of the 1930s.[8]

Finally, what about our builder, George Ball, and his company, George Ball (Ruislip) Ltd, or its subsidiary, Manor Homes? Is there more information to be had about their activities? There are references in the local Urban District Council minutes of the 1930s to other developments by Ball in the area, for example in Hillside Road, between Northwood Way and Pinner Hill; but other than this there is little to be had about him or his other building work. The mid-1930s sales brochure lists his firm's directors, who, other than Mr Ball himself, were T. F. Nash, Francis G. C. Jackson, and A. C. C. Thorne. Here other books on the area, and on the suburban expansion of Middlesex, offer some clues. Francis Jackson had his own development company, and had built at least one large estate near by, at the Glebe estate in Ickenham. Nash, though, is the big fish. His principal business, T. F. Nash Ltd, was at the time one of the largest private development companies operating in London's suburbia, laying out enormous estates amounting to about 4,000 homes at Tithe Farm and Rayners Lane in south Harrow. He was also at the same time building houses in Havering Park, near Romford in Essex, and another large estate outside London, in Sevenoaks. Nash employed over 1,000 workmen on these projects, using wood from his own joinery works in Wealdstone, and mass-produced materials and fixtures to keep costs and prices down.[9] George Ball's Manor Homes seems to have been part of the greater T. F. Nash organization, and Ball's methods by and large were Nash's methods – standarized designs, mass-produced materials, low prices. Nash Ltd houses in Rayners Lane, for example, look very similar in plan and appearance to Ball's at Ruislip Manor: three-bed houses in a mock-Tudor style, arranged in 'terraces' of four, with long parades of shops near by, *à la* Victoria Road. In

fact, what little documentary evidence there is about the workings of his company points to Ball being something of a 'sleeping' partner. When Ruislip–Northwood UDC members asked to discuss the Ruislip Manor estate development in some detail with representatives of George Ball Ltd in May 1934, it was Nash and Jackson whom they met, not Ball; and when the local paper mistakenly printed a report that designs for houses by an architect not associated with the firm had been 'disapproved' by the council, it was Jackson who wrote within the week to point out the 'gross misstatement', adding that the account was already proving detrimental to sales.[10]

One other area where Ball's company followed Nash's methods was in the field of promotion. Both used courtesy cars to ferry buyers, and regular adverts in the *London Evening News* to tempt the weary London workers, as did many suburban builders; but more unusual perhaps were their elaborate fireworks displays. In September 1933 a huge display was held on the Ruislip Manor estate, ostensibly in aid of local hospitals, but no doubt planned by the developers as a promotional opportunity *(ill. 124)*. Special cheap train tickets were issued by the Metropolitan Railway, to lure Londoners to the area. In addition to themed 'sets' of fireworks – including 'a glory of ancient Egypt' and 'the Defence of London' – there were searchlight displays, a treasure hunt, open-air dancing, music by Eric Crosby and his band, and a Variety programme featuring stars of the stage and radio, including Clapham and Dwyer. Promoted as the greatest fireworks display 'ever seen outside the Crystal Palace', it attracted a crowd loosely estimated at between 20,000 and 80,000, all of whom would have got the message loud and clear — 'Remember Manor Homes'.[11]

Summary

Although the Manor Homes estate's development at Ruislip Manor is not entirely typical of London's 'between-the-wars' suburban growth, the documentary sources used here to help explain its history — such as OS maps, ratebooks, electoral registers, local archive holdings and (where they survive) UDC minutes — should also be applicable to almost any other outer suburb of the era. The way in which the capital's former villages and rural settlements were swallowed up by metropolitan expansion, and the experiences of suburban living, are today important aspects of our capital's history.

NOTES AND REFERENCES

1. Advertising slogan of George Ball, the developer of the Manor Homes Estate in Ruislip, quoted in Alan A. Jackson, *Semi-Detached London: Suburban Development, Life and Transport, 1900–1939*, 1991 edn, p. 161.

2. The ratebooks for the Ruislip Manor area are available on advance order at Hillingdon Local Studies and Archives Service, Uxbridge (hereafter HLS&AS).

3. HLS&AS, Manor Homes Box (ref MUS 25A)

4. HLS&AS, Ruislip–Northwood UDC Council Minutes, 15 May 1933, p. 64; 12 June 1933, p. 79; 14 May 1934, p. 19.

5. *Ibid.*, 12 March 1934, p. 437; 14 May 1934, p. 26; 12 Aug 1935, pp. 222–3; 6 Dec 1937, p. 558.

6. A copy of the Ruislip Manor Ltd company prospectus of 1910 is at London Metropolitan Archives, Acc/1819/069; and the Soutars' plan was published, along with written details of other competitors' schemes, in *The Builder*, 6 Jan 1911, pp. 17–19.

7. See W. Thompson, 'The Ruislip–Northwood and Ruislip–Manor Joint Town Planning Scheme', in *Town Planning Review*, vol. IV, No. 2, July 1913, pp. 133–44.

8. Eileen M. Bowlt, *'The Goodliest Pace in Middlesex'*, 1989, p. 260.

9. For T. F. Nash Ltd see Alan A. Jackson, *Semi-Detached London*, 1991 edn, pp. 66–8, 81, 100, 155, 164, 170–1, 255; and Dennis F. Edwards, *Harrow. A Pictorial History*, 1993.

10. HLS&AS, Ruislip–Northwood UDC Council Minutes, 14 May 1934, p.19; *Middlesex Advertiser and County Gazette*, 28 July 1933, p. 5.

11. *London Evening News*, Oct 1934; *Middlesex Advertiser and County Gazette*, 29 Sept 1933, pp. 4, 15; 6 Oct 1933, pp. 9, 21.

FURTHER READING

Walter W. Druett, *Ruislip–Northwood Through the Ages* (King & Hutchings Ltd), 1957

Alan A. Jackson, *Semi-Detached London: Suburban Development, Life and Transport, 1900–1939* (Wild Swan), 2nd edn, 1991

James H. Johnson, 'The Suburban Expansion of Housing in London 1918–1939', in *Greater London*, ed. J. T. Coppock and Hugh C. Prince, 1964, pp. 142–66

David Massey, *Ruislip–Northwood: The Development of the Suburb*, 1967

W. Thompson, 'The Ruislip–Northwood and Ruislip–Manor Joint Town Planning Scheme', in *Town Planning Review*, vol. IV, No. 2, July 1913, pp. 133–44

David Tottman, 'Ruislip–Northwood. An Early example of Town Planning and its consequences'. Ruislip Northwood and Eastcote Local History Society Occasional paper No. 2, June 1982

Victoria County History, *A History of Middlesex*, vol. iv, 1971

INDEX

Pages marked by an asterisk denote an illustration or caption

INDEX